They Chose To Live

Also by J. Herbert Gilmore

When Love Prevails:
A Pastor Speaks to a Church in Crisis

I would rather die for a principle that
is going to live, than to live for a
principle that is going to die

They Chose To Live

The Racial Agony of an American Church

J. HERBERT GILMORE, JR.

WILLIAM B. EERDMANS PUBLISHING COMPANY
Grand Rapids, Michigan

Dedicated
to the Members
of
The Baptist Church of the Covenant
Birmingham, Alabama
a
people of God
committed to love all people
and through disciplined discipleship to
"sum up all things in Christ"

Preface

This is a tragic and heroic story. Tragic—because the majority of the members of the First Baptist Church of Birmingham, Alabama, chose to live for a principle that is going to die: racial segregation. Heroic—because more than two hundred fifty members of this historic old church chose to die for a principle that is going to live: brotherhood in Christ.

I had originally entitled the story *They Chose To Die*. But this title was negative, backward looking, and bereft of hope. The events described in this book speak of creative action, lively hope, and courageous faith. This awareness prompted me to change the title to *They Chose To Live*.

Although this is the story of a Baptist church in the South, the denomination and the geography are really incidental. Racism plagues all religious groups in every section of America. The racial agony of this particular church mirrors the racism present, more or less, in most churches—North and South, East and West. Swift-moving events on the American scene remind the thoughtful observer that no one section may point a finger at any other. Racism often appears to be strongest in the South because it is expressed in raw vehemence by the rank and file. But suave and sophisticated racism in other parts of the country is equally difficult to dislodge. In any case, racism is unworthy of the Christian church and unworthy of America, with its avowed commitment to "liberty and justice for all."

Baptist churches in the South frequently seem to be strongholds of racism. I do not wish to minimize our severe shortcomings or our almost total captivity to the culture, but it is true that the democratic polity of Baptist churches lends itself to washing dirty linen in public. As a result, our worst mentality, rather than our best, is revealed in the public press. The

7

story that this book tells demonstrates that clearly. In Christian groups with a hierarchical structure, pronouncements are made by the best leaders. Yet at the grass-roots level all denominations suffer about equally from the terrible malady of racism. So the subtitle of this book refers to *The Racial Agony of an American Church*, not of "a Southern church" or of "a Baptist church."

The sermons I preached during this racial crisis have been previously published under the title *When Love Prevails.** The present book complements that one by describing the results of that proclamation of the Christian gospel. The story is told from my perspective. Its documentation comes from recorded tapes of the church conferences, from my diary, from conversations with many—friend and foe—involved, and from my memory of the events as I lived through them. It is suggested that each appendix be read as the text calls attention to it. I have tried not to intrude personally as I tell of the heroic faith of my friends who left the First Baptist Church of Birmingham to pioneer in a new one. I was, however, the scapegoat on whom the rage of segregationists was laid; and so there are passages in what follows where the personal pronoun is more prominent than I should have liked. I trust the reader will remember and forgive this.

Several people have assisted me in various ways in preparing the manuscript for publication. First, I thank Miss Betty Bock, my Minister of Education, and Mr. H. Hobart Grooms, Jr., the attorney who was my first contact with Birmingham, for reading the manuscript and offering many helpful suggestions. Secondly, I thank my other colleagues on the staff of The Baptist Church of the Covenant for their encouragement—Mrs. Sarah Wilson, Dr. John N. Sims, and my secretary, Miss Erin Nation, who also demonstrated great patience and competence in typing the manuscript. Finally, I am grateful to my wife Joyce and to my children—Victor, Dale, Winston, and Marie—for their gentle push to write the book.

If this story can inspire and encourage Christian ministers and laymen to give leadership where they are in helping the church correct racist patterns and attitudes, my purpose in writing it will be realized, and I shall be very happy.

*Wm. B. Eerdmans Publishing Company, Grand Rapids, Michigan, 1971.

Contents

Prologue

On September 27, 1970, two black people, a mother and her daughter, were presented to the congregation of the First Baptist Church, Birmingham, Alabama, to be received into membership according to the policy of the church. They were rejected. I went to the pulpit and told the people: "I have said that I would not be the pastor of a racist church. I meant what I said! So, this morning I respectfully request that you accept my resignation, effective November 1, 1970."

How could one reared in the ways of the old South, the pastor of a church similar to all other Southern Baptist churches, come to such a position? I recall certain incidents and events in my life that helped bring about such a radical change in me. One of them dates back to a June night in 1936 when, as an eleven-year-old boy, I was permitted to stay up with some twenty to twenty-five men, gathered in a neighbor's home, to listen to the radio broadcast of the heavyweight fight between Joe Louis, a black American, and Max Schmeling, a German whom Hitler used as a model to buttress his claim to German superiority. The community in which I grew up was typically Southern. Most of the citizens would have denied that they were against the Negro. Yet, so far as I can remember, everyone that evening was for Max Schmeling for the simple reason that he was white.

As we sat in the living room listening to the fight, there was deep concern on the part of these white men that Louis might win. When Schmeling knocked out Louis in the twelfth round, some of the men leaped to their feet shouting: "We did it, we did it! We whipped that 'nigger!' " Though I did not understand the subtle dynamic of racism, I sensed that something was wrong with that.

I remember, too, the vivid impression made on me when, as a lad of ten, I was invited into the shack of a Negro family, one of the customers to whom I delivered the newspaper. The mother explained that she could not afford to pay her paper bill, a mere twenty cents per week. During her embarrassed speech I caught glimpses of the degrading squalor in which this family was living. "Though I can't pay you in money," she said, "I can give you some blueberry muffins." On this basis I continued her paper for some two years. But I could not understand why the black people lived in the poorest homes in the worst sections of town, wore the dirtiest clothes, and held the poorest jobs.

My wonderment occasionally embarrassed my mother. Once when she took my twin brothers and me to shop with her in Knoxville, we rode the streetcar. As we boarded, I noticed a large sign reading "Colored sit in rear." A growing resentment was building in my young head. I asked my mother why this was done. Though she had deep sympathy for the feelings of the black people, she could not explain adequately to her young son this enforced separation.

Nothing was more thrilling to me as I was growing up than baseball. I played it every chance I had; and, since our family budget did not allow for much entertainment, my mother often took my brothers and me on Ladies' Day to Caswell Park to see the Knoxville Smokies play. I noticed at the ball park that the black people were seated in the bleachers in left field with no protection from the sun, though there were many empty seats out of the sun. Once again, I troubled my mother by asking her why the Negroes could not sit where we were. Again, her explanation did not really explain anything.

During my high school years my concern that the treatment of black people was not right continued to grow. Though my church did not address itself directly to the racial problem, the pastor did, to his credit, arrange for black groups to come to our church and for our church choir to go to black churches. (This is the more significant when one remembers that it was in the thirties.)

When I entered college in 1942, I began to realize how thorny and pervasive America's racial problems were. As a young man preparing for the Christian ministry, my conscience was pricked by an increasing awareness of the gross injustice done to the Negro. Most troubling was the fact that there seemed to be little or no awareness of this in the Christian church. The college pastor did sound an authentic note against racism, but no action was taken by the church, and his preachments were angrily resented. Even at the Christian college I attended there was nothing more than tokenism: an occasional invitation to the principal of the Negro high school in Jefferson City, Tennessee, a man of culture and refinement, to speak to a literary society or in chapel. There was a tremendous gap between the proclamation of love and justice in the Christian church and the actual practice of churchmen. By my junior year in college I vowed that if I ever had the chance, I would try to do something about this inequity.

An incident a year after my graduation from college deepened my resolve. Newly married, I was moving what few possessions my wife and I had to our new place of service in Springfield, Tennessee, where I was to serve as the Associate Pastor of the First Baptist Church. A Negro was driving the small truck. When it was time for lunch somewhere between Knoxville and Nashville, I was naive enough to suggest that we stop to get something to eat at a roadside hamburger stand. The owner told us, in language not repeatable, that he did not "serve ——— niggers." Embarrassed, humiliated, and righteously indignant, I declared: "If he cannot eat here I do not want to eat here," and walked out. As we walked out the owner said: "If he wants to come around to the back I'll sell him a ——— hamburger." I think then for the first time I really understood the hideous life black people were forced to live. I saw the awful effects that the denial of dignity for the Negro had, not only on the blacks, but equally on the whites.

These experiences caused me to raise questions about this in youth groups in my early pastoral ministry. Church leaders were unwilling to discuss the issue. Most people were not only ignorant of the situation but hostile toward anyone who raised the issue.

In September 1947, I entered the Southern Baptist Theological Seminary in Louisville. I had just become the pastor of a small rural church in middle Tennessee, to which I commuted on weekends. One Sunday morning, I expressed in a sermon the wrong we were guilty of, as a Christian church and as a nation, in our treatment of the Negro. That night one of the pillars of the community told me: "The KKK is interested in you, boy." The man who said this was not a "bad" man; in fact, he represented the great majority of the church people.

In the ensuing years I have learned that one cannot separate brotherhood from all other phases of personal religious living. A Christian cannot so much as say the Lord's Prayer without bumping up against this fundamental matter of racial justice, for its opening words are "Our Father." We are all—black or white—children of a common Father.

Some of the greatest hypocrisy in the contemporary church is in the area of evangelism. There are churches that send buses, in the name of evangelism, to pick up people to bring them to the church—a worthy thing to do—but studiously avoid nearby black communities and white communities where the economic level is not up to their own. In order to avoid the poor whites, these churches may establish a mission to take care of them. But evangelism becomes a mockery when it is concerned, not with the redemption of *all* men, but with those of our own choosing. It violates the great commission at the very heart of the church's existence: "Go ye into *all* the world and preach the gospel to *every* creature. . . ." The church cannot say to a black person or to a poor white: "God loves you. We want you to be saved, but we do not want you in our church." Even on the most rudimentary basis of Christian understanding, this practice is a sacrilege.

Christians should know that love is personal. Condescending paternalism is not Christian love. Segregationists often say: "I love the Negro. I am willing for him to have just as good a house, just as good a car, just as good an education, just as nice clothes, *but* I don't want anything to do with him personally." Such an attitude is a gross misunderstanding of the universal and personal characteristic of Christian love.

If it were not so pathetic, it would be comical how racists use the Bible to buttress their ideas of segregation and racial superiority. Often people who have been members of the church for half a century see no contradiction between segregation and the Christian Faith. Such people talk about Christianity in terms of the first century, but do not apply it to the twentieth. They read and teach the story of the Good Samaritan—a classic exposé of racism haloed by religious snobbery—with great enthusiasm. It never occurs to them that if they applied the dynamic expressed in this story to contemporary expressions of racial prejudice, they would have to give up their racist ideas. The biblical teachings on racial justice are not seen as relevant for twentieth-century America.

14

One cannot read the Bible, even devotionally, without seeing the contradiction between enforced racial separation and biblical teachings. According to Amos, the Lord asks: "Are you not like the Ethiopians to me, O people of Israel?" (Amos 9:7). The biblical record says that the man who lifted Jeremiah from his cistern prison was an Ethiopian. In ancient Israel, there were many nationalities that wanted to be grafted into the tree of Israel and become sharers in the covenant. Their great concern was that they would not be treated as full persons and assimilated into the life of Israel. This concern called forth these searching words:

> Let not the foreigner who has joined himself to the Lord say, "The Lord shall surely separate me from his people. . . ." And the foreigners who join themselves to the Lord, to minister to him, to love the name of the Lord, and to be his servants . . . these will I bring to my holy mountain, and make them joyful in my house of prayer; . . . for my house shall be called a house of prayer for *all* peoples (Isaiah 56:3-7).

The New Testament tells of the cowardice of Peter, who was willing to eat with the Gentiles until certain prominent Jerusalem churchmen arrived, when he removed himself to another table. Paul rebuked him to his face for his hypocrisy. Such an integrated meal was doubly difficult for the Jews because of dietary practices and the belief that Gentiles were unworthy. But Paul was championing a Christianity that was universal in nature. His indictment of Peter has much to say to the contemporary church. So, too, Jesus' treatment of the Samaritan woman is very significant. To her Jewish contemporaries she was of the wrong race, the wrong religion, the wrong sex, and, over and above that, a moral vagabond. But Jesus leaped over all of these artificial barriers to treat her as a person with dignity and respect.

Our racial attitudes affect everything from prayer to politics. What passes for Christian faith is often no more than a folk religion that uses the Bible to buttress segregationist customs and mores. The Southern mystique is buttressed by Fundamentalism, which consists of biblical literalism, puritan piety (at least in public), and an other-worldly hope. After one Sunday service in Birmingham, a man came up to me accusingly and said: "You have no right to come down here and change our way of life." For this person, it was not Christ who determines

15

what is right, but what the majority of the people think. Ultimate ethical questions are irrelevant: what matters is not what is right but who has the power to say what is right.

Sooner or later the Southern minister who would try to change this Southern mystique must face the sad reality that most of his peers cannot be counted on for support. Indeed, most of them are prisoners in their own ecclesiastical houses. As the struggle in Birmingham intensified I became increasingly aware that the decisive force would not be the Klan or the White Citizen's Council or the John Birch Society or any other extremist group, left or right. Rather, I would lose out to the cautious deacons and ministers—respected and moderate in all things—who put a pseudo-peace and the counting of noses above the truth of Christ.

I do not tell the story of the events in Birmingham to embarrass any person or to heap ignominy on the First Baptist Church. Indeed, I have a deep feeling of Christian love for the people who remain there. One cannot long minister to a people without becoming emotionally involved with them. My purpose in telling this story is to encourage other churches and ministers—wherever they are—who will be embroiled in the effort to secure racial justice. I believe that the incidents surrounding the racial struggle in the First Baptist Church of Birmingham form a microcosm of a larger whole. There is no way to prevent the coming of racial justice for the black people apart from the destruction of us all. I could hope that the Christian church, long tardy in its response to this elemental matter of justice, could assume in the days ahead the role of leading in the fight for equal dignity and worth of all men. I could hope that the church would never again say "separate but equal," but "equal!"

1

If there is no broad basis of fact beneath my assumptions in the life of this congregation, this pastorate will certainly be disastrous. (Inaugural Sermon, September 22, 1968)

A New Ministry and a New Minister

I

The haunting and tragic events that form the heart of this story cannot be understood without some knowledge of the recent history of the First Baptist Church of Birmingham, Alabama. At the time of the racial explosion in September 1970, the church was ninety-eight years old. For the first fifty years of this century, the church had had three pastors. These were stable and prestigious years, but when the last of that triumvirate resigned in 1953, a new era began, which is not yet over. In the next fifteen years there were six pastors. An element had arisen within the church that was consistently hostile to the minister. While I served as the pastor of First Baptist, I heard several of my predecessors dissected — none too kindly — by some members. This one couldn't do this, that one couldn't do that. This one "couldn't preach"; that one "wouldn't visit"; one was "too sociable"; one was "too evangelistic"; another was "not evangelistic enough." Some of my predecessors had left under great duress.

A new era in the struggle for racial justice began in May 1954 with the Supreme Court decision regarding desegregation

17

of public facilities. To the credit of the First Baptist Church it adopted two months later, under the leadership of its young pastor, a policy that no one would be denied the privilege of worship because of race, color, or national origin. With this decision, an exodus of the members began, and the pastor was criticized for this. Whereas there were more than 3600 members in 1953, fifteen years later the membership was less than half that figure.

In 1963, Birmingham experienced its racial convulsion. The civil rights movement was gaining tremendous momentum. Under the leadership of Dr. Martin Luther King, Jr., who had begun his work in Montgomery a few years before, the downtown churches were "tested" on Easter Sunday 1963. Significantly, First Baptist Church seated the black worshippers that came as they would seat anyone else, true to its resolve made nine years before. National television cameras showed the pastor of the First Baptist Church shaking hands with the blacks. Wire services flashed the picture around the world. Again, this was the occasion for many people to leave the church, and prompted cruel harassment of the pastor until he resigned a few months later.

When my immediate predecessor resigned, after only eighteen months as pastor, a crisis of identity faced the church. With a declining membership and budget, with fewer young people, the church was aware that something was desperately needed to reverse the process. But what should the church do? More importantly, what should the church be? During the eight months prior to my coming, without a pastor, a committee of lay people studied the situation intensively. Consideration was given to moving the church to Mountain Brook, the most affluent suburban community in Birmingham. There were problems with this course. It would be very expensive to build the facilities needed, and there was a question of whether the entire membership would go along if the church was relocated. Another option was for the church to remain where it was and minister to the downtown community. This occasioned some soul-searching on the part of the committee. They were quite familiar with the past response of the church to the matter of racial confrontation and integration. They were aware that directly across the street from the church was a large government housing project that had been recently integrated. They

18

were keenly conscious that the membership had halved in fifteen years, and that of the eighteen hundred members on the roll, only seven hundred participated in the life of the church, and approximately two hundred fifty manned ninety percent of the places of leadership and contributed about fifty percent of the budget.

There were some who thought that the way to recover former strength was to do the same thing that had always been done, but to do it with more vim and vigor. Many members had little or no awareness of the new cultural and community developments that had transpired in recent years.

Against this background the committee concluded that the church must remain downtown and minister to the needs of the people there, while not forgetting its larger ministry to the whole city. Knowing that this was a tremendous venture, the committee made certain that the membership considered carefully the *Commitments* it suggested. First of all, these *Commitments* were presented by a federal judge, the Planning Committee, and several other laymen in the youth and adult Sunday School classes. They were then printed in the church paper. After the congregation was given notice that the *Commitments* would be presented at a given worship service, they were discussed at length. On July 31, 1968, the *Commitments* were adopted unanimously.

This is very significant in the light of subsequent events. The records reveal that there was not a single dissenting vote to the *Commitments* when they were adopted by the church. In fact, a committee member, Dr. Byrn Williamson, a local surgeon, was asked to comment on the spirit in which the church approved the *Commitments*. The congregation's response was so positive that he "made some inspiring comments about . . . future plans as outlined by the Planning Committee Report."

The Planning Committee Report is very significant and far reaching in scope, effect, and understanding. The report was divided into two parts, the first presenting the basic commitments and the second making some proposals by which the commitments could be implemented. Because of the importance of it, the Planning Committee Report is cited here in its entirety:

> The Planning Committee, after extensive study, submits the following commitments and proposals for adoption by the church:

19

Commitments

(1) We, the members of the First Baptist Church, recognize and accept the responsibility of a Baptist Christian ministry in downtown Birmingham. We recognize that the acceptance of this ministry involves, to some extent, giving up the usual concept of a neighborhood family church in favor of a ministry to the special groups around us, such as the medical center, internationals, Y's, Central City, downtown apartment dwellers, deaf, elderly, and so forth.

(2) We give ourselves to that ministry with the full realization that it requires not only our most dedicated efforts, but also requires our giving up some of the fruits of labor which are commonly considered the signs of success.

(3) We accept the fact that our downtown location is not easily accessible to most of the residential areas of our city.

(4) On the other hand, we recognize that there are people in our area who need the love of God as expressed through the church of our Lord Jesus Christ, and a city which needs spiritual leadership.

(5) We believe we cannot abdicate the responsibility of giving what we have of dedication, of leadership, and of love, to the situation immediately around us.

(6) We do not deny our responsibilities to other communities, and other nations and other continents, but we accept, as our primary obligation, downtown Birmingham, and we will direct our efforts, both physical and financial, primarily toward discharging that obligation.

(7) We recognize that much of our membership will be made up of people with an unusual dedication to the cause of Christ and who will continually ask not what "easiest" thing can I do, but what "most important" thing can I do for the church.

(8) Our members may differ in nationality, birth, position, possessions, education, or affinity, but we do not differ in our unswerving desire to be more Christlike; not than any other living soul, but more Christlike today than we were yesterday.

(9) We are maintaining here a small part of God's great democracy, and we ask courtesy and tolerance for all alike. On

20

these stern terms, we invite all who will, whether they be young or old, proud or plain, rich or poor, to partake with us of the love of God, and to give themselves to the task that is before us.

Proposals

We recognize fully the hazards involved in making specific long-ranged commitments and we know that we cannot be rigid in our plans. However, we believe it imperative that a definite direction be established and a target date be set for major steps in our ministry.

We, therefore, make the following proposals:

(1) That we make a firm decision to remain in our present downtown location.

(2) That the church call the best leaders available to form an adequate staff. The staff should consist of a pastor, associate pastor, minister of education, minister of music, youth director, children's worker, social worker, and other staff members as may be deemed necessary.

(3) First priority of the income of the church shall be given to the development of an adequate staff and program; second priority to the general maintenance of the facilities; third, to property payments; fourth, to our outreach, cooperative program, missions, so forth.

(4) That our present facilities shall be maintained in usable condition as reasonably as possible.

(5) That a target date of 1973 be set for the commencement of a major building program to consist of
(a) a new sanctuary—the size to be determined by the projected need at that time;
(b) such other supporting facilities as the ministry requires.

(The present indebtedness of First Baptist Church as of July 31, 1968, is $282,711.13. At the present rate of liquidation, the debt on July 31, 1973, will be $149,179.74.)

(6) That a definite building fund be established and funds solicited from the membership of the church as well as other interested individuals and groups.

21

At the time I was contacted about accepting the pastorate of First Baptist Church in Birmingham, I was serving as minister of the Chevy Chase Baptist Church in Washington, D. C. Like many others across America, I had deep misgivings about Birmingham, but I was tremendously impressed by the quality of the person who first contacted me. Since I indicated that I would be willing to talk with the committee, they came to Washington; and again I was deeply impressed by the members. I asked immediately about the racial situation. With pride, Mr. H. Hobart Grooms, Jr., handed me a copy of the Planning Committee Report. As I read it I was amazed at the insight and the maturity it revealed. I could scarcely believe that a church anywhere—least of all in Birmingham, Alabama—could understand that there were measures of success other than statistics. I found it incredible that a church would be willing to lose its life in order to minister to a community.

At the invitation of the Pulpit Committee, I came to Birmingham to preach a "trial" sermon. That afternoon we discussed in great detail the scope and implications of the Planning Committee's Report. After some three hours, we had dinner together and then began to discuss various other matters related to the report. Our discussion lasted again for several hours.

The Planning Committee Report spoke of "all . . . young or old, proud or plain, rich or poor. . . ." It did not say "black and white." However, I was told by the Pulpit Committee that it was the intention of the report that anyone was welcome and that everyone—regardless of color—who had need would be ministered to by the church.

I spoke very carefully to the committee, both in Washington and in Birmingham, pointedly stating that I could not and would not fit the segregationist pattern of the South. I emphasized that I would preach racial justice. My racial views would not be held privately: I would declare them openly and would work for racial justice in the Birmingham community. I was assured by members of the committee that they did not want a racist pastor, nor did they want to follow a segregationist pattern. In short, my understanding was that the church was committed to ministering to the need of any human being— white, black, or otherwise—and that the fruit of such ministry would be welcomed.

On the basis of this Planning Committee Report, as discussed ever so carefully with the Pulpit Committee, I accepted the pastorate of the First Baptist Church of Birmingham.

Let me emphasize here that I do not want to leave so much as an implication that the Pulpit Committee did not mean what it said or that it misled me in any sense. In the succeeding years, I have discovered that most of the members of the committee meant exactly what they said and have backed it up with their lives. They simply did not understand the depth of the racial prejudice of the majority of the members of the First Baptist Church.

II

I began my ministry in Birmingham on September 22, 1968. It was intriguing to ponder the possibility that here was a church in the "heart of Dixie," as the automobile license plates say, really trying to be the church. My ministry began with high hopes that something very significant could be done for the cause of Christ.

My first sermon set forth the basic assumptions upon which I began my ministry. I prefaced them by saying: "It is imperative that the pastor and the people work together from the same basic assumptions. If there is no broad basis of fact beneath my assumptions in the life of this congregation, this pastorate will certainly be disastrous." Little did I know how prophetic this statement was to be. I expressed my delight with the *Commitments* the congregation had made. I began, I told them, with the assumption that the church was prepared to minister to all and that they would be hospitable to the effort to make Christ Lord of all—from prayer to politics; that they would welcome all people regardless of color, class, or condition. In essence, the sermon was a résumé of my conversation with the Pulpit Committee, stated in terms of the gospel. The entire sermon was couched in terms of the principles of the gospel with specific applications not defined.

Usually a new minister is granted a honeymoon period of six months to a year, depending on how rapidly he projects his new program. During this time he can do no wrong in the eyes of the membership. As soon as he begins to suggest that the church chart out new courses of ministry, the honeymoon is abruptly over. I was not given even this luxury. Within my first month in Birmingham I had two visitors sent officially by a large men's

Sunday School class. I was told that what I had preached "may be all right in Washington, D.C., but we are here to remind you that you are now in Birmingham, Alabama." They added that they were sure that I wanted to "get off to a good start and be loved by all the people."

Immediately I called the Pulpit Committee together and informed them of this visit. Various members of the committee gave me in detail a history of this kind of action in the church. Still, the members of the committee were obviously distressed by this turn of events. Their counsel was to ignore it, inasmuch as the church had adopted the *Commitments* unanimously. I made a mental note of reservation as to whether the church as a whole really understood what had been adopted.

The nature of genuine Christian discipleship was the central theme of some of the first sermons I preached in Birmingham. In a sermon on "The Role of the Church," the suggestion that the church should be "the spiritual 'home of room enough' to include any person who is a follower of Jesus Christ" brought a strong reaction from a hard-core few. Despite the fact that the universal nature of the church is evident from its very beginning, as shown in Paul's great statement that "there is neither Jew nor Greek, bond nor free, male nor female, for you are all one in Christ Jesus," I was charged with preaching "the social gospel" instead of the Bible.

It was becoming more and more apparent to me that many—how many I did not know—did not understand the spirit of the *Commitments* the church had made, nor the implications of the kind of ministry the *Commitments* called for.

My first "visitors" had intimated that I should preach what the people wanted to hear. A sizable group wanted the pulpit to be an echo of the pew. While the members of the Pulpit Committee had indicated that they wanted a minister who would speak prophetically to the real issues of the day and lead the church to engage itself with these issues, a large number of church members seemed to want no more than a priest to keep the temple fires burning. They wanted a man who could be controlled, who would keep everybody happy.

A significant factor in the emergence of criticism was the expansion of the community ministries that the Woman's Missionary Society had begun before I came to the church. The very fact that the lay leadership had already begun these programs underscored for me the sincerity of the people and the

24

integrity of the *Commitments*. One of the persons instrumental in launching this work in the community was Miss Betty Bock, the national director of the Young Women's Auxiliary of the Southern Baptist Convention, who was working voluntarily in these ministries as a member of the church. Her work was so excellent and received such enthusiastic praise by the church at that time that I began a year-long effort to persuade her to join the staff as the Minister of Youth.

One of these ministries (which were all integrated) was a tutoring program designed to help the children of the inner city with their studies. These children were not only poor economically, but even poorer in motivation. The school they attended was two blocks from the church. Our trained personnel would meet with them two afternoons a week for two hours at the church. The principal of the school told us that this ministry was most helpful to the children.

Another effort was begun to aid the large number of people in the urban area—most of them black—who could not read or write. A warm human interest story emerged out of this ministry. Five black illiterates were found working at a lumber yard. The Jewish owner, Mr. J. B. Mazer, asked Mr. W. B. Rogers, Jr., what the people from First Baptist Church were doing with his employees. Mr. Rogers explained that we were trying to help people in every possible way, and one of our ministries was to teach people to read. Mr. Mazer was so impressed that he wrote a letter to the editor of the Birmingham *News:*

> In my experience I have rarely seen any supposed religious person pledge himself to the betterment of his fellowman without any other benefit than to the heart. . . . I cannot contain my admiration; and so in the small measure of this letter, I want to publicly thank them for being true Christians.

He sent the church a check for $250 to help in this ministry.

Birmingham has an expanding medical center that draws internationals from all over the world. A ministry was begun to help these people. Each Monday evening a dinner was provided for them, and, under the skilled supervision of our leadership, they were taught conversational English and aided in their understanding of America. An average of fifty to sixty, representing twenty to twenty-five nations, came each week.

All these ministries were in line with the spirit and purpose of the *Commitments* that the church had adopted. My goal was to

25

strengthen and expand these ministries and add others. To do this, a capable staff was necessary. The first year of my ministry was given over to understanding the mind-set of the people, the needs of the church and the community, and securing a staff in the light of these considerations.

One of the results of these developing ministries was to make the membership aware of the implications of the *Commitments*. For example, one afternoon, as the black children came into the educational building of the church for a tutoring session, a member of long duration said to me: "I had no idea that we would have these black children come *here.*" There was a growing uneasiness over this involvement. The ministries did not yet come under judgment, but their results began to raise the haunting specter of racial integration of the church. Community leaders, however, were excited by the ministry of the church.

This queasiness on the part of some members was reflected in the budget campaign in the fall of 1968. The long-range program, as stated in the *Commitments*, called for an enlarged staff to lead the church in expanded ministry. This required a sizable increase in income; but when the campaign ended, we were $41,000.00 short of our budget goal, even though more money was given than ever before. The deficit was almost exactly the amount needed to add the new staff members.

Reaction to this report revealed to me for the first time that the deacons themselves were not in unanimous support of the new ministries. One deacon stated that "there is a lack of communication on the part of some of our membership as to what the church is trying to do." Nevertheless, the deacons voted unanimously on January 20, 1969, to "ask the membership to help raise $41,739.00 to subscribe the full budget." When this special fund drive was recommended to the church by the deacons, the Budget Committee, and the Finance Committee, it was adopted unanimously. These additional funds were subsequently raised and the church settled down in relative harmony.

This harmony was shattered in the first week of April 1969. Dr. Foy Valentine, Executive Secretary-Treasurer of the Christian Life Commission of the Southern Baptist Convention, came to lead the church in the Crusade of the Americas, a denomination-wide evangelistic thrust. Dr. Valentine preached winsomely and prophetically, and those who were in favor of the new ministries of outreach responded to him very positively. How-

26

ever, those who were beginning to feel uneasy about the involvement of the church in social ministries spoke very critically about him. I was unaware that there were some in the church who had a negative attitude toward Dr. Valentine already because of an article he had written for a mission magazine that had "stirred the waters." The common theme of the criticism was: "He doesn't preach the Bible; he preaches the social gospel." Here was vivid evidence that there was a cleavage in understanding of the nature and mission of the church.

Two other events added intensity to the growing apprehension. Because the percentage of the membership that was actively involved in the life of the church was low, and had been low for many years, a Membership Committee recommended changing the procedure for accepting new members in April 1969. The new method involved careful counseling with prospective members by the committee and the pastor before they were inducted into the membership. Though this proposal was adopted without opposition, it started some rumors that served to aggravate the fears of those who thought we were moving toward integration. Some felt that this was a ruse by which "the pastor and the Membership Committee can say they have talked with the 'niggers,' and that they are all right and we ought to take them in." Others interpreted it as a safeguard: "By screening new members we can keep the 'niggers' out."

The second event took place in May 1969, when the Woman's Missionary Society sponsored a Missions Emphasis Seminar. Miss Marjorie Jones, director of the society, told the members of the church in promoting it that "we hope to learn what we can do about caring for people right here around our own church. We believe this will get us going with our downtown mission." Dr. C. W. Brister, Professor of Pastoral Ministry at the Southwestern Baptist Theological Seminary in Fort Worth, conducted one of the finest seminars I have ever attended. But there was sharp criticism in the church from those who saw it as another example that we were moving toward the "social gospel rather than winning people to Christ." Again, the conflict was between narrowly conceived evangelism and the Christian gospel, which seeks to win persons to Christian discipleship through ministry to the total man. The fact that we were developing ministries by which to minister to the abysmal distress—social, physical, emotional, economic, educational, cultural—of persons in our community was a sure sign we were not

27

interested in "spiritual" matters. We were, it was said, "not interested in people's souls," only in the "social gospel."

Among the fundamentalist element in the church, an event of some months earlier came to be seen as further evidence that I did not believe in evangelism. Two children, both under twelve, had come seeking baptism. When I counseled with them, I asked them a number of elementary questions about Christianity, which they could not answer adequately. So I suggested that their baptism be postponed for a time, while I counseled further with them. One of the fathers, whom I shall call Mr. Dodd, was incensed at this; and this was later to become an important factor in his opposition.

The charge that I was opposed to evangelism was totally misguided. What I have always opposed — and always will — is the practice, all too common in the South, of baptizing very young children as the fruit of a high pressure revival. There is, of course, no fixed age at which a child is sufficiently mature to choose to follow Christ, but it is necessary that the child who makes a decision to do so understands what he is doing, and is not just responding to group pressure.

On June 1, 1969, the first member of the new staff was called. The Rev. Mack M. Goss came to serve as Associate Pastor. His coming was to give bodily form to the church's resolution to serve in new and fresh ways. From the beginning, Mr. Goss related well to the people, particularly commending himself to the older members of the congregation.

I left for my vacation during the month of July, keenly aware of an ominous undercurrent that, unless corrected, would cause great difficulty in the days ahead.

III

My assessment of the situation was accurate. When I returned from vacation on August 1, I found that the opposition had been working overtime while I was away. The phone rang almost incessantly, carrying the news that during my absence a petition, with two hundred eighty names on it, had been circulated calling for my dismissal. Several members had joined other churches in the city. One caller explained this exodus by saying that "they are afraid about the program." It was said repeatedly that I had misinterpreted the Planning Committee Report; that

28

it did not mean for Negroes to be involved in our church, because the church had not voted to integrate.

I have nothing but contempt for the cowardice that prompts some people in Baptist churches to undermine while the pastor is away. In the name of democratic procedure, many Baptist churches engage in partisan politics that would make the proverbial "smoke-filled rooms" appear pure and tame by comparison.

At the deacons' meeting on August 4, I informed them of what I had heard from numerous callers and suggested that a time be found at the forthcoming deacons' retreat to restudy the *Commitments* of the church. It was the responsibility of the deacons to scuttle the rumors making the rounds by bringing the issues out in the open, enlightening the people and alleviating their fears by providing a correct interpretation of the issues. I pleaded with the deacons to interpret the Planning Committee Report for the congregation in order to make clear whether or not Negroes could be involved in our various ministries and whether, if they presented themselves for membership, they would be received.

In response to my plea, one deacon, long a highly respected leader in the church, who had seen the church in this condition several times before, said: "I simply do not have enough physical energy to go through another church fight." Another deacon, whom I shall call Mr. Brown (not his real name), a fundamentalist lawyer who was to accuse me later of not preparing the church spiritually to face integration, argued against making any statement. "Why should we divide the congregation now? We don't have any Negroes asking for membership. Let's wait until we do have. It is all hypothetical now." My response was that if the deacons did not unequivocally declare their position, as the lay spiritual leaders of the church, the church would be at the mercy of the rumor-mongering racist element.

The discussion that followed revealed that a group in the church who feared integration had compiled a list of four hundred members opposing the stand made by the church, and were demanding that the deacons make a decision that night as to what the church would do. Several deacons voiced resentment at this threat. The chairman stated that "the leadership [of the church] was not only in the pastor, but in the deacons and other leaders of the church." He requested each deacon "to

29

go home and pray about this matter." There was no disposition on the part of the deacons to make a decision on this thorny issue.

The rumors grew with the attendance of Negroes at the worship services on August 17. So bitter had the charges become that the deacons called a special meeting on August 26. The discussion became quite heated immediately. It was said that a group in the church was considering immediate withdrawal if the church did not reconsider its programs and actions regarding the seating of Negroes.

This intimidation prompted Dean Byrd to speak. "Our church has committed itself to receive and seat Negroes if they come to worship; if they are Christian, they should be received . . . for membership. We should be concerned about the lost, no matter the race. . . ."

An older deacon retorted that "the church has never voted to integrate as such."

Federal Judge H. H. Grooms, Sr., replied that "the church has reaffirmed its action three times in fifteen years. The church voted to seat Negroes in 1954, 1963, and again in 1968."

When it was apparent to the deacons sympathetic with the segregationist line that the diaconate as a whole would not be intimidated, they shifted their attack to the pastor. The usual charges were brought against me. One said I "preached too much on social issues." Another reported comments he had heard from members: "Dr. Gilmore has Betty Bock out trying to enlist Negroes as members"; "Dr. Gilmore is out to integrate the church"; "Dr. Gilmore has not sold himself to the membership."

David Bamberg responded, "This same group has led this turmoil in our church every time. If they don't like it here, they should go somewhere else."

After further criticism and more charges that I was responsible for the situation, Mr. Marvin Prude stated: "This session has developed into a trial of the pastor. We are the ones on trial because we have not let ourselves be leaders. Our pastor was called to have freedom in the pulpit." At the request of several of the men that I respond to the charges that had been mentioned, I dealt with each of them,* concluding with a plea that the deacons interpret the Planning Committee Report and

*The text of the response appears as Appendix 1.

30

clarify the position of the church. Dr. Byrn Williamson responded by saying that "sooner or later, we are going to have to decide on the question to integrate or not integrate." He offered the following policy statement:

> In the past, members have not been rejected or accepted on the basis of color or any other physical characteristic. The basis for membership has always been a simple statement by the applicant of faith in Jesus Christ as Savior, and a desire to worship and work with the other members of the church, for the cause of Christ.

> It is recognized that in our culture in the past Negroes have not been considered acceptable socially, and have not applied for membership in the First Baptist Church. Social patterns have changed in the recent past, and it is possible that Negroes will apply for membership in the future. If this does occur, each applicant will be considered, as in the past, on an individual basis and will be neither rejected, nor accepted, because of his color.

> It is recognized that many of our people have deep emotional feelings, both pro and con, concerning the involvement of our church in the racial issue, but it is our belief that the love of Christ is sufficient to encompass us all. We, therefore, make this statement of policy unfalteringly, believing that if our leadership in and ministry to this community is to be meaningful, we must take a position on the vital social issues facing our church, our community, and our nation.

No action, however, was taken on this motion. One deacon's response was that "our rearing is one thing and our Christian conviction another." A young deacon said that "the world knows how this church stands on seating Negroes. This church does not need to make a statement every time a group wants to bring up this matter."

The chairman called on the men to "not add to the problem, but to support the pastor ... so that the church can move forward together." Mr. Harry Baker, Chairman of the Planning Committee, then moved that "we go from this meeting to continue to promote in a positive manner the pastor and program of the church as adopted by the church on the acceptance of the *Commitments* and *Proposals* of the church membership." This motion passed, and the chairman declared that "there will be no change in our process of seating Negroes. Any person who comes to worship will be seated."

31

I felt then—and feel even more strongly now—that, even though the deacons reaffirmed the *Commitments* adopted in 1968, their failure to deal forthrightly with the matter of integration in the way that Dr. Williamson's motion had called for, was a monumental error of tactics. Their indecisiveness intensified the opposition toward the pastor and the church program. Since the *Commitments* were not interpreted, but only reaffirmed, uncertainty about the racial integration of the church increased, only to express itself with a vengeance a short time later. There was further polarization of the church into two camps, each declaring its interpretation of the *Commitments* to be the correct one. At this juncture, through default of the lay leadership, there was no way for the church to express itself as to its understanding of its mission in the light of its prior commitment.

IV

As hostility grew in the church in the fall of 1969, the unquestioned assumption of the majority was that the peace, harmony, and unity of the church were ultimate considerations. The church's purity of life, faithfulness to Christ, and fidelity to the truth were forgotten if they threatened the tranquility of the church. The institutional church as the members wanted it—not the church as Christ intended it—became the ultimate, to be saved even if it meant losing its own soul.

It was said *ad nauseam* that "we need a pastor who can make us love everybody." (Ironically, that was precisely what I was trying to do—love *everybody!*) The element of the church who talked this way wanted a religious pitchman who would be all things to all men without offending any. I recall having lunch with a member of that group. He suggested that I change my ideas regarding the new programs. "We can and will do a lot for you," he said. He made it very clear, however, that if I persisted in championing integrated ministries, my association with the First Baptist Church of Birmingham would not last long.

Many members had already resigned themselves to my becoming the scapegoat of the racist element in the church. There was, however, a growing number determined that this would not be repeated again. They began acting on Christian principle rather than absolutizing the unity of the church. This tension produced agony in all of us. We wanted "to keep the unity of the Spirit in the bond of peace," but not at the expense of denying what is basic to the Christian faith—love and justice for all men.

At this juncture the church called three highly competent people to join the staff—Miss Betty Bock as the Minister of Youth, Mr. Carlisle Driggers as the Minister of Education, and Dr. John Sims as Associate Pastor — Minister of Music. Their coming put us in a position to intensify and enlarge the ministry of the church as set forth in the *Commitments* of 1968. An effort was made by the small fundamentalist element of the church to dictate the theological views that these new staff members must hold, particularly the Minister of Education and Minister of Youth. At the session when Dr. Sims and Miss Bock were called, these questions were asked: "Do they believe in the blood?" "Do they believe the whole Bible is the Word of God?" "Do they believe in Christ's atonement?" "Do they believe in soul-winning?" Such questions served as clues to me—and to some deacons as well—that those who opposed the church's programs and its pastor were gaining strength. Everyone on the staff could have answered all of these questions positively. The fundamentalists, however, insisted that *their* methods and understanding of these matters be followed. Even though the questioners were assured the two people did answer these questions affirmatively and did believe, they voted against their coming.

With the addition of the new staff, the church took an upswing, and the servant-minded of the membership were encouraged. The Mission Action Committee of the Woman's Missionary Society stepped up its community involvement. Enthusiastically, Mrs. W. B. Rogers, Sr., reported to the church in October 1969 that the women had been busy in the total church program, "in visitation, working in the Baptist hospitals, tutoring young people, aiding in work with disadvantaged children, conversational English work with internationals, literacy work, and specific prayer groups." The significance of such involvement is that it revealed a persistent determination to minister, even in the face of a growing hostility.

In September, my wife and I invited the church family to our home for an open house that had become an annual tradition for us. Though many came, it was noticeable that a certain segment of the church did not. Even so, a wonderful sense of unity could be observed among those who were there.

As the reaffirmation of the *Commitments* in August became known in the church, several began to transfer their membership to other churches in the city. A few instances symbolized rejection of the program and stance of the church. But there was also movement in the other direction: several joined First Baptist Church from other churches in the city *because* of the stance and program. The ministry and position of the church was becoming known in the city.

It is usual for Southern Baptist churches to engage in the raising of the budget for the upcoming year in the late fall. Because the new staff members had just arrived and had not had a chance to get their programs underway, and in order not to conflict with other programs in November and December, I recommended that the stewardship program be postponed to January. This budget was the largest in the history of the church, reflecting the desire to serve more effectively in the inner city. This budget was recommended to the church by both the deacons and the Finance Committee, and adopted *without opposition* in January 1970.

This was a false reading of the situation, however. Many of the opposition refused to pledge to the budget and began to withhold their money. It is a fact of church life that the financial condition of the church is used by many laymen to judge the success or failure of the minister. Withholding funds is one devastating way in which people express displeasure with the minister. The financial boycott was intensified as the church sought to perform its mission in the succeeding months.

At the deacons' meeting in February 1970, I stated that because of the evident withholding of funds, First Baptist Church was near a crossroads, and I asked the deacons to set an example for the church to follow in both attitude and sacrificial stewardship. The chairman also spoke out of deep concern, saying that "it will take the laymen of the church to get the job done."

All pleas were ineffectual and it became necessary to revise the budget downward. At a meeting of the deacons called for this purpose later in February, the first open expression to scuttle the new program was made. A motion was made to veto the proposed two new staff positions—the Social Worker and Children's Director—and the proposed new programs from the original budget. (At the next deacons' meeting the man who made this motion said that he had meant "until money is available for new employees and programs." But his actual motion—without the explanation—expressed the sentiments of the opposition.) The motion lost. An amended budget was recommended to the church and passed *without opposition.* The financial boycott, however, would continue, with the intent of causing the church program to collapse, the pastor to be blamed, and subsequently dismissed.

Clearly, a strong commitment marked those who wanted the church to be a servant-body. Many of them gave far more than they had pledged; several even gave a double tithe. These people insured that the financial boycott would not succeed in destroying the church program. By this magnificent action they thwarted what the opposition had thought was an unbeatable strategy and encouraged the progressive group who were determined to make the church a vital, redemptive agent in the city.

This demonstration of commitment, however, stiffened the resolve of the opposition to rid itself of the pastor in a direct manner. Such an effort, with a vengeance, was not long in coming.

V

While the financial struggle was taking place, a significant event took place on February 1, 1970. Negro children, most of whom had been involved in our tutoring program for more than a year, attended our Sunday School that day. (It is interesting to note that this was the same day the Federal Court had ordered the end of Birmingham's dual school system.) There had been Negro children who visited the Sunday School before, but after one visit they would not return. This time it was different: they began returning in ever larger numbers on succeeding Sundays.

Moreover, in the middle of March Negro adults began to attend both our Sunday School and worship services. The ministry of the church to the community was beginning to reap visible response. Our ministry was sufficiently authentic to evoke a response from the Negro families to whom we had ministered.

The reaction of the opposition was immediate. We lost six families to neighboring churches, and they made very plain their reason for leaving. One of these women who left said angrily to a group: "I am not going to let my children attend Sunday School with 'niggers.' " The appearance of Negroes in Sunday

35

School and church supplied the arsenal of the opposition with new fire-power. Here was vivid, concrete evidence of what they had feared from the beginning. The new programs that had been undertaken would mean the integration of the church. There was no understanding on their part of the universal mission of love to which Christ had commissioned his church. Many of those who left had been serving in our nursery and elementary departments, so that these were seriously crippled.

I have been asked frequently: "Why didn't the Negroes sense the hostility and cease to come?" The reason is that the majority of those in places of leadership, especially the educational leadership, were delighted, not offended, by their coming and treated them with dignity and respect. It was evidence to them that our efforts to be the church were succeeding.

I was advised by the segregationists to stop these ministries immediately. It was not worth upsetting the church, they argued. "It takes time for this kind of thing to be done." When asked how long, they had no answer, except to affirm that it was not worth splitting the church. In a committee meeting one segregationist stated that "we ought to tell the Negro people not to come." Asked if he would tell them, he replied that "since the pastor and staff got them to come, they can tell them not to come." I responded that I could not tell Negro people not to come to First Baptist Church without crucifying my conscience and violating everything I knew about the Christian faith. His only reply was to say that "it is tearing the church apart."

It is part of the life-style of segregationist churchmen to fear discord like the plague. Controversy is the unpardonable sin. They could not understand why I would risk causing controversy because of my commitment to a Christian principle. This was totally alien to their notion of a minister as a man of peace. Indeed, one of the deepest tragedies in the racial struggle of the churches today is the revelation it gives of the common image of the minister held by those in the pew. He is not to follow Christian principle, no matter how kindly; he must not be prophetic, for this will disrupt. It really does not matter whether or not the minister is a man of truth, only that he "keeps the peace." This, of course, means, if not embracing the segregationist pattern, at least not challenging it.

The segregationists were encouraged by the comments of some other Baptist ministers in the community. One was quoted to me by several persons as saying that I "should have taken at least five years to integrate the church." He himself has been in his pastorate far more than five years. To him, it is "a mark of maturity to recognize what you cannot change." With this philosophy his church goes unchallenged as a bastion of racial segregation.

In fact, the church, unless it violated its conscience, had no choice in the matter of Negro attendance at its meetings. We did not set the timetable; we had merely ministered creatively and helpfully. Now we were seeing the fruits of that ministry: an honest response from the Negroes to whom we had ministered. It is a curious paradox that some of those who were most concerned about evangelism, and who accused me of not being "evangelistic," were most adamantly set against receiving this evangelistic fruit of our ministry. Apparently their evangelistic concern was colored white.

What the segregationists—both within and without the church—ignored or overlooked was that integration was not the real issue. There was no effort—either on my part or on the part of the progressive members of the church—to integrate the church as an end in itself. What was at stake was *the very nature of the church.* What concerned us was that *the church be the church;* that the church be faithful to its charter from Christ. What was at stake was whether the church was to be an exclusive religious country club requiring its members to be white, or to be the body of Christ preaching *and* practicing an inclusive and universal love toward all God's people. We were trying to minister to human need; the face of need knows no color. Integration was the natural by-product of such love, of a church being faithful to its own nature.

It is failure to understand this that causes Christians to think that their church can be Christian while practicing racial exclusivism. The truth is that the deliberate attempt to make the church "all white" or "all black" or "all anything" is a contradiction in terms. To be true to itself it must embody the spirit of Christ, Lord of the church, who loves all men equally.

In the spirit of the *Commitments* it had adopted in 1968, First Baptist Church had sought to minister to human need wherever it was found. The color or condition of the person in need did not matter. Now—after a year and a half—a response from the black people had been secured. It was impossible to minister in the name of Christ and to show his love in personal

37

action without calling forth such a response in due time. To have tried to prevent it by ministering to whites only would have violated the Great Commission to go into *all* the world and preach the gospel to *every* creature.

Segregationists, however, can interpret this commission in a strange and contradictory manner. During the financial campaign of early 1970 a segregationist deacon urged that "we cut out these new-fangled programs and give this money to the Cooperative Program for world missions." He saw no contradiction at all in his attitude. He was all for sending missionaries to Africa to convert the black heathen, but "new-fangled programs," designed to reach the blacks and others in an integrated community across the street from the church, were bad. Such is the pattern of many churches in America. That kind of hypocrisy cannot continue without the church's incurring the contempt of men, and—what is far more serious—the judgment of God.

VI

As these significant events swirled around the leadership of the church, and the insistent demands from the segregationist element of the church that "something be done about it" continued, it became inevitable that the deacons would have to face up to the direction the church would take and what disposition would be made of the racial issue in the life of the church.

At the deacons' meeting on April 6, 1970, concern was expressed over the loss of members to other churches in the city. (There seemed to be no awareness that several people had joined our church from other churches in the city.) It was suggested that a study be made of the causes of the members' leaving, in spite of the fact that several of those who left had made their reason for leaving very clear: the presence of the Negroes in our church life.

An unholy alliance was formed at this time within the deacon body between Mr. Brown, the fundamentalist lawyer, who took exception to the pastor's supposed "liberal" theology, and Mr. Dodd, a segregationist. They tried to force the chairman of the deacons to call a special deacons' meeting while I was away on a preaching mission, in order to discuss my relationship with the church. As a matter of principle, the chairman refused to call such a meeting. He promised, however, that it would be done when I returned.

The meeting was called on April 14. To the surprise of many of the deacons, there were many non-deacons present, among them the two men who had visited me shortly after I came to the church to inform me that I was "now in Birmingham, Alabama." All the visitors were asked to leave by the chairman, but a motion to permit them to stay was carried. The chairman then asked that "the meeting be considered an executive session with no discussion with others outside about the meeting." This request was ignored and tragically violated.

For the first time, Mr. Brown openly charged me with theological heresy and biblical unsoundness. He spoke at great length, documenting to his own satisfaction my supposed "liberalism," "humanism," and "unbiblical preaching." Mr. Dodd, who had earlier been offended by my counsel with his young daughter relative to her conversion experience, joined forces with the lawyer. He asked me either/or questions, designed to ensnare me no matter how I answered and charged that I did not believe in child evangelism. A few others, who had no real interest in theology and less knowledge of it, joined in, adding their contention that "if the gospel had been preached the church would not be in such conflict; that the church is not getting Bible preaching, but the social gospel and the opinions of men."

The charges were broadened to embrace other criticisms, expressed with great bitterness. I was seen as the cause of the church's difficulty: I had misinterpreted the *Commitments* made in 1968; I was responsible for people's leaving the church, low morale, money's being withheld, and no new members. Further, I was guilty of not visiting the elderly and shut-ins. "The church can never achieve unity," they said, "under the existing program and pastoral leadership." One man who was withholding his money said that "the church cannot continue because the money is not coming in." He blushed when asked, "Is yours?"

The opposition never so much as mentioned the race issue as the cause for the malaise in the church. When deacons who were in favor of the new program that had been instituted suggested that this was the real issue, not the pastor or his theology, the opposition denied it. Several of the deacons spoke in defense of

39

the pastor and championed our programs. Indeed, they categorically positioned themselves as in favor of an integrated church, and they gave theological and biblical reasons for such a stance. This incensed the opposition.

It became a very hostile session. I felt as if my bones were showing and my mind was being spied upon. The spirit expressed against me was so obviously hostile that when I was asked to speak (I had said nothing during the meeting), the deacon sitting next to me whispered, "Be kind to them, pastor."

I spoke very briefly, trying to be as conciliatory as possible, refuting the false charges that had been made against my theology, my preaching, and pastoral care, and setting forth the motivation for my ministry as trying "to sum up all things in Christ." Once again I stated my understanding of the *Commitments* of 1968, referring to the decision of the deacons in special session in August 1969 that we continue to minister to Negroes. I requested the deacons once more to clarify the *Commitments* to the church.

As the meeting closed a motion was made "that we as deacons rededicate ourselves to God and his teachings and to the ministry of First Baptist Church." Mr. Dodd refused. I sensed at the time that his action was symbolic of the attitude of the opposition.

What went on at the April 14 deacons' meeting soon became common knowledge to the church family, though it was supposed to have been an executive session. Misinterpretations and misinformation were bandied about. The charges that I was biblically unsound and heretical were picked up by those offended by the issue of race. A vicious collusion began to grow between the segregationists and the fundamentalists, who used each other to accomplish their common purpose—the removal of the pastor.

Mr. Brown declared to the deacons—and I have no reason to doubt him—that he had no difficulty with my racial views and that he believed the church should not reject black people. But he entered into a compact with those for whom the whole issue was race, who had no concern about theology, in order to rid the church of a pastor whom he deemed heretical. It was an unholy alliance, even though Mr. Brown stated that the Holy Spirit prompted him to do what he did. Alas! how the Holy

Spirit, who speaks of the Christ, can be appealed to to condone what is at loggerheads with the mind of Christ!

Members continued to join other churches in the city, and members from other churches continued to join our church. More left than came, but it was not a one-way street, as the opposition believed. The breach was widening—much to my sorrow. The Negro children came in ever larger numbers, though in comparison with the total number, they were never a large group. Black adults also continued to attend our Sunday School and worship services.

At the May deacons' meeting, the chairman, Mr. Marvin Prude, indicated that "he would appoint a committee to study, update, clarify, and interpret the 1968 *Commitments and Proposals* of First Baptist Church in light of the experience the church has had since then." The urgency of the fast-moving crisis events is reflected in his letter of May 22 to the members of the committee:

> It is expected that this committee will counsel with the pastor on its work and progress. The importance of the committee cannot be over-emphasized. Therefore, it is expected that you will work diligently and with ordered haste. Expediency should not, however, be sacrificed for a thorough and proper study of the future of First Baptist Church.

The concern and earnestness of the progressive people was very intense. They were as determined that the church would fulfil its mission in line with the commitments made as the segregationists and fundamentalists were determined that it would not. The polarization of the church into these two distinct groups became more obvious with the response made to every new event confronting the church.

2

"In the admission of members, it is desirable that the vote should be unanimous, but if in any instance objection is made, the case shall be referred without debate to the pastor and deacons for investigation and report...." (By-laws, First Baptist Church, Birmingham)

The Moment of Truth

I

For three and a half months, Negroes had been attending various activities of First Baptist Church. On Sunday, May 17, Mrs. Winifred Bryant, one of the Negroes who had been attending, marked on her visitor's card: "I am interested in becoming a member of this church." When I read this I knew that the moment of truth had come.

During the following week I visited Mrs. Bryant, as I did any person who indicated a desire to be a member of the church. She lived two blocks from the church in Central City, a large, integrated government housing project. Her daughter, Twila Fortune, had been in the first group enrolled in our Tutoring Ministry in September 1968, and her other children had been involved in other church activities. The church had been helpful to this family in many ways during this time. Mrs. Bryant's interest in the church had been quickened by authentic Christian ministry expressed in varied ways; it was not something

42

contrived, artificial, or unnatural. She and her family had not been bused from some ghetto across the city. She had seen much evidence to convince her that we meant what we professed. In her Sunday School class she had been accepted as a person and treated with love and respect.

I told her I was delighted that she was interested in becoming a member of our church. After talking with her at great length about her Christian experience and spiritual pilgrimage, we discussed the congregation's reaction. Candidly, I said that many of the members would rejoice—as I would—for her to be a part of our fellowship, but that many might reject her. I apprised her of the two distinct attitudes held by the members and said, "If you feel that you are spiritually and emotionally strong enough to take possible rejection, then come." We prayed together, both of us asking for the guidance of God, and that his will might be done in this decision. I asked her to call me if she had further questions or desired to talk more in detail about the matter. I visited with her two other times—around June 1 and June 15. According to my usual practice, at no time did I put any pressure on her. We were both conscious of and sobered by the historic uniqueness surrounding her decision.

My visits with Mrs. Bryant greatly impressed me. Hers was a transparent sincerity and a humble Christian strength. A divorcee, she was trying to provide for her children by working as a charwoman. She had chosen to work a night shift in order to be home when her children came from school. She was determined to provide for her family because she did not want to be on the welfare rolls. It was obvious that she was a genuinely Christian person with great strength of character, one who would be a blessing to any congregation.

While Mrs. Bryant was deciding whether to present herself for membership, several other things happened in June that added to our difficulty. First, the Building Superintendent resigned. This would have had no bearing on the struggle in the church, except that one of the segregationists reported that the resignation was tendered because the Negro maids were kept from their work one entire morning each week. Because of such interference, attributed to the pastor, he could not do his job. The superintendent had never spoken to me about any difficulty. He did state to a staff member that he was not "going to clean up after 'niggers.' "

The truth is that we tried to indicate to the janitorial staff that they were a real part of the church team. Once a week, prior to our staff meeting, they would join with us for some refreshments and a period of prayer and meditation together. Each staff member, including the maids, took a turn in leading us in a brief period of worship. It was a very meaningful time for us all, never lasting more than thirty minutes, and bound us together in real friendship. The Building Superintendent had been invited repeatedly but would never attend. This "racial incident," as it was interpreted by the segregationists, was further proof that I was determined to integrate the church.

At the June deacons' meeting, Mr. Brown, the fundamentalist lawyer, went to great lengths to extol the virtues of the Building Superintendent and moved that a resolution of appreciation be approved by the deacons. In the face of the rumors attached to his resignation, such action was a slap at the supposed "integrationist" pastor and applauded by both the fundamentalists and segregationists.

A second event that added fuel to the fire also took place at the June deacons' meeting. Mr. Brown, still smarting from the failure of his attack on my alleged biblical unsoundness and theological heresy the previous month, presented a resolution that the deacons go on record disapproving any change pertaining to the Scriptures in the *Baptist Faith and Message*. This doctrinal statement was a live issue in the Southern Baptist Convention at the time. Mr. Brown's resolution failed, but the fact that I spoke against it—on the ground that no doctrinal statement should be absolutized as the rule of orthodoxy—was taken as further proof of my "liberalism."

I have never held a doctrinaire theological liberalism. But because my views regarding racial justice were "liberal"—from the segregationists' viewpoint—I was a liberal to them. The gospel I preached undercut the Southern mystique, with racial segregation at its center, and that was proof positive to them. They did not concern themselves about doctrinal technicalities. And so, the fundamentalists and the segregationists were strengthened in their resolve to rid the church of the pastor.

Furthermore, at this June deacons' meeting the Educational Task Force Committee recommended that the church adopt for fall 1970 the new educational program sponsored by the Sunday School Board of the Southern Baptist Convention. The deacons endorsed it, and their recommendation of it was passed by the church with only two dissenting votes, but there were

44

those who were sure that the new program meant "less Bible training."

Deacons' meetings had become the launching pad for rumors. Whatever the deacons did was the basis for embroidered tales. Approval of the new educational program was viewed by some as fresh evidence that the pastor and staff of the church were not committed to real Bible study, in spite of the fact that the Minister of Education, Carlisle Driggers, had carefully explained the new programs and procedures, and had distributed to the members an explanation of these changes prepared by the Executive Secretary of the Sunday School Board.

At the morning worship service on June 27, Mrs. Bryant presented herself for membership, and her daughter Twila came to profess Christ publicly as her Lord and Savior and to be baptized into the membership of the church. Unlike most Baptist churches, our custom was not to ask the congregation to vote on their acceptance at that time.

The gauntlet was down. There were many eyes filled with tears of joy. Several members openly and unashamedly embraced them. Many members expressed to me their great delight that this day had come, but spoke wistfully of their doubts that the two would be accepted into the membership. There were other eyes squinted in hate, however, and several of the members vilified and harangued me for allowing such a thing to happen. Some were beside themselves in anger.

From this moment on, until the bitter end, I could do nothing right in the eyes of the opposition. Every conceivable method was used to downgrade me as a minister. Hate calls began to come at all hours of the day and night.

I was eating lunch at home when the Birmingham *News* called. A caller had reported to them that "two 'niggers' just tried to join the First Baptist Church. I guess you will want to make something out of that." Mr. Wallace Henley, the *News* Religion Editor, was assigned to write a story, which appeared the next day and was picked up by the major news services and spread across the newspapers of the nation.

The appearance of this story incensed the segregationists and a few of the progressive group. I was accused of using the incident for personal publicity. In fact, during the entire struggle, which was subsequently featured in *Newsweek* twice, *Time*, *The Christian Century*, *The New York Times*, and the

Washington *Post*, I did not initiate any coverage or try to use the news media.

I said earlier that one of the most far-reaching practices in the renewal of the church had been the adoption of a Membership Committee responsible for counseling and guiding candidates for membership, and making certain that each person understood the nature and work of the church and was committed to bring his unique abilities and resources to strengthen its redemptive mission.

The new members were presented on the first Sunday of the month, after they had been in conference with the pastor and the Membership Committee. Since I had already counseled with Mrs. Bryant and Twila, I asked the committee to counsel with them so they might be presented on July 5. Even though another member of the committee had been assigned to visit with them, Mr. Brown took it upon himself to visit Mrs. Bryant and question her at great length about her theological beliefs. After conferences with them, the committee concurred that they should be presented.

During the week between June 27 and July 5, the segregationists launched a telephone campaign to urge all inactive members to be present "to vote against the 'niggers.'" All during the week the rumor mills worked overtime. When I walked into the sanctuary on July 5, I was not surprised at the large attendance. I saw many faces I had never seen before. Obviously the segregationists had done a good job of "getting out the vote." A Baptist church that has forgotten that it belongs to Christ and must order its life in obedience to him can become the most ruthless political machine imaginable. Matters of morals and faith are then decided by the counting of noses. No single dynamic in Baptist life is in greater need of change.

I preached that morning on "Christ and Conflict."* When I had projected my preaching for 1970 the preceding summer while on vacation, I had no idea that this event and this sermon would coalesce on this day. I considered changing the sermon because the title might be misunderstood. But as I went over the sermon that week I could not escape the conviction that I should preach it. Its appropriateness was sobering, confirming my conviction that God uses imperfect human instruments to do his work and causes the obedient minister to become his prophet, declaring his Word. The text for this sermon was Jesus'

*The text of this sermon appears as Appendix 2.

46

statement: "Do not think that I am come to bring peace on earth; I have not come to bring peace, but a sword."

The six candidates for membership were presented, each affirming his commitment to be faithful to Christ through the church. Mrs. Bryant spoke very simply, saying that she would "do her best to be a good member" if she were accepted. When the vote was taken, a majority of the people voted to receive all of the candidates into the membership. However, an older deacon, whom I shall call Mr. Long, objected verbally. According to the by-laws of the church, the matter now had to be referred, without debate, to the pastor and deacons. If after hearing the objection we deemed it invalid, the rejected person could be recommended again and received into the membership, but this time a two-thirds majority, not just a simple majority, was required.

One of the most unforgettably tragic scenes I have ever witnessed transpired after the benediction was pronounced. In controlled silence Mrs. Bryant wept. Twila looked dismayed and stunned. The four white candidates were visibly shaken. Members of the church surrounded the prospective members, embracing them and seeking to console them. As I spoke to the people at the door of the sanctuary as they left, many wept, both men and women, so that they could only grip my hand firmly and nod in response. As Mr. Long passed by me, he said in livid anger: "You have no right to come down here and change our way of life." I replied, "Mr. Long, you shamed Christ and your church today."

The event exploded in the local and national newspapers and media. No doubt the segregationists would have thought twice if they had known how much publicity their actions would get. A local television station asked for an interview on Monday. I expressed my conviction that "the church must be in the forefront, not the rear, of the effort to secure justice and dignity for all men; that the church was the one place under heaven where rich and poor, learned and unlearned, crude and cultured, black and white, should be able to sit side by side because they had one great treasure in common—Jesus Christ; that the church must be Exhibit A of the way the world ought to be." I expressed the hope that the deacons would declare the objection invalid at their next meeting and that the church would accept these persons into the membership. That meeting was already set for July 6.

II

The regular monthly deacons' meeting on July 6 was a bristling and historic session. A large number of people from the church-at-large were in attendance.

From the beginning, the segregationists—with the aid of Mr. Brown—tried to cloak the meeting in secrecy. One segregationist moved that the voting on any motion that evening be by secret ballot, and later, "when the candidates are presented, the vote be in secret." The lawyer moved "that members not speak of the meeting to anyone for report or publication in the news media." During the entire struggle, this dynamic of secrecy was always the first order of business, at the insistence of the opposition. They did not want to vote in any way that would reveal *how* they voted.

I spoke against the effort to block legitimate reporting of what went on, arguing that the world was already watching us:

> If we think that we are going to serve a good purpose by saying—to men who have a legitimate right to know—that we have nothing to say to them, that is not going to stop their reporting, either with their pen or with their voice. It is simply going to be a bad report, and the only conclusion they can draw—or that the world can draw—of what we do is that we are ashamed of what we have done. . . . I think we will make a serious mistake, because we do not have the right or authority to say to anybody, "you cannot speak."

Concern about the news media grew out of a newspaper article the week before and the coverage given that very day to the events of Sunday. The Birmingham *News* reporter had attended the worship services. Mr. Long, the deacon who had objected to receiving the Negroes, was incensed, because he thought that I had given his name to the reporter. I told him I had not; that the reporter had been present at both worship services the preceding day, but not at my invitation; and that he had gotten the name of Mr. Long from a member of the congregation. I rehearsed the sequence of events by which the *News* had been tipped off to the event of the week before. When the vote was taken, the motion to vote by secret ballot carried, but the motion to prevent speaking to the news media failed.

Mr. Long said he had objected to receiving the Negroes into membership for two reasons: (1) the procedure of presenting the candidates had been improper and (2) the church had not

48

voted to integrate. The chairman asked me to respond to the charge that improper procedure had been followed. I cited that portion of the church by-laws pertaining to receiving members:

> In the admission of members, it is desirable that the vote should be unanimous, but if in any instance objection is made, the case shall be referred without debate to the pastor and deacons for investigation and report, and should the church, upon hearing their report, regard the objection as invalid or unscriptural the applicant may be received by a two-thirds vote.

My understanding of this was that it was not *necessary* but *desirable* for a person to have a unanimous vote in order to be received into the membership. In other words, a majority vote gave membership—otherwise why did the rules state that if an objection was made, it would later take a two-thirds vote? Thus, a mere vote against accepting a person as a member did not constitute an objection. The opposition had held that a vote against was an objection; I argued that an objection must be verbalized, and emphasized that the by-laws did not say that unless a person received a unanimous vote he was rejected. The chairman ruled invalid the objection that there was improper procedure in presenting members, but stated that the second objection could be considered.

The objections cited by the several persons who spoke during the lengthy session boiled down to the same thing: admitting Mrs. Bryant and Twila would split and ruin the church. Typical was a letter from a member about integration, which was read by Mr. Long. Using the same tired, cliché-ridden language, the writer expressed racism of the crudest sort.

The scapegoating process was very much in evidence. The pastor was to blame for the troubles besetting the church. Rather than raising the question of the rightness or wrongness of it, rather than grappling with the issue in the light of the Christian faith, the rationale of the opposition went no further than this: There was difficulty, difficulty was bad, and the pastor was to blame for it.

Again, the objection was voiced that the church had not been "properly prepared to accept integration." What might have been considered "proper" preparation is problematical. Any pastor in a time of crisis agonizes in his soul about what he might have done or not done. I was painfully aware of these haunting questions, but I was also aware that I was not the first pastor to lead the church to face up to racial justice. A number of pastors before me had worked at it with integrity. To act as if this experience had stealthily slipped up on the church for the first time now was to ignore the recent history of the church, which was full of encounter with the stark reality of the racial issue. Three times in its recent past—1954, 1963, and 1968—it had positively affirmed that it would minister to Negroes. Each time it had lost members, but it had confronted the issue with increasing earnestness and determination.

At the deacons' retreat in September 1969, this issue had been at the center of our discussion—sometimes heatedly. For that retreat I had written a lengthy paper on the nature of the church. Grappling with this central theme had confronted us in every session with the matter of the racial integration of the church.

Some of the ablest men in the Southern Baptist Convention had spent time among us to help the church be the church in facing up to the demands of ministering to all men. Dr. C. W. Brister had addressed himself brilliantly to this matter in a seminar designed to help the church to minister. Dr. Foy Valentine had spent a week in the church preaching and lecturing on various aspects of this reality. Dr. Findley Edge, one of the most informed and reliable leaders in church renewal, had led the church to confront this reality, both publicly and in private conversations.

I had dealt with this matter from many perspectives in preaching. Only one sermon prior to July 5 had dealt entirely with the race issue, but many sermons had spoken about the nature of the church, the universality of Christian love, and the Christian understanding of justice. These themes were not dealt with theoretically or academically, but applied to our own situation. Many had heard and responded positively. Many heard but responded negatively. I am convinced that, in large measure, people see and hear what they want to see and hear.

As the meeting progressed I was asked to give a brief résumé of the events leading up to the Negroes' presenting themselves for membership. When I finished with my overview, I was charged with having "hounded" Mrs. Bryant, and with visiting her repeatedly. I explained that I had visited her three times, and if that was "hounding," then I had hounded some of the sons and daughters of those present, for I had spent more time with them than I had with Mrs. Bryant. I stated that "in sincerity of purpose, believing that the church meant what it said—that it wanted to minister to the community—I did invite this woman to come, and she, of her own volition without any pressure from me, made the decision that she made."

After hearing at great length the objections and my role in the Negroes' coming, it was moved and seconded that "the deacons recommend for acceptance the candidates for church membership." A segregationist succeeded in amending this motion so that the vote was on each of the six members individually. The motion as amended passed. *All of the candidates would be recommended for membership.*

It is instructive to note the breakdown of the deacons' vote on the respective candidates. The four white candidates received the following vote: 31-1, 31-1, 30-2, 27-5. Mrs. Bryant was recommended by a vote of 18-14; Twila by a vote of 19-13. It is hard to avoid the conclusion that race had something to do with this, though it was increasingly denied as the struggle unfolded. The white woman who received the lowest vote had been quoted that day in a newspaper article as saying: "If Mrs. Bryant and her daughter are not good enough for membership, then I don't want to be a member." Apparently this statement affected some deacons' votes.

When the chairman asked me if I would like to comment, I made the following recommendations:

1) That a church conference be called for the express purpose of discussing and considering the acceptance of Negroes as members of First Baptist Church.

2) That the church conference be called on Wednesday night, July 29, and continued on as many subsequent Wednesday nights as may be necessary for the thorough consideration and discussion of the subject. The conference on each Wednesday night shall last no longer than one hour, and the chairman of the deacons shall be moderator.

3) That Mrs. Bryant and Twila Fortune remain under the watchcare of the church [all the rights and privileges except voting rights] pending a decision by the congregation.*

*This was subsequently changed to include all six candidates.

51

No man alive takes the business of being pastor more seriously than I do. My purpose, Ladies and Gentlemen, is to build up and not to tear down, but, as several here have said tonight, the ultimate criterion is that we seek to know the mind of Christ. I do not want to be one who rams something down somebody's throat, although some apparently interpret this that way.

I want to ask respectfully that you consider the recommendation I have made to you in order that the air of hostility, and suspicion, and misrepresentation, and ugliness, and even hatred may abate, and we may talk and pray, and talk some more and pray some more, and open our minds to the Scriptures again and again,—and talk some more and pray some more—until no one could think that fairness, and equity, and honor, and good will, and fair play have not been evidenced from the housetops.

I want this congregation to make up its mind. I will be leaving this week to attend the Baptist World Alliance meeting in Tokyo, Japan. I want this congregation to make up its mind, so that when I return six weeks hence, perhaps in the grace of God we shall know what it is, in order that all of us together, pastor and people, can chart our future course.

I felt that it was imperative that no hasty judgment be made. It seemed to me it would be salutary for the church, under the lay leadership, to decide the matter relative to the acceptance of Negroes while I was away. With prayer, Bible study, and discussion, the issue itself could be dealt with. With the pastor gone, the people might better be able to concentrate on the issue instead of on the personality of the pastor who many felt was responsible for the integration issue.

Someone asked whether the issue of integration as such could be dealt with, rather than the two specific black candidates? This was precisely the sense of my recommendation, and I repeated that I thought it would be a mistake for the church to make a hasty decision that would lead one group to think that the other was taking advantage of the situation.

The question was then posed whether we would vote on the Negroes the following Sunday. So that the church would not give even the appearance of racism, I recommended that we not "vote in the whites but exclude the blacks" on the following Sunday. "That would be just another slap in the face of the blacks," I said, "and, whether we mean to or not, it would be a racist action." The chairman stated that no vote would be taken the following Sunday.

The recommendation passed, and the meeting ended with a definite plan of action agreed to by both sides. I left two days later to attend the Baptist World Alliance in Tokyo, after which I would continue on a trip around the world. I had some misgivings about leaving, but the key leadership of the church urged me to do so. We agreed that they were capable of handling any emergency that might arise. Little did we realize that within three weeks, at the quarterly church conference on July 22, while I was halfway around the world, a carefully planned attempt to fire me would be made by the segregationists.

III

After the July 6 deacons' meeting relations between the two sides deteriorated steadily. I have relied on several well-informed members and on the professional staff for insights into what happened while I was overseas.

The deacons' recommendation of the Negroes for membership had infuriated the opposition, as had been apparent from the comments that could be heard when the meeting was over. As the July 22 quarterly church conference approached, ugly rumors were bandied about with increasing frequency. First, the Nominating Committee's work would be sabotaged. The by-laws required this committee, which was responsible for recruiting leadership for the various ministries of the church, to bring its report to the July church conference, so that the leaders who were chosen could be trained for service in the new church year, which began on October 1.

Some said I would be asked to resign; others had concluded that I must be fired, since I would not resign. Still others spoke of planned motions to fire the pastor and the Minister of Youth, Betty Bock, or even the entire staff. The opposition felt that they would have a better chance of sacking the pastor without considering the whole staff.

The air was electric with apprehension. Since a stenographer transcribed what went on at the meeting, an accurate account of the actions taken is available. I have drawn on this record and on the impressions of those present in relating the chain of events that follows.

53

After the meeting was opened with prayer, a telegram I had sent from Tokyo to the chairman of deacons was read: "My prayers are with you and the church. Let us be faithful to Christ and he will give us victory. With love." In the light of what happened that night, the telegram turned out to be rather ironic.

The rumors that had been making the rounds now became stark reality. After the report of the Nominating Committee had been read, the segregationists presented an opposition slate, in a bold bid to capture the leadership of the Sunday School and control of the Staff, Finance, and Long Range Planning Committees. Mr. H. Hobart Grooms, Jr., a young lawyer who was to play a creative role in the entire struggle, moved that this rump slate be considered as an amendment to the Nominating Committee's report, thus requiring a separate vote. He urged defeat of the amendment, pointing out the diligent efforts of the duly elected committee. But the amendment carried. The segregationist opposition now controlled the major levers of power in the church.

This was but an omen of things to come. Ordinarily, the report of the Nominating Committee was the major item of business at a July conference. With this item now taken care of, a motion was made to adjourn the meeting. The majority, however, voted to stay in session. "Now is the hour," reflected my wife; "it is about to happen." In the face of the swirl of rumors Joyce—like many others in the church—had prayed prior to the meeting for strength to endure. It was an appropriate prayer.

The opposition had planned very carefully for this coup. For example, they made a motion to include those they had already chosen to serve on the tally committee to represent them, and these had been assigned aisles. These persons counseled their followers on how to vote on each motion as they handed out the ballots. Moreover, all of the motions made by the segregationists were read from cards prepared prior to the meeting.

When the moderator called for new business, a former high school football coach rose to declare that:

> When a football team has a losing season, the coach is blamed. The way this is corrected is to get a new coach. First Baptist Church has had a losing season. People are leaving the church, finances are down, attendance is down. The way to correct this is to get a new coach.

54

He then moved that "the position of Pastor and the position of Youth Director be declared vacant as of this date, that salaries without allowances be continued through September 30, and that the Treasurer and Financial Secretary be instructed that the church will not be responsible for any debts or expenses incurred after this date."

The moderator ruled the motion out of order and referred it to the deacons for consideration and a later report to the church. An elderly and influential businessman, a staunch segregationist whom I shall call Mr. Adams, appealed the ruling of the chair—and won. In supporting the motion to discharge his pastor and a talented youth worker, this long-time deacon remarked that:

> Every man is entitled to his opinion and every group is entitled to its opinion, but when those opinions begin to drive wedges between friends who have been friends for thirty or forty years, and when those opinions begin to separate mothers and fathers from their children and their grandchildren, and when it separates a church right down the middle, then there is something wrong with those ideas, because I do not believe that the type of religion we have been receiving is the type of religion that I have been accustomed to, and many other people around this church feel this way.

> I, like you, regret this decision this evening because these people are wonderful people. But there are certain privileges that we have here and we do not want to lose them. And we read in the papers and we read in articles about how a certain type of religion is taking over this country, and we know that we may just be buying time, but we need to buy all the time that we can. I know a house that's divided cannot stand, and I think that would be agreeable to each and every one here. And I believe the Bible in its entirety ought to be preached. I have heard very little of the Bible being preached from this pulpit in the last several years.

> We have a great responsibility as Baptists to remain true to the Baptist cause; not only to the Baptist cause, but to the Christian cause in this land in which we live. We need to maintain it, and stand up and enforce it, because as I have said before, I think the trouble with this church and this land of ours is that the silent majority just does not want to become involved. If we had, then this situation would not be upon us today.

> Please keep an eye on every employee we employ around here as you would in your own business, because this is the largest business

55

we will ever have anything to do with. With that, I would like to second the motion.

Mr. Adams' assumptions are revealing. If the pastor was fired, he argued, unwanted opinions would vanish. But what of the fact that many of the lay people agreed with their pastor? He was making a pathetic effort to cling to the segregationist racial pattern, to "certain privileges that we have here," which he did not want to lose. The type of religion he had been accustomed to was obviously the kind that buttressed segregation. Religion that challenged that way of life meant that the Bible was not being preached. Mr. Adams did not understand that authentic biblical preaching could be most disruptive, as Jesus taught.

According to Carlisle Driggers, this speech "left a host of people angered and upset. He left no doubt in anyone's mind, not only by the words he spoke, but by the expressions on his face, that he was leading an effort to turn the church back in every way to where it used to be years ago."

After this speech, Federal Judge Hobart Harlan Grooms, Sr., was recognized. In eloquent and masterful fashion this well-known jurist and long-time Bible teacher cautioned his brethren about taking such drastic action.* Arguing that summarily dismissing the pastor, as Mr. Adams suggested, would be catastrophic for the church, he moved that the motion to dismiss me be referred to a special church conference on August 19, when I would have returned from overseas. When the vote was taken, Judge Grooms' motion carried by two votes—188 to 186. It was close—too close! But several of the progressive members were optimistic. They had at least bought time; ultimately, they felt, the matter would be resolved in a positive manner.

IV

When this was going on, I was thousands of miles away in Hong Kong. Awakened at 6:00 a.m. by a transoceanic telephone call on Friday, July 24 (it was Thursday the 23rd in Birmingham), I was told by Mr. Prude, the deacons' chairman, of the close scrape the previous evening. He asked me to return immediately, as my family and my staff sorely needed me.

The earliest available flight left Saturday afternoon, and the

*The text of Judge Grooms' speech is printed as Appendix 3.

56

earliest flight from Honolulu to the mainland left Monday. So I had a long weekend for thought—and many serious questions to think about. How would my wife react to this pastoral crisis? How would she be affected by this rejection of her husband? Though I had implicit confidence in the mature faith of my wife and never doubted her unfailing support, I could not help asking what this would do to her.

If I were fired, how would I provide for my family? My oldest son Victor was to begin college in the fall. Even more important, where would we live if soon I was to be jobless and homeless? How could I cushion the shock to my family by this irrational uprooting? How could I interpret these events to my children, so that they would not despise the church? How could I be most helpful to the members of my staff and their families? Any pastor feels this responsibility keenly; and I felt it more keenly, because I had the best staff I could have imagined.

The sobering realization came to me that if I were fired, most Southern Baptist churches—and even those of other denominations—would not touch me. I was guilty of the unpardonable ministerial sin of troublemaking. The possibilities of pastoral service were sharply narrowed. Teaching in a Southern Baptist seminary or college was equally remote, for such institutions would not run the risk of incurring the wrath of the constituency and face possible financial loss. Moreover, little secular work is available to a dismissed pastor. (This is a reality that needs serious research.) Such a man is viewed with suspicion by secular employers; and if race was involved in his dismissal, he is tabbed "unclean" by both religious and secular leaders.

"The dark night of the soul," as St. John of the Cross described it, was a vivid reality to me. I was under no illusions as to the seriousness of my position. At the age of forty-five I was at the prime of my career as a minister, but no realist relishes starting a new career at forty-five.

Still, I was in no mood to pick up my things and run. Whatever happened, I would see it through because what I was standing for was right. Of this I was sure. All my parental training and Christian convictions anchored me at this point. No matter what, I would not compromise my belief that the church is the ample home for all Christlike souls, regardless of race, color, or condition.

Arriving in Birmingham on Monday, July 27, I met at my home Marvin Prude, Billy Austin, the vice-chairman of the deacons, and Dr. Byrn Williamson. After they had briefed me carefully on what had happened while I was away, I asked them what they thought I should do. All three thought that I should resign, because, they said, the situation was hopeless. I asked if they meant to be asking me to resign. All three responded that they were not, but that they were suggesting it for my own good. "In that case," I said, "I will never resign. They can fire me, but I will not resign." I was determined that I would not resign, because this church had pressured an earlier pastor who had incurred its wrath over the race issue to resign and then continued its racist practices. I shall never forget their response. Mr. Prude spoke their sentiments: "Then, in that case, we will stand with you." Dr. Williamson said, "I have been waiting for a minister with guts."

I knew first-hand how churches can pressure ministers with a New Testament view of race to leave quietly by the side door "for the good of the church." Under such a hypocritical guise embarrassing publicity is avoided. Then it is back to business as usual and the word goes out that "race never had anything to do with it." My pastoral pilgrimage has painfully convinced me that it is only *the truth that matters*. No Christian purpose would have been served by my resigning if the truth were to be hidden. The integrity of the Christian ministry and the Christian church was—and still is—everywhere at stake. The gauntlet had been thrown; I would see it through.

Reaction was not long in coming. Telephone calls bombarded us at all hours, night after night, day after day, many punctuated with veiled threats and couched in vicious and vile language. One man snarled, "You know what happened to Martin Luther King," then hung up. I was also swamped with an avalanche of mail—more than five thousand letters and wires in the next two and a half months. To my surprise, ninety-eight percent of the letters praised my stand. Many of the rest were unprintable examples of congealed hate and prejudice. Missionaries from all denominations wrote from distant lands to underscore the importance of an unequivocal Christian stand on the race issue in America. *Newsweek* wanted to tell of our travail. A story in the August 10 issue made the progressive forces aware of the importance of our struggle and strengthened their resolution to face it firmly, but the publicity incensed equally the diehard opposition.

While most of my fellow ministers watched my struggle from

58

the sidelines, a few did not hesitate to show their support. The Reverend Louis Wilhite, pastor of the West End Baptist Church, rallied several ministers and laymen from all faiths in a show of support. As the struggle unfolded, this unique gesture of friendship and support grew to mean more and more. The Reverend Otis Brooks, pastor of the Vestavia Hills Baptist Church, wrote an excellent article for the Birmingham *News*, identifying himself with me and affirming the principles for which the church was struggling. As there were just a few ministers who were willing to identify with me in my struggle, there were a few who spoke openly and bitterly against me. Later, however, the Greater Birmingham Ministerial Association passed a resolution commending my stand. This action was triggered by the conviction of Rabbi Milton Grafman of Temple Emmanu-El. He said to the Executive Committee of the Ministerial Association:

> I know that this is a Christian matter, but I am injecting myself into it. Have you fellows read that series of books called the New Testament? I have! Have you fellows read about a man named Jesus Christ? I have! He has settled this matter, Gentlemen!

Since my family had had no vacation, and my next involvement in our struggle would not take place until August 19, I decided to take my family to the Great Smoky Mountains for the first two weeks in August. Here we were spared from the hate calls and got some needed rest. I used this time to prepare myself physically and spiritually for the ordeal to come. New perspective came through long walks and lengthy periods of prayer and meditation deep in the forests.

I do not want to romanticize this. The physical and emotional beating, the unrelieved tension, had been terrible. My nerves were taut and my stomach soured. Events of past days were re-enacted over and over again. There was the haunting question: "Could I have prevented this?" Anxiety, anger, and frustration fought for control of my emotions. How painfully I was reminded of my human limitations! Yet I experienced as never before what Paul meant when he spoke of the "peace that passes all understanding." God's peace can come in the midst of violent controversy when one knows at the center of his being that he is doing what is right.

At their July 6 meeting, the deacons had approved my recommendation that a series of discussions about accepting Negroes as members begin on July 29. After the July 22 conference, it was clear that meaningful dialogue would be impossible. There could be no helpful discussion in the midst of an attempt to fire the pastor and the Minister of Youth. There was, however, still a meeting scheduled for July 29, and, according to Carlisle Driggers,* that evening turned out to be the angriest of all the public confrontations during the entire controversy.

Mr. Prude learned that an effort would be made by the segregationists that evening to do away with the series of discussions entirely and simply vote *not* to accept Negroes. To avoid this, he quickly called a deacons' meeting at 5:30 p.m. for the purpose of canceling the business session. A number of the segregationists stood out in front of the church before this deacons' meeting and made an unsuccessful effort to persuade deacons not to enter, for if the deacons could not get a quorum, the business meeting later that evening could not be called off. While this maneuvering was going on, Mr. Driggers telephoned the educational secretary to call and urge the young people of the church to come back from Shocco Springs, where they were attending a music week retreat, in case their votes would be needed at the business session.

The deacons voted to postpone the business meeting. When the time for the meeting came, then, Mr. Prude made an announcement to that effect and turned the floor over to Associate Pastor Mack Goss, asking him to proceed with the worship period. Still weak from recent surgery, Mr. Goss rose to walk to the microphone, but before he could get there, one of the segregationists, whom we shall call Mr. Kelly, took it and demanded that Mr. Prude call a business session. As Mr. Driggers tells it:

> At that precise, tense moment, the young people from Shocco Springs came rushing into the sanctuary and seemed to startle a number of people, including Mr. Kelly. Finally, Mr. Goss seemed to persuade Mr. Kelly by telling him very quietly to go back and be seated. Then Mr. Goss went up to the pulpit and began to speak to the people. He said he was not going to proceed with the brief message which he had prepared, but instead called the congregation into a time of prayer and confession. He asked anyone who would to come down to the front and kneel for prayer.

*The information in the paragraphs that follow is taken from Mr. Driggers' account of the meeting.

60

About 150 people came forward, several of them praying aloud. Among those who remained seated, some made open remarks of contempt. When the time of prayer ended, Mr. Goss dismissed the congregation. Most of those who had been praying in the front left the sanctuary; the rest remained in their seats. There was a brief effort by the opposition to call a business meeting anyway, but an eloquent speech by Mr. Brown, the lawyer, counseled against that idea on the grounds that it was legally dangerous. According to Mr. Driggers:

> ... the actual division at the First Baptist Church came that night. When the group walked down to the front to kneel and pray, and the remainder of the congregation sat in their pews, and then, when the people who had prayed walked out of the sanctuary and left the others sitting there, it is my judgment that the split came. From then on it was simply a matter of time as to when the announced division and the parting of ways would take place.

When I returned to Birmingham on August 15, I discovered that several "dirt sheets" were being circulated in the city. The most vicious one, emanating from the "Concerned Christians of Alabama," purported to prove that I was a Communist, in league with the Kremlin, paid by the NAACP, and—for good measure—the anti-Christ. The entire city was now embroiled in our struggle. To my pleasant surprise, many citizens from all walks of life were in sympathy with what we were trying to do. Many said they were tired of having Birmingham identified with racial injustice. They appreciated our efforts to correct this image. The progress Birmingham has made in the area of racial justice in recent years has been heartening. Though the city has sinned, it has also been sinned against.

What does a pastor say when he returns from vacation to address a congregation that has tried to fire him in his absence? I filled a wastepaper basket trying to answer this question. My concern was to address myself responsibly to the issue before the church so that the people might respond creatively to the meeting on August 19. The sermon for August 16 was entitled "With Christ at the Crossroads," based on Paul's magnificent statement in Ephesians 1:10 that the task of the church is "to sum up all things in Christ."*

In the sermon I repeated that I had sought, in twenty-three

*The text of the sermon appears as Appendix 4.

months at First Baptist Church, to take seriously the *Commitments* of 1968. Despite apparent setbacks—lower Sunday School and Training Union attendance, budget difficulties, declining membership—there was, I felt, progress. I shared with the congregation some of the motives that led me in my ministry as I sought to work out the belief that in Christ Jesus all things are to be summed up. I had tried to live and preach by the American dream of equality for all men, by the reality of conscience and judgment, and—most important—by the reality and integrity of the gospel. I pleaded that the members and pastor of First Baptist Church join together to risk being the people of God in Birmingham.

When the worship service was over, many of the progressive members of the church gathered around me and wept openly. They spoke to me and to one another of their intention to be faithful to Christ at this time. A few of those who had been in the camp of the opposition embraced me and said they now realized they had been wrong in their racial attitudes. They asked me to forgive them for the hurt they had done me, and promised to be faithful to Christ in the days ahead.

But the opposition, a larger number, hardened in its antipathy toward me as the pastor and renewed its determination that the church be closed to Negroes. One woman was so convulsed in hate that she had difficulty getting her hate-filled emotions out of her mouth. She heaped ugliness, indignity, and vindictive hate upon me. All attention was now focused on the forthcoming church conference set for Wednesday, August 19. To that historic episode we now turn.

3

"When a great church in a great city stays up until three o'clock in the morning debating whether they will fire their staff because it has brought in two blacks, we are not as far along as I thought we were." (Dr. Ken Chafin, Director of Evangelism, Home Mission Board, Southern Baptist Convention)

The Marathon—The Attempt To Fire the Pastor

I

The church conference was a marathon session, beginning at 6:45 p.m., Wednesday, August 19, and continuing until 2:30 a.m. Thursday. The speeches were taped, and the transcripts required fifty-three single-spaced, legal-size pages. Though the meeting was significant, with its results reported around the world, it was in many respects a travesty and mockery of churchmanship. Democracy at its worst was frequently in evidence. Often the conference seemed more like a town-hall meeting, with cheap political maneuvers used to win arguments, than like a gathering of Christians concerned to know the mind of Christ so that they might do it.

It was quite apparent from the beginning that two major camps were arrayed against each other, since these two groups sat as separate entities. It was evident who were the major spokesmen for each group, though the progressive spokesmen did not caucus nor constantly compare notes with each other nor speak out to disrupt the meeting, as did the opposition. Many members were present because they had been contacted by the opposition, even though they had not attended the church for years. Some of them were unfamiliar even to those who had been active members for a long time.

Every seat in the church sanctuary and balcony was taken. The recent publicity given to the First Baptist Church made this meeting a common topic of conversation and interest in the city, and we knew that many people would be present who were not members of the church. In order to make sure that only members of the church voted, numbered ballots were distributed by tellers, who checked the church rolls before granting them. Only members of the church would be allowed to speak unless there was a unanimous opinion to let someone who was not a member speak.

Since the meeting was called to determine my future relationship to the church, I had asked Marvin Prude to serve as moderator, rather than exercise this prerogative myself. Mr. Prude set the stage for the meeting very carefully by making it plain at the outset that all motions and behavior would be in keeping with Christian conduct, or he would exercise his authority to rule anyone violating this out of order, or call a recess or adjournment. Anyone who wanted to speak was to go to a microphone, so that every person could hear. Throughout the arduous evening, Mr. Prude presided with great dignity, fairness, and strength.

After an opening prayer by Dr. Gaines S. Dobbins, a beloved former professor of mine, Mr. Prude stated twice the motion before the meeting—the motion first made on July 22:

> That the position of Pastor and the position of Minister of Youth be declared vacant as of this date; that salaries without allowances be continued through September 30; and that the Treasurer and Financial Secretary be instructed that the church will not be responsible for any debts or expenses incurred after this date.

The meeting began with explosiveness. Dr. Byrn Williamson was first to speak. He stated that he objected to a "consideration of this motion at this time," and set forth the reasons for his objection.

> I do not believe that we are ready at the First Baptist Church to blame one or two people for our problems. We were told that we

64

have had a losing season; that this was the reason for this motion. If you will think back with me for seventeen years, every other year somebody has felt we had a losing season and somebody was blamed for it. I don't believe this is the way you build a church. I don't believe this is the way you do the work of the Lord.

Now, we have many problems at the First Baptist Church and we have many things that we ought to do. We have a lot of things that we ought to say to each other; we ought to have a lot of discussion. We ought to have a lot of work, but I don't think one of them is blaming one person or two persons or half a dozen persons for our problems. . . .

I'm not willing to judge you and I hope you are not willing to judge me. And so, Brother Moderator, I think we are not ready; I think this is the wrong time and the wrong question, and that we are going about it in the wrong way. And so I object to consideration of this motion at this time.

An almost comical parliamentary hassle ensued, triggered by Mr. Brown, the fundamentalist lawyer. The moderator explained that Dr. Williamson's objection was in order and not debatable and would require a two-thirds vote of the congregation to carry. Mr. Brown asked to speak before the vote was taken; Mr. Prude repeated that the objection was not debatable. Mr. Brown then moved that the motion be laid on the table. The moderator once again explained that the objection was not debatable; that a "yes" vote sustained the objection and the main motion pending would not be considered. However, a "no" vote would defeat the objection and the main motion would be considered. Again, Mr. Brown moved that the motion be laid on the table. Mr. Prude insisted that the motion was not debatable and that we would proceed to vote. Mr. Brown countered that any motion yields to a motion to lay on the table.

When Mr. Prude attempted to proceed with the voting, Mr. Brown asked if that meant that his motion to table the objection was being ruled out of order. The moderator said yes, and Mr. Brown immediately appealed his ruling. Mr. Prude informed the congregation that Mr. Brown's appeal was legitimate according to *Robert's Rules of Order*. After considerable discussion of the intricacies of correct procedure, much of it serving to confuse the issue further, the vote was taken, and the chair was overruled, 310-249.

The chair then asked Mr. Brown to state his motion. "I move," he said, "to table the objection to the consideration of the main motion at this session." Again, there was considerable confusion as to the effect of this motion. The moderator explained that a "yes" vote on this motion would table Dr. Williamson's objection to considering the main motion, and the body would then consider the main motion. A "no" vote would mean that Dr. Williamson's objection to the main motion would be voted on. The motion to table carried, 324-222. The moderator explained that Dr. Williamson's objection was no longer before the body, and the main motion would be considered.

The consideration of the main motion began in earnest with Mr. William B. Rogers, Sr., setting the issue in bold relief. He referred back to the analogy of the "losing season" that had been raised at the July 6 meeting:

> I believe that this drastic action ... needs more than "a losing season" explanation, whatever that might be. ... I'm not convinced it has any relevance to the Lord's work here on this corner.

> I wonder ... if there were not some people who stood around at the foot of the cross and said, "We have had a losing season; let's get another coach!" I wonder how these two staff people's ministries here have brought about, as it is hinted at, "the losing season." I think this needs lots of answers.

> For instance, how do you score these sort of things? What kind of a score sheet do you use to put down what has happened in the lives of young people here in this church? How do you put down what has happened in the lives of people who have needed the pastor, and he has gone to them at their command? When they have needed him, he has gone to their rescue. In the times of stress that I know about, I don't have any score that I could put down about it. What do you put down when a man is offered a free pulpit to deliver his sermons as God has led him to prepare and deliver them to us, in the light of what we need? The "losing season," brethren, has no application in the ministry of the First Baptist Church here on this corner.

> In his second to the motion, I remember the gentleman said he wasn't getting religion like he used to when he came here. Well, I don't know what Betty Bock and the pastor had to do with that either. I can't see myself coming here expecting these two people to give me religion that I didn't have, maybe, when I came in the door. They could inspire me to help others to find Christ, and they can inspire me to go out and help somebody in his endeavor to be

66

whatever he might be—to seek the Lord, to improve himself—but I don't know how they could be expected to hand me religion when I come in and sit down.

Therefore, I think the charges have to be made. They have to be specific. The charges as to these people's responsibilities in these matters need to be spelled out. And I, for one, am asking the chair to ascertain who wants to make these charges and what they are. Mr. Chairman, I submit this request for clarification.

The moderator stated that he was sure both sides agreed that this was a reasonable request. Many people in the congregation had questions about precisely what was taking place, and he would recognize the one who made the original motion, or anyone who would like to speak to it and bring specific charges.

II

Mr. Brown was the first to speak in favor of the motion and to bring charges against me. He spoke from a prepared text at great length concerning my alleged "liberalism."* He began by emphasizing that he was in favor of continuing all the programs initiated by the church, and in favor of admitting to membership all those persons who had been presented. His reasons for favoring dismissal of the pastor were twofold: his belief that I was scripturally unsound and his belief that I was responsible for much of the disunity and disharmony in the First Baptist Church.

One of the grounds for his believing that I was scripturally unsound was my suggestion to him at one time that he read Harry Emerson Fosdick's *A Guide to Understanding the Bible.* Mr. Brown cited evidence from a newspaper clipping at the time of Fosdick's death that he was a liberal, who denied such doctrines as the virgin birth, the inspiration of the Bible, the atonement of Jesus, and the return of Christ.

Mr. Brown suggested that the major ways to test my belief should be the criterion of Scripture and the criterion of historic Baptist tradition. I did not, he said, "believe that the Bible is the infallible Word of God, . . . that the Bible is free from error." Specifically, he focused on the Book of Genesis, alleging that I did not affirm the historicity of Adam and Eve or of the account of the flood. In other words, he argued, I was denying

*Mr. Brown's comments appear as Appendix 5.

the authority, accuracy, and inspiration of the sources of the major doctrines of the Bible, of the "scarlet thread of man's need for redemption." Furthermore, to do this, he said, is tantamount to giving each person the right to decide what parts of the Bible he wants to believe as authoritative and what parts he wants to reject.

Mr. Brown further stated that I had told him that I did not believe man was born a sinner, but that man became a sinner under the influence of sinful culture. This, he said, "is contrary to the teachings of the Bible."

As an indication that I fell short when tested by the standard of historic Baptist beliefs, Mr. Brown cited my membership in the E. Y. Mullins Fellowship, which *Newsweek* magazine had referred to as the liberal group of the Southern Baptist Convention. Also, I had stated, he said, that I found nothing objectionable in the Broadman Bible Commentary on Genesis and Exodus, which had been rejected by a vote of more than two to one by the Southern Baptist Convention as not consistent with traditional Baptist beliefs.

Mr. Brown did not speak at such great length about my role in the disharmony of the church. He argued that, in his judgment, "we have no hope of harmony in this church if the pastor stays as the pastor of this church." He reiterated his support for the programs we had undertaken, but emphasized his opposition to the pastor.

The charges of the fundamentalist lawyer brought swift and sharp response from many members. Mrs. E. O. Edney, a member since 1922, an elderly saint beloved by all, rebutted Mr. Brown's contention that the church had not previously had dissension and controversy. She recalled that when Dr. Slaughter, the last of the long-term pastors, came to Birmingham in the late thirties, he met with the committee who "had the reins in their hands." He asked them if there was a clique in the church. They responded, "Oh, no!" According to Mrs. Edney, Dr. Slaughter told his wife that night: "Margaret, I met the clique tonight." "I have seen times in this church," Mrs. Edney said, "when my heart was almost breaking for the dissension. . . . We know that there has been something wrong with our church for years because we could not keep a pastor. Something is wrong with the people of the church."

She repudiated the lawyer's charges of heresy pointedly. "Now, we have a pastor as good as I have ever heard in all my life . . . and I have never, Mr. Brown, heard him preach anything like you are talking about! Not one time!" This statement evoked clapping and amens from some of the people, prompting the moderator to request that the congregation refrain from any such demonstrations—positive or negative.

Mrs. Edney then said of my work at First Baptist: "I have grown spiritually under his preaching. I am a better Christian today than I was when he came to this church. . . . I beg you tonight, before you vote to dismiss such a man as this from our church, that you do a lot of praying and a lot of thinking, and remember that some day you have to answer to your Heavenly Father for the fault you have found in a man that I believe was sent to our church."

Dr. Harry Dickinson, head of the Sociology Department of Samford University, made the point that Mr. Brown as a lawyer knew the difference between the law and the interpretation of the law. "Now, what you have heard is not what Dr. Gilmore believes, but what Mr. Brown has interpreted Dr. Gilmore to believe." He turned to me and asked: "Dr. Gilmore, do you believe that the Bible contains the Word of God unto salvation through Jesus Christ?" When I responded, "With all my heart," he said, "That is all I need to know."

A middle-aged businessman whom we shall call Mr. Porter spoke next. Although by his own admission he had attended the church only twice since I had been pastor, he spoke of those two occasions with bitter criticism. The first time was Easter Sunday 1969, when Dr. Foy Valentine, Executive Secretary-Treasurer of The Christian Life Commission of the Southern Baptist Convention, had preached. Dr. Valentine, a very capable preacher, is the able—though much maligned—leader of Southern Baptist efforts to apply Christian principles to the ethical and social problems of America. In an excellent sermon on that Sunday he had spoken meaningfully of the Christian hope. Mr. Porter, however, was greatly offended. After his mother had passed away in November 1968, it was a long time, he said, before he and his wife were able to bring themselves to attending the church again, not because of the pastor but because of the associations the place had for them. Finally, on Easter 1969, they had decided to attend:

> The sermon that day was done by a Mr. Foy Valentine. In fact, I don't think frankly the man deserved to be called "mister" in my

opinion. He got up and he started his sermon—and this was Easter Sunday—he started his sermon off very quickly by saying: "Death is returning to little white worms." He was quoting George Bernard Shaw, at the very least a socialist and an atheist.

Dr. Valentine in fact had quoted from Shaw's *Back to Methuselah*. In that drama, Adam and Eve come upon a dead fawn, and the following dialogue takes place:

> Adam: Dead? What word is that?
> Eve: Like that. I call it dead.
> Adam: There is something uncanny about it.
> Eve: Oh! It is changing into little white worms.
> Adam: Throw it into the river. It is unbearable.
> Eve: I dare not touch it.
> Adam: Then I must, though I loathe it. It is poisoning the air.

In his sermon Dr. Valentine had said:

> What is death? *It is not just "little white worms."* It is facelessness. It is perverted vocation. It is missed calling. It is squandered time. It is life unlived. It is wasted talent. It is lost joy. It is unfound peace. It is prostituted personality. It is three meals a day and a suit of clothes. It is pride, prejudice, and the acquisition of things. . . . It ill behooves us, in the face of mankind's ultimate enemy, to try so frantically and pathetically to cover it up with rouge, fingerwaves, formaldehyde, Cadillac coaches, bronze and walnut boxes, lovely flowers, and plastic grass. . . .

His sermon had spoken profoundly of the Christian hope through the resurrection of Christ: "God has destined us for something better than death, so 'Death, be not proud. . . . Death, thou shalt die.' "

All that Mr. Porter had heard in this moving sermon, faithful to the deepest insights of the Christian faith, was one sentence from George Bernard Shaw, and he had misunderstood the fact that Dr. Valentine had refuted that very sentence.

Mr. Porter went on:

> I wrote a letter to Foy Valentine and enclosed a copy to Dr. Gilmore, in which I stated that I thought he could read the Bible a little more and George Bernard Shaw a little less, and I also stated that if this was the type sermons coming from First Baptist Church, I was sorry but I could not return. I didn't expect a reply from Foy Valentine, but I did expect a reply from Dr. Gilmore. I never received one, which either meant to me one of two things—that he

70

didn't want me to come back to this church, or he condoned what Foy Valentine said, one of the two. Well, we started going to another church.

Mr. Porter's second visit was on Veterans' Sunday, November 9, 1969.

That Sunday we received a sermon by Dr. Gilmore on patriotism, and in this sermon Dr. Gilmore castigated quite a group of conservative organizations that I believe are trying to uphold the Constitution of the United States, and for which I am very much in favor. But he started off by castigating one particular organization, I think it was the National Association of Manufacturers, and went ahead and quoted their magazine, saying: "[The] Free Enterprise system is the backbone of the United States." I am just old fashioned enough that I still believe this. I don't want to give personal experiences, but friends in World War II got killed protecting this, and I still believe in the free enterprise system. In fact, I feel more salaries are being paid by the free enterprise system—and these young children going to school—their parents have sent them to college on money they've made from the free enterprise system.

As a matter of fact, I had not spoken about the free enterprise system at all. I had referred to an advertisement of the National Association of Manufacturers that stated that "free enterprise is the backbone of America," and commented that *no* economic system was "the backbone of America," that it was the values of freedom, justice, mercy, and righteousness that constituted the backbone of America. The part of the sermon to which he took exception went as follows:

What is loyalty or patriotism? Let us state first what it is not. Patriotism, seen in Christian perspective, is not unreflective conformity. It is not championing America as it now is or has been. It is not sanctifying the status quo. It does not overlook the present difficulties in American life, such as inadequate housing for many of our people, racial discrimination, and the lack of adequate medical facilities for our elder citizens. It is not loyalty to any particular economic system. Authentic, genuine patriotism never says, "My country, right or wrong." It is not guilty of passive acceptance of the status quo. True patriotism does not selfishly prefer everything American over everything foreign. Christian patriotism is not a particular creed, not a particular version of history, not a particular economics, not a fixed and static philosophy. True patriotism must not assume a fixed content of patriotism. . . .

71

Who are those who would define, who would set the standards, of patriotic loyalty? They range over the whole spectrum of our American life, all the way from the extreme right to the extreme left. They are the John Birchers, the George Wallaces, the Carl McIntires, the D.A.R., the American Legion, the National Association of Manufacturers, the Ku Klux Klan on the right, and the Black Panthers and anarchistic students on the left. In every instance, they would fasten on the minds of Americans a fixed content of what it means to be loyal. But what do these know of patriotism, who make a mockery of our Constitution and Bill of Rights, who stir racial hatred and contradict the American spirit? What kind of patriotism is it that would ignore present difficulties and look toward the past in defining what it means to be American? Or, on the other hand, would arrogate to itself the right to determine what is loyal in the future?

Mr. Porter also argued that politics should be kept out of the church pulpit. Once again, it was a case of his not having heard what I had really said. Regarding politics I had stated in that sermon:

There is desperate need for a vocal, active, determined Christian citizenship which will express itself in the halls of Congress and the politics of this nation. It is time for Christian men and women to become involved, at every level, in the decision-making processes that affect our common life. If we do not, we may expect evil men to enforce their ideas and attitudes on America. The consequences will be disastrous. One of the saddest spectacles in our common life is the way many Christians never even take the time to vote.

Mr. Porter summed up his support for the motion by stating that he came to church to praise God, not to get angry; but that on the two occasions when he had attended First Baptist Church in the last two years he had become angry. So, he concluded:

I'm not coming back under the present leadership, because I come to worship, not to get a lecture on politics or to hear an atheist quoted from the pulpit. . . . I have heard it said that we might tear this church apart, but frankly, I think it's better that this church be torn apart stone by stone than to become a temple of Baal. And I really think that's what it would be under the present leadership.

A new member, Mr. Hal Griffin, spoke against the motion. The pastor and a few others, he said, were the main reasons he and his wife had become members. They had been interviewed by Mr. Brown (as chairman of the Membership Committee)

72

before they became members, and he now wondered whether Mr. Brown had recommended them for membership. When Mr. Brown said yes, Mr. Griffin replied: "I don't see how you did that, Mr. Brown, in all good conscience, because when you left our house that night, you had to know how we felt about the very same things you've accused the pastor of—being (scripturally) unsound. And to me it is unbelievable that you would accept us, and be up here condemning him for the very same thing." Mr. Brown responded that he had "no recollection of talking about the authority of Scriptures" with them, and *that*, he said, was the basis of his charge against the pastor.

Mr. Griffin then touched on a matter that was to be a source of great embarrassment to the opposition. If the charge against the pastor was heresy and biblical unsoundness, what were the charges against Miss Bock?

> I submit to you that if this congregation is really concerned about the scriptural background of this preacher, then Betty Bock should not have been involved in this motion. However, if there is something else that this congregation is really interested in—like race— then I can see why Betty Bock is involved in this motion, because she has spearheaded drives in this church which have said, "Let's minister to this community."

The fact that at no time did anyone ever bring a single charge against Betty Bock was a serious tactical blunder on the part of the segregationists. By attempting to fire her along with me, they lent support to the contention that the issue was race, not theology. None of them knew what Miss Bock's theology was, but all were aware that she had given leadership to the community ministries that culminated in the Negroes' coming to the church.

Another dimension of the struggle was introduced by Miss Dorothy Scott, a nursing supervisor at the Baptist Medical Center and a former missionary to Africa: "We pat ourselves on the back for going overseas, but it is different when we minister to the black person here. . . . I think we need to look at our own lives and see what really we are doing to ourselves." She was touching a vital nerve, since some of the most generous contributors to foreign missions were the most thoroughgoing segregationists.

A senior at Samford University, whose father was identified with the segregationists, introduced a new twist. He said that he disagreed with me on many points because he was more liberal than I. "If the pastor is voted out of this church on these points," he went on, "those who believe like him or believe that he is too conservative . . . must also submit our resignations as members of this church."

He amused some and angered others by saying that the majority evidently wanted to make everyone

> believe every point in the Bible exactly as it is written without taking into consideration recent scientific facts, of which I am afraid the man, Jesus, had not heard of at that time. . . . That is a serious charge. I seriously doubt that Christ had ever heard—the *man* Jesus—had ever heard of the splitting of the atom, of flights to the moon, though he might have envisioned these. I fail to see why the Holy Scriptures should be used as a scientific text book to test my faith in my Savior, and his ability to save me from my sins. Therefore, I ask if these are the only charges, because they are inconsistent; they must be defeated.

Some began to clamor for the vote to be taken, but the moderator stated that no vote would be taken until everyone who wanted to speak had been heard, unless a two-thirds majority wanted to cut off debate. Mr. Nash, an older member, now responded sharply to the remarks of the university student:

> I think a pastor is supposed to bring the congregation together, not separate them. I think a pastor should minister to the needs of his people, give them the Holy Spirit, teach them the Word of God. Christ knew from the beginning everything that was going to happen and when it was going to happen. Don't tell me He didn't know about the splitting of the atom. He knew more about that than this boy will ever know.

This last statement drew applause. After the moderator once again requested that the congregation refrain from such demonstration, Mr. Nash continued:

> I'm speaking right now to try to keep these people together and not separate them. I believe in a unified church, not one that is separated. And I think we are splitting wider when we listen to some of these talks. And I think we need to have a chance to vote on what we came here for—let's do it!

Many, many others wanted to speak, however. The clock ticked on.

74

III

As the debate wore on, tensions—physical and emotional—grew. Since some of their number were leaving as the hour grew late, a restlessness marked the segregationist opposition. They had come for a very specific purpose, and they were anxious to get on with it.

Feelings were calmed somewhat when Dr. Mabry Lunceford asked to speak. A professor of religion, he had served the church several times as the interim pastor during recent years and was beloved and respected by many on both sides of this struggle. When he rose to speak I heard some people around me wonder aloud which side he would support. With quiet dignity Dr. Lunceford told of his distress at the current state of affairs in First Baptist Church. But the crucial question the church had to face on that evening, he said, was "what is the Christian thing to do?" And he could find no reason whatever to justify considering the motion on the floor as a response to that question. There was no room in Christ's church, constantly watched by skeptics on the outside, for factions and party spirit. "Let me appeal by everything we love in Christ," he concluded, "that we search ourselves and act as in his presence, in which we are."

The president of the Woman's Missionary Society of the church, Mrs. Luther Easterwood, was the next to take the floor. She stated that in her many years in the church she had never seen greater unity among the young people; and they attributed this, she said, to the fact that "our 'leaders'—plural— have led us to see that Christianity is a business of activity as well as belief, and we have come to see that by doing our faith grows."

She addressed herself specifically to the women of the segregationist opposition, many of whom were members of the WMU:

> The principles upon which the Woman's Missionary Union was formed and which have been its driving factors through the years . . . have been the principles of missions in action, and certainly missions in action has to involve the "here" as well as the "there." We do not need an organization in this church or any other church which is just a meeting place to listen to a program, and then have a very nice luncheon, and chat and enjoy fellowship, and call this a mission enterprise in the name of our Lord. If Woman's Missionary Union is to continue in the purposes for which it was founded, it must continue in mission action.

She spoke about the staff's involvement in leading the church in mission action, which had occasioned the immediate difficulty:

> We have solicited the help of our staff in the past. This was nothing but right. Our staff is here to help us grow. They are here to help us succeed in our program. As I see it, they have done nothing more than exactly this.
>
> If our programs are wrong, then let us rethink them, but let us be very careful that we do not do a sacrilege to those holy saints who helped us form the Woman's Missionary Union in the first place. I would ask you to think very carefully, very literally, into what fields we may move here in the city of Birmingham in this next year. What fields of mission can we expect to be successful in the name of our Lord if we do not continue in those in which we are now engaged? Please think carefully because your whole future in Woman's Missionary Union stands on this.

The growing restlessness and physical tiredness prompted the moderator to declare a brief recess. When the meeting resumed, anyone who had additional charges to bring against the pastor would be given an opportunity to speak. Mr. Prude noted that "there has been nothing said at all concerning the activities of Miss Bock in this motion, other than to have her made a part of it. Would anyone like to speak to those charges?"

A short silence preceded another knotty parliamentary hassle. A motion was made and supported to cut off debate; this was followed by a motion to table that motion. The latter motion failed, then the former motion gained a majority, but less than the two-thirds required. So the debate continued.

Two young people now spoke in favor of the pastor and Miss Bock. Miss Jeanette Wilson, a teen-ager, stated that "there has never been a youth program like there is now with Betty Bock. . . . I just think you ought to consider the young people when you decide what your vote will be." Miss Yvonne Selby, a young nurse, said that since she had been a member of First Baptist, she "had grown as a Christian as never before." She remarked that when she traveled recently to Oregon and Washington, she had met many people who knew about First Baptist Church of Birmingham. Everywhere she had been, she went on,

> People have told me about Dr. Gilmore and how much respect they have for him. Truly, tonight he has my respect and so does the rest of the staff. I have heard some people get up all night and say, "If

we keep Dr. Gilmore and the staff, what's going to happen to the church?" They keep saying there is going to be more disharmony and more dissension and more splitting down the middle. But I haven't heard anybody say: "What's going to happen if they have to leave?" I always hear that the young people are the future of the church. You have said that to us here tonight, you have said it to me many times since I have been a member here at First Baptist. Don't destroy the future of the church.

Though a number of efforts had been made to get the opposition to bring charges against Miss Bock, no one was willing to come forward. The pastor had been charged with biblical unsoundness, theological liberalism, and dividing the church. What had Miss Bock done? Why dismiss her? Why the reticence to speak against her?

Finally, a motion was made, supported by Mr. Brown, that attempted to get the opposition out of this embarrassing dilemma by dividing the question and voting on the two separately, the pastor first and then the youth director. Miss Bock now rose to a point of personal privilege on the ground that she was involved in the motion and thus had a right to speak of it.* Miss Bock said she opposed the motion on the basis that there was only one issue involved here—the issue of race. A chorus of "no's" greeted that remark. As evidence, Miss Bock cited the events of recent months, beginning with the Sunday in February when Negroes began attending Sunday School regularly, and concluding with the meeting of July 22 when the first attempt was made to fire her and the pastor. She explained in brief the involvements she initiated in the tutoring program before I arrived in Birmingham, and took full responsibility for this. Finally, she agreed, it was extremely difficult to believe that only theology was involved in the main motion under consideration, or even that theology was a fundamental issue at stake.

Someone then requested the person who made the motion to clarify his reasons for making it and show what benefit would come from its adoption. The reply was as follows:

> Dr. Gilmore has been here for twenty-three months—and, in saying the things I do, I say them in Christian love as much as I am able to say them, and I'm not judging people because I don't think that's

*The text of Miss Bock's comments is printed as Appendix 6.

77

my responsibility to judge individuals. But I think the Scriptures tell us that we do have the power to discern, and this is my discernment that—this is what I have written to Marvin, to Billy, and Dean, and I'm going to read the whole thing because this is in answer to their letter of August 17. Part of it has already been said, but it says: "My interpretation of what the Scripture teaches about the Holy Spirit leads me to believe you are wrong in your statement that Dr. Gilmore uses as his basis for direction the Holy Spirit. Galatians 5:23 tells us: the Spirit produces love, joy, peace, patience, kindness, forgiveness, faithfulness, humility, and self-control. Of these, I can only detect faithfulness and self-control in Dr. Gilmore." Now I want to tell the things that you have heard these young people say tonight as a result of. . . .

Here the moderator interrupted to ask if what he was saying was germane to the motion to split the vote on the pastor and Miss Bock? Assured that it was, Mr. Prude urged him to continue.

So I feel like that Betty Bock is living her life under the direction of the Holy Spirit. And I believe that what's happening in the lives of these young people is a result of the Holy Spirit. I've heard Betty Bock's testimony, her personal Christian testimony, and in twenty-three months I haven't heard Dr. Gilmore's personal Christian testimony. I don't know what it is even though I have sat in quite a few sermons. So for this reason I think they should be voted on separately.

The motion to vote separately failed, 252-282. The significance of this vote should not be overlooked. Had the real issue been biblical unsoundness, theological liberalism and/or heresy, and causing division in the church—charges that had been brought against me—there would have been no reason for not voting on Miss Bock separately, for she was not charged with these faults—or any others, for that matter. The church had the opportunity to vote on me separately and fire me for the alleged reasons, while sparing Miss Bock. The fact that it refused to take such action is weighty testimony to the contention that *the* issue was race. In refusing to split the main motion, the segregationist element of the congregation was expressing its true feeling of hostility toward anyone who had given leadership to programs that had resulted in this racial confrontation. If the segregationist element had followed their heads, they would have had to acquit Miss Bock. But, following their heart—their true feelings—they had to get rid of her, for along

78

with the pastor she was guilty of bringing the " 'niggers' into the church." As the debate continued this was to become ever more apparent.

IV

After the defeat of the motion to separate the voting on the pastor and the Minister of Youth, the debate continued. A surprising participant was Mr. John Chandler, who had resigned several months before as Minister of Music (a post he had held for ten years) to take a position with the Baptist Sunday School Board. He was still a member of First Baptist Church, however. Mr. Chandler brought to the debate insights drawn from a larger perspective:

> My heart aches with all of you. There is confusion. But what you do tonight is not your doing alone, for the eyes of the Convention are on you.
>
> Three weeks ago in Albuquerque, New Mexico, this church was used as an example by a man I had never seen. I would like tonight, with real kindness, but with real clarity, to take my stand with Dr. Mabry Lunceford, and ask you to prayerfully consider before you dismiss any staff member. There are churches around this Convention that are envious of you. They say that the finest staff in the Southern Baptist Convention right now is at First Baptist Church, Birmingham, Alabama. You may agree or you may not agree. But there ought to be an awareness that people who are not emotionally involved as you and I are pass this judgment.
>
> I am aware that we all have friends on both sides of the fence tonight, and there is a deep yearning in all of our hearts to come back together and to be Christian brothers. Think prayerfully!

Mr. Chandler's statement was significant because he was held in high esteem by both factions. His testimony, however, angered many of those who were opposed to the pastor.

As the debate continued, it was noticeable that people from different walks of life, of different ages, and having different interests spoke their mind. Mrs. Lou McCracken said that she was "a very conservative Baptist" and did not always agree with the pastor, but that she listened to the pastor preach with "amazing regularity," because, she said, "I feel blessed every time that I hear him preach." She addressed herself to those present who had not been involved in the church for years:

There are many here tonight that I have never seen before in this church until there was an occasion to vote. It makes me wonder if what you have to give to this church is a vote. I would ask that if you are committed to this church that you give your funds, your service, your attendance; that you listen to this pastor, not to people who tell you what he says, but listen to what *he* says and decide for yourself whether it is scriptural or not. I, for one, stand with this staff totally, and completely committed to their ministry to this neighborhood.

An older teen-ager, Mary Jane Easterwood, spoke with startling clarity about her spiritual pilgrimage in the church:

I have grown up in this church, as most of you know, so I am going to be completely honest with you tonight. Until about two years ago church didn't mean much to me. I came because I had grown up in the church, and my parents had grown up in the church, and my parents brought me. And so I just came and I sat, and I was in choir, and I guess I was in all the programs, but I didn't really do anything.

When Dr. Gilmore came I started to sit up and take notice that this man is preaching something that applies to me and my life *now* in 1970. It's something that I can live and really believe. And I guess the young people will agree with me on this, he has inspired us to carry out the programs that Betty Bock is helping us carry out now in this church. To me this is the only way that I can live as a Christian.

An exchange then followed between Dr. Harry Dickinson, Professor of Sociology at Samford University, and Mr. Nash, a rabid member of the opposition. Mr. Nash agreed that the charge against the pastor voiced with the greatest conviction was that he has divided the church. Dr. Dickinson then asked Mr. Nash if he thought getting rid of the pastor under these circumstances would bring the church back together. Mr. Nash replied:

Doctor, all I have to say is that a person is entitled to his own beliefs and I don't think I need to tell you my personal beliefs. Now, you believe like you want to, you live like you want to, and you profess your own beliefs. My beliefs are sacred to me, and I don't think I owe you to tell you exactly how I feel about it. I have expressed myself by saying that I think and I believe that he has separated this church, and I think that his program will separate this church more if it is continued on the road it is now traveling.

80

Dr. Dickinson responded:

> I think, perhaps, we are coming to the true picture, which I think has been hidden heretofore. There are some of us here in this church who are present tonight who are convinced that they are following Jesus Christ as they follow this pastor. I think I can speak with conviction about the great mass of the young people. But this is [true], not only for the young people, because I know my own heart. I have heard the voice of Jesus Christ more clearly from this pulpit in the last two years than I've ever heard it before. I'm not speaking for some of us; I know that. But do you realize that if you vote under these circumstances to get rid of this pastor, for many of those in this church, it is not the pastor that you are getting rid of, it is Jesus Christ.

This last statement evoked a loud chorus of disagreement. Dr. Dickinson repeated that he was aware he was not speaking for everyone in the church.

Up to this time, the only member of the staff who had spoken was Betty Bock. Now Dr. John N. Sims, who had served with excellence as the Associate Pastor — Minister of Music since November 1969, took the microphone.* He told of coming to Birmingham under the leadership of God's Spirit, eager to work in the church that had—while without a pastor—adopted the *Commitments* of 1968. Now, he said, if that church was trying to fire its pastor for his theology or social outlook or its youth minister for reaching out to the community without respect for persons, the church probably would not want him either. He assured the congregation that he was going to continue to minister in his role without respect to a person's race or color and if someone should charge him with trying to integrate the church, his response would be that "Christ's church *is* integrated. We just haven't got the word yet."

A young deacon, Dean Byrd, then spoke at some length against the motion to dismiss the pastor, concluding with a letter from the deacons of the Oakhurst Baptist Church of Decatur, Georgia, who identified with the struggle in First Baptist Church, having gone through a similar one in their own church in the recent past. They had elected to stay in a neighborhood that had become virtually all black, welcoming all who wanted to share their witness to Christ's reconciling power.

*The text of his speech appears as Appendix 7.

Like you we have been swayed by our own fears, our own struggle for alternatives, and multiplicity of seemingly rational reasons why the development of this inclusive ministry was not the proper direction for our fellowship. However, through it all, we have come to see time and again that there is really only one issue at stake: do we have the courage to be the church of Jesus Christ, even when it means standing with Christ over against the values of our culture? We were forced to the conclusion that the rejection of any person as a prospective member of our fellowship on any other basis than his willingness to affirm his faith in Jesus Christ as Lord is tantamount to the rejection of Christ Himself. We covet your participation with us in this pilgrimage and earnestly pray that you will join with us in offering to the world a visible demonstration of the gospel's reconciling power.

For me, this was one of the most meaningful events of that seemingly interminable evening. I thanked God for the thoughtfulness of these men and the witness borne in their letter, and I took heart.

Though the hour was already past midnight, there was no disposition to discontinue the debate. Mr. Luther Easterwood, the church treasurer, spoke of his experience in the church for nearly twenty years.

Since I have been here I have grown to love this church, and I believe that I have matured as a Christian a great deal. It hurts me to see the divisions that now exist within the church, but I want to tell you one thing: if you think that these divisions were created after Herbert Gilmore came here, you have an awfully short memory. . . . I will say one thing for him—he has, perhaps, furthered the divisions a little bit, which exist because of race in this church, because he has taken a forthright stand. . . .

Mr. Easterwood dealt incisively with the real issue that was before the church.

I don't . . . believe that Herbert's theology is really what is bothering us as a church. I don't really believe it. What I believe is that what is bothering us as a church is this simple question: what kind of church do you want, and what kind of church are we going to have? Now, that is very simply stated the essence of what we are discussing here tonight. . . .

Now, Herbert has advocated a service church in every way he could. I'm standing by Herbert. I believe that if the First Baptist Church exists, it will exist as a service church, or it will die. . . . I want to impress on you in all sincerity that when you vote tonight you are casting a vote for the type of church that First Baptist is going to be.

Mr. Easterwood also defended Miss Bock unequivocally, pointing in particular to her tremendous influence on his children. He suggested that the program that Miss Bock was executing very successfully was one for which the Woman's Missionary Society should probably be blamed. In effect, if the church voted to fire Betty Bock, it would be like sending a message to the Woman's Missionary Society loud and clear: "Ladies, be careful what you get into."

Two ministers who were members of the congregation offered their insights into the situation. Howard Goodwin, a student in the School of Church Music of the Southern Baptist Theological Seminary, had driven down from Louisville just for the meeting. He spoke first of his very favorable response to the pastor's preaching, noting that it had helped him find "a strength on which to base my life and to stand as a Christian." His words were sobering to many:

> I am going to the seminary on your recommendation. I stand in full support of Herbert Gilmore and Betty Bock, two of the finest friends that I have ever known, who have helped me more than any other two living souls in my knowledge of Christ. Please do not make me regret that my recommendation to the seminary came from the First Baptist Church, Birmingham, because I do not think that I could quite stand it.

The other minister, the Rev. Mr. Charles Worthington, Executive Director of the Crisis Center in Birmingham, warned the congregation of the consequences of carrying the motion on the floor:

> I want to issue a warning to you—this is not just some janitor that you are firing or just some lady. This is God's man and this is God's woman. I'm really afraid of some of you, you're so vicious, and you're so judgmental. I'm trembling right now to think what God said: "Vengeance is mine, I will repay." This is God's job, not ours. So I want to warn you tonight that you seriously think of what you are doing when you take it into your hands to fire God's man and God's woman. . . .
>
> Think seriously of what you are doing, because if the Bible is true, it says you reap what you sow. If that is true, some of you folks have

83

got a rough row to hoe, because you are going to be treated just as ugly and nasty and judgmental as you have been here tonight. And God be our witness, that whatever we measure will be measured right back to us again. I would hate to think that I was going to be judged as some of you have judged these people here tonight.

At this juncture, Mr. Hobart Grooms, Jr., a law partner of Mr. Brown, asked to speak.* Mr. Grooms had grown up in First Baptist Church, and thus he provided a historical perspective to his remarks about the contemporary issue. Forcefully, Mr. Grooms charged that everyone present knew what the real issue was—not the pastor's theology nor the actions of the youth minister, but race. Why else would First Baptist Church of Birmingham blindly entertain a motion that would dismiss "one of the finest young women of our Convention, in an attempt to rid our staff of this 'troublesome' pastor?" Furthermore, he said, First Baptist Church did not seem to recognize a good pastor when they saw one. It was the church that had passed the *Commitments*—unanimously, after considerable discussion and explanation. And it was the church that was now risking God's judgment on itself by trying to dismiss a pastor who was working to implement these *Commitments*.

An older member suggested that, since the church had lost 90 members and its revenue was down $6,000, it would not be long before the staff would be lost—"not because we want to but because we have to." He noted that the pastor had not said a word as yet in defense of himself. Then he moved that the debate be postponed until the following Wednesday. This motion died for lack of support. The moderator asked if there was anyone else who wished to speak to the issue. For the first time during the long evening, no one responded. It was time for me to speak.

V

The air was charged with emotion. As I stood to speak, my silent prayer was that I would speak clearly, firmly, and without rancor. I reminded myself that I was the pastor of *all* the people, and prayerfully hoped that I could speak redemptively to them all. There were no illusions as to my ultimate fate at the hands of the First Baptist Church. The issue was too grave,

*The text of Mr. Grooms' speech appears as Appendix 8.

84

the enmity too deep, for me to expect any future in the church. I could only hope that some seeds might be sown that would ultimately bring forth "the fruits of the Spirit." To speak in such a setting was necessarily to speak extemporaneously, and to speak extemporaneously is to risk overstating the case or overreacting. But such speaking does have the advantage of coming from the depths of genuinely held convictions, and so it reveals a man very accurately. My resolution was to deal with the issues as forthrightly as I could in a spirit and manner that no one could fault.*

I began by answering in detail the allegations against my theology that Mr. Brown had made. I recalled the circumstances that surrounded my coming to First Baptist Church, the lengthy sessions I had had with the committee about the exact meaning of the *Commitments* of 1968 and their application. My effort in the twenty-three months I had been in Birmingham had been merely to implement these *Commitments.* The issue now, I alleged, was race—not theology.

I denied the ludicrous allegations that I was an agent of the NAACP or the Communist Party, and the rumor that I was being paid by the Home Mission Board of the Southern Baptist Convention. To the charge that I had created disunity, my response was that there are two kinds of disunity. Surely the disunity in First Baptist Church was not a result of my "human cussedness"; rather, it was the disunity that results when people are disturbed by the truth of the gospel. In conclusion, I said:

> My dear people, I am deeply concerned as to what is going to happen to the cause of Christ here. Leave me out of it and let's face the issue at hand. To vote in such a way that we position this church as a racist church, or to vote in such a way that we position this church as being a rank fundamentalist church that is concerned about dotting every "i" and crossing every "t" theologically, is to mean great loss to the cause of Christ here in this city, and around the world. A letter came to my desk just a few days ago from a friend I made in Japan. She said, "I am praying for you and your church as you meet next Wednesday night." All over the world! I make no plea for myself—I come to you not in weakness, not in begging—but I come to you in great moral strength and earnestness, simply asking you to *be the church.* And may God have mercy on our souls!

*The complete text of what I said appears as Appendix 9.

85

When I had finished speaking, Dr. Byrn Williamson rose to amend the motion on the floor as follows: "We at First Baptist Church commend Dr. Gilmore and Betty Bock for their courageous leadership in this community and in this church, and pledge to them our wholehearted confidence and support as they continue to lead us." His amendment was defeated, 256-243. The moderator then read the main motion again. Mr. William B. Rogers, Sr., now moved the meeting be adjourned for one week. The opposition felt that this motion was dilatory, and asked the moderator to rule on it. Mr. Prude replied: "Recognizing the integrity of the men who made the motion and the second, I would have to rule the motion is not dilatory, and that we have to vote on the motion." He explained that a "yes" vote would adjourn the meeting for one week; a "no" vote would continue the meeting. The motion was defeated, 300-191.

The ugly spirit that had manifested itself particularly in the voting on this last motion convinced the other staff members that they had no future with the church if Miss Bock and I were fired. The spirit in the church that sought our dismissal would also seek theirs if they were faithful to their convictions. Following that vote, therefore, Carlisle Driggers moved to amend the main motion so that the other staff members would also be dismissed:

> This is something on my heart that has not been prearranged, nor is it any action to keep us from voting on the main motion, but is offered by Mr. Mack Goss [the Associate Pastor], Dr. John Sims [the Minister of Music], and myself. In a conversation we have just had, the three of us have agonized tremendously since July 22. At times we have felt almost envious of Betty Bock and Herbert Gilmore because, at least something definite was there that they were dealing with, and we were hanging in suspension. But we come now to offer an amendment, and I speak for all three of us, Mack and John and me, in saying that we would very sincerely request of you to add our names to the list of those to be dismissed, Betty Bock and Herbert Gilmore. We feel a very deep sense of covenant relationship with them, and in good faith and sincerity we make this amendment at this time.

Dr. Sims seconded this amendment. It carried by a vote of 356-130.

Since the opposition had carried every one of the eight votes taken, it seemed quite apparent that the whole staff would be dismissed. In order to make some provision for them, Mr. Luther Easterwood rose to speak: "Brother moderator, I would like, in all fairness to the staff, to say this. When this motion was first made, there was more time involved to allow them to be relocated. We have eaten up a month in the postponement. What I would like to do is amend this motion, to be fair to all the staff, to make their period of ministry pay go through December 31, 1970."

This amendment evoked loud yells of "no!" The moderator responded: "Order, please, or you will get adjournment in a hurry." The spirit expressed in the boos and yells of "no" was difficult for all. Mr. Easterwood expressed the sentiments of many when he said: "Brother moderator, could I make a comment? I want to tell you people something. That is the most unkind and ungentlemanly conduct that I have ever seen in a church. For a minute I'd take off my coat with any of you! I really feel that." At this moment, Mr. Porter—the man who had heard but two sermons during my pastorate, and violently disliked both—responded vehemently: "I just want to say one thing. These people in opposition to the [main] motion call themselves Christians. I have seen less display of Christianity on their part tonight. Every motion they have made has been dilatory. If they call themselves Christians, I don't know what I am."

The vote was finally taken, and the motion to extend pay to the staff to December 31, 1970, was defeated, 239-235.

The moderator then read the main motion again, explaining that a "yes" vote would pass the motion, which would mean that as of that date, the church would not have any ministerial staff. While the ballots were being counted, many of the progressive members sitting around me wept. Knowing that the opposition was more numerous, they waited with heavy heart for the announcement that all the staff had been dismissed. There was a jocularity, however, among some of the hard-core opposition—even laughter as they conversed with one another. I had already resigned myself to being fired.

When the tellers entered the sanctuary, a deathly silence fell over it. The moderator announced that the motion had been defeated, 241-237. There were many who wept for joy; some clapped; others embraced each other. The opposition left the sanctuary sullen and angry. I felt like a condemned man who has been given a brief reprieve. The sentence was still hanging over me, and I knew it was just a matter of time. While I was happy for my colleagues, in my heart there was a pervasive sadness, not for myself, but for the church, for I knew this was but an interlude to the final tragic drama that was yet to come.

The meeting adjourned with prayer at 2:30 a.m., Thursday, August 20, 1970.

4

"Can it be that a segment of the community of faith has deteriorated to such a level that it will not trust those who wish to become part of it?" (Wallace Henley in the Birmingham *News*, September 5, 1970)

Church Politics—The Take-over of Leadership

I

The results of the August 19 meeting let loose all the fury of the segregationist/fundamentalist opposition. My secretary, who had served the church for several years, resigned the next morning in sympathy with them. During the remainder of August and all through the month of September and part of October there was one long church conference after another. At the deacons' meeting on July 6, which had dealt with the objections to the request by Mrs. Bryant and Twila for membership, the deacons had approved the recommendation that the church engage in Bible study, prayer, and dialogue at the mid-week Prayer Hour beginning on July 29. These sessions were to be limited to one hour and continue for an indefinite period of time. As recorded above, this possibility had been undercut by the attempt to fire the pastor and the Minister of Youth on July 22. The meeting scheduled for July 29 had been postponed by the deacons until August 26.

The events of the marathon meeting on August 19 produced such a climate of hostility, however, that members on both sides of the controversy asked the deacons to postpone the meeting indefinitely. Letters like the following began to appear:

SOCIAL GOSPEL OR CHRISTIAN RELIGION

Our beloved preacher and especially this church seem to make the headlines in the *Birmingham News* quite often these days. On February 8, July 6, 7, and 29 our church was in the *News* and then on August 5 little Otis Brooks (Minister of the Vestavia Hills Baptist Church) put in his two cents worth.

Dr. Gilmore tells us the government best knows how to run the schools and what is best to teach our children. How long will it be before the good Doctor tells us the government knows best how to run our churches? Sounds impossible? Well, do you recall the history of England when the king dictated to the church and the dedicated pilgrims came to this country to worship Christ?

Isn't it strange how the *Birmingham News* is able to obtain news about our church and attempts to spotlight activities of this congregation? Since Dr. Hall, Dr. Christian and H. H. Grooms are members here, doesn't it seem that something strange is taking place between the Samuel I. Newhouse-owned *Birmingham News* and somebody in the congregation? Just a thought. Who is playing the part of 'Judas' and keeping the church activities funneled into the New York-owned *News?* Is Samuel I. Newhouse a Christian? Has he accepted Christ and been baptized in the water of salvation? This would be good to know.

As members of this church you will recall that Christ was murdered to further the cause of a special interest of a 'so called religious group' of his day. Are we going to stand by and let a 'special interest group' do an injustice to this church and its good standing? The good name of this church was built by our fathers and grandfathers and should not be shakened [sic!] or blotted by a special few.

A federal judge may issue orders of tyranny from the federal bench but he has no authority to spout out anti-Christian phrases from within the walls of the sacred church.

The preachers of this area are telling the good church people if they don't fall down and worship the DEVIL they are not doing the will of Christ. Remember when the devil took Christ to the high mountain and promised him the world if He would fall down and worship him—the devil? It looks as if some of these 'so-called preachers' in Birmingham and Vestavia have been taken to the high mountain.

90

Half-baked politicians and federal judges are now stooping so low as to inject the works of the devil into the church house. Christ will in no way permit this. Watch and you will see how Christ deals with his enemies. Beware of the *Birmingham News*, it is the enemy of the people and Christians in particular.

Now comes the big test: Those who are following Christ will withhold their $$$$$$$$$$$ for the next three months. This will determine if the preacher is preaching for the love of money or to spread the Gospel of Christ. Don't let the devil use your own $$$$$$$$$$$$ to pave the road to hell for you!

STAND FAST AND THE LORD OF HEAVEN AND HIS SON JESUS CHRIST WILL DELIVER US FROM THE MIDST OF THE EVIL DOERS. PRAY AND BE STRONG IN THE FAITH OF CHRIST.

The chairman of the deacons called a special deacons' meeting on Sunday, August 23, and recommended that the August 26 session be postponed indefinitely. His recommendation, however, was defeated. The August 26 meeting lasted nearly four hours, most of it in parliamentary haggling. I shall describe this at some length, because it is a favorite strategy of segregationist churches unwilling to change. Perhaps an analysis of this kind of behavior will benefit other churches facing up to the same issue.

The moderator began the meeting by asking the secretary to read the recommendation adopted by the deacons on July 6:

That a church conference be called for the express purpose of considering the acceptance of Negroes as members of the First Baptist Church.

That the church conference be called on Wednesday, July 29, and continued on as many subsequent Wednesday nights as may be necessary for the thorough consideration and discussion of the subject. The conference on each Wednesday night shall last not longer than one hour and the chairman of the deacons shall be moderator.

That all six candidates remain under the watchcare of the church pending a decision by the congregation.

The secretary explained that at a subsequent meeting of the deacons, an amendment to these recommendations had been added, according to which the church would be given a notice

91

of one week before voting on acceptance of the blacks. He explained further that the special church conference set for July 29 had been rescinded by the deacons and reset for August 26, to consider the question: "Shall Negroes be accepted into the church?" He moved that these recommendations be adopted as the order of business for this special church conference.

It is important, in the light of subsequent discussion, to note that when I had made these recommendations to the deacons on July 6 I had deliberately avoided any mention of voting. In fact, I had stressed that *no* vote should be taken. My hope was that honest dialogue over a period of time would ready the church to act responsibly. Ultimately, of course, the church would have to vote, but I wanted to postpone this indefinitely so that the church could, I hoped, vote responsibly.

Mr. Nash immediately amended the motion:

> I move that at this time the First Baptist Church decline to accept Negroes into the membership of the church due to the fact that the majority of the membership are not prepared to accept Negro members into the First Baptist Church of Birmingham. Also, that the membership vote on this motion before the time suggested is up and the meeting is adjourned, and both sides be given equal time to speak on the subject.

The moderator asked if he were "making this motion as a rule of the church." Mr. Nash responded that he was making an amendment to the motion. This set off a long and involved dispute over the interpretation of the church by-laws.

The chair ruled Mr. Nash's amendment out of order on the ground that it was contrary to the by-laws, which read: "Those applying for membership shall be received by vote of the congregation at the regular services." The force of Mr. Nash's amendment, he said, was to change the by-laws "to decline to accept Negroes as members of the church." The by-laws, as the chair interpreted them, did not deny arbitrarily membership to anyone. To amend the by-laws required written submission of the change at a regular church conference and adoption by a two-thirds majority at the next one.

This prompted a rank segregationist, whom we shall call Mr. Gates, who had previously tried to interrupt the moderator, to say: "I have seen some fast tricks pulled in this church but this is the fastest one. We have just made a motion, and if he [the moderator] wants to rule us out of order for making a motion,

I think we should ask the congregation to vote on whether to abide by the decision of our moderator. I so move."

The moderator replied that he was simply following the rules under which the church had operated for years. The original motion was subject to amendment as it related to the discussion for the conference on that night, but the by-laws as such could not be changed except according to the prescribed procedure.

Mr. Nash asked if the by-laws had been approved since they had been changed. The moderator stated that he knew of no change and called on Judge H. H. Grooms, who had done a great deal of work on the by-laws, to speak.

Judge Grooms stated that "this rule . . . has been in the Blue Book [the by-laws] since 1942. . . . I do not think we can change the by-laws of a governing body by simply getting up and voting on the thing. It is provided in the by-laws how we can change it. Now you can amend the motion, but to adopt a permanent policy changing the by-laws, you have to go through the procedure. . . . We cannot accept those we like and disregard those we don't like. That is fundamental."

Mr. Nash retorted: "I think you will notice that I made an amendment to the motion that was already made. I didn't make any amendment to change the constitution."

The chair responded: "But it is relevant to that and that is out of order."

Mr. Brown launched into a lengthy and involved parliamentary harangue, contending that the conference was a special one to consider a single question and that it could not consider any other one. The moderator replied: "Not without unanimous consent." Mr. Brown said that, as he understood *Robert's Rules of Order*, the motion was for a special order; and, without previous notice, it required a two-thirds vote of the membership in order to carry. The conference, he said, was called to consider this one question only: "Shall we admit Negroes into the membership of this church?" He asked the chair to rule on this.

The moderator replied: "Our order of business is merely for discussion and consideration. To use your words, to consider the acceptance of Negroes as members of this church. In our consideration that is what we will be talking about. There can be no conclusion. We can get the consensus of the people. We can understand what the pros and cons are of this thing, and, perhaps we will go away better educated as to what our problem is. This was the sense of the deacons and this was the idea for the call."

Mr. Brown came back strong: "The call for this church conference did not include any rules pertaining to the discussion for one hour, nor did it give any rules pertaining to one week's notice, nor did it pertain to any rules concerning no vote in this conference, and I would like to have a ruling on what the call for this conference is."

The moderator responded by reading a full explanation of the action of the deacons taken on July 6, which was printed in the church paper dated July 9 and mailed to all the members.

Mr. Brown charged that the action of the deacons on July 6 was not the action that had called this conference. The moderator reminded him that he—Mr. Brown—was the one who had made the motion on July 29 to delay the meeting until August 26.

The lawyer countered by saying: "I made the motion to call this conference to consider one question. My point is that we cannot consider any other question other than that one question, and in the call of this conference there was nothing said about discussion for one hour; there was nothing said about no vote being taken; and there was nothing said about one week's notice being given for a vote to be taken. Those rules applied to a conference which was rescinded. This conference is the result of another call and a specific vote of the deacons." He asked the chair again to rule on what the call of this church conference was, and what was the motion to be considered.

The moderator spoke very carefully: "I rule that the delay of this conference from July 29 to August 26 was in the same sense as the original called meeting of the deacons, and that we go back to that original meeting of the recommendations of the deacons at this time, which the secretary read to us. I rule that that is what we are here tonight to consider and that is the order of business."

Mr. Brown's whole case rested on a technicality. Because his motion at the deacons' meeting on July 29 to rescind the church conference on that day and reset it for August 26 did not specifically verbalize the provisions of the original recommendations he argued that those provisions did not apply to this meeting. He, therefore, appealed the ruling of the chair.

This turn of events set off another lengthy discussion.

Mr. Brown then spoke at some length to explain his position, concluding:

> In parliamentary procedure, when you consider a question, you open it for discussion and action; that means to vote. Now it is my position—and this is why I appeal from the decision—it is my position that we do not in this conference go back and pick up all the rules of the previous recommendations of the deacons in the previous conference which has been rescinded. It is my position that the call for this church conference contemplates the consideration of that question to its ultimate action, which is a vote. I would ask you to vote not to sustain the decision of the chair.

Was it his understanding that this would be a permanent action on the part of the church? He replied:

> We are not amending the by-laws of the church. We are just voting on action in church conference as we take any action in church conference. We are not voting on the six members tonight. They are not here. They are not to be considered tonight. This is a vote on a motion and that would be the business of the church as any other business of the church. It is not an amendment to the by-laws. I will ask you to vote "no" when he puts to you the appeal from the decision of the chair.

There was a clamor from the segregationists to vote immediately. Mr. Prude, however, spoke with urgency, explaining his position:

> I feel compelled . . . to point out some of the characteristics of our [deacons'] meetings leading up to this one tonight. I presided at both meetings [July 6 and July 29]. It was the sense of the deacons that we were merely delaying action that night [July 29]—the same action—to this other [August 26]. I am sorry . . . that we are getting into semantics, but Mr. Webster has this to say about "consideration" or "consider": "to turn over in your mind, to look closely, think of attentively, contemplate carefully, reflect, meditate upon, to consider a matter in all of its aspects." So if we are going to get into the legalistic, semantic side of this thing, there is no basis for an appeal, and I am still ruling that we are amending the by-laws if we try to vote . . . some change in our method of receiving people, whether they be of one race or of any other race. I think the best thing we can do is to get on to the business of this body. I know there is no other business to come before it because this is the sense of the deacons in calling it. For us to consider anything else would take a unanimous consent, and I dare say we would have a hard time getting a unanimous consent even on adjournment tonight.

Mr. Prude's statement called forth a bitter response. Mr. Nash, who had spoken often, said vehemently: "I think you will railroad this thing. You ought to have a vote on this to see whether we agree with your motion or not."

The chair replied that he was simply "trying to carry out the rules that [the church] had made."

A former minister, whom we shall call Mr. Dunn, spoke harshly: "You are forgetting that the body of the members is the last word over yours or anything. What this body of members votes, that's what it's going to be. You're forgetting that."

The chair ignored this remark and asked if there was any discussion of the motion. Mr. Long, who lodged the original objection to receiving the black people on July 5, asked for Mr. Brown's motion to be read again. Before this could be done Mr. Brown chided the chair: "We have an appeal before the house."

The chair, however, would not be intimidated. "The appeal is out of order," he said, "because it has to do with other business, and it takes unanimous consent to do it."

After the full recommendation had been read again, Mr. Brown said: "I appeal the decision of the chair in ruling that the call of this church conference includes the recommendation for the call of the church conference on July 29, 1970."

The chair responded: "I don't see how you feel that this congregation, whether they feel one way or another, can rule on the sense of the deacons in making this recommendation."

The lawyer persisted in demanding that the chair rule on his appeal, and sought to buttress his position by alleging that when the pastor made his recommendation, which the deacons adopted, "it called for a vote on the very same question" that he was now asking the chair to conduct a vote on. He had either forgotten or chosen to change the facts. I had not called for a vote; indeed, I had stressed that a vote should not be taken until the issue had been carefully weighed, and then it would have had to follow the prescribed rules laid down by the by-laws.

The moderator, trying to be fair, asked some of the deacons present at their July 29 meeting to give their impression as to whether or not the sense of the rescinding was simply to postpone the meeting. Though he was doing this in an effort to be fair, it brought forth a charge from Mr. Nash that he was out of order, because there was already a question to be voted on. The chair was not bullied. He responded that Mr. Nash was the one out of order, and called on deacon Lou McCracken.

Mr. McCracken spoke pointedly: "It was the consensus of the deacons there, and my thinking in setting the date, that we were carrying forward the same thoughts that were set forth by the deacons in the July meeting."

Mr. Chance, a segregationist deacon, had a different interpretation. He spoke very harshly:

> I was one who boycotted that meeting and I am glad I did it because we got the word just before we came down here on Wednesday evening that there was a called meeting. Some of us smelled a mouse and refused to go to the meeting. The meeting was for 5:30 p.m. and at 5:30 they could not get a quorum. They came into the dining room at 6:00 p.m., and of all the hustle and bustle you ever saw, it was during the supper hour. So after supper they came back for another meeting, and they corralled enough people to carry the motion that was presented. It was not unanimous. We have not had a unanimous vote among the deacons, just as we did (not) originally on this motion. It was 17-14.* Fourteen voted against it. Just as they tried again last Sunday morning to postpone this meeting tonight at the called deacons' meeting, fourteen deacons were there and voted not to cancel this meeting tonight and only ten voted to cancel it. So I submit to you, Gentlemen and Ladies and Christians, and people of this church, that we are just being subjected to a lot of hogwash, if I might say so.

The chair responded by explaining that he had called the special deacons' meeting because people from both sides did not feel that any positive contribution could come out of a church conference. He emphasized that he called the deacons together to consider these suggestions without putting any pressure on them; he simply wanted their guidance. Once they had voted not to suspend the conference, he said, their meeting immediately adjourned.

Mr. Milton (not his real name) stressed that the word "rescind" was the crucial word to understand. It means, he said, "to wipe out, to forget all about what has gone before. . . . Now that word 'rescind' means to do away with all the recommendations made by the deacons' meeting when they voted 17-14. Now the word 'rescind' was authentic because it was read by Mr. Byrd. When you rescind, that means forget it, wipe it out, erase it, start all over."

Another segregationist, whom we shall call Mr. Hough, spoke

*The actual vote was 24-8.

97

with tongue-in-cheek to ask the chair if the sense of the motion was for the discussion to continue indefinitely. When he was told that this was the intent, he asked if the chair could give an approximate date when there would be a final vote. There was applause and raucous laughter from the segregationists.

The chair now spoke to the congregation with deep earnestness:

> Friends, I appeal to you, we must have order, we are in the Lord's house. We allowed some things last week that we should not have. But I am asking you to keep your emotions in bound—whether they be for or against—and let us act as Christian gentlemen. . . . We must conduct ourselves with Christian decorum. I'll do my best to do it even though you think I am not always in order—and perhaps I may not be. But let us restrain our emotions and our demonstrations.

Mr. Luther Easterwood suggested a new insight that was germane to the appeal:

> Dr. Gilmore's motion and Mr. Brown's motion both would change the substantive rules because our present rules just say application or members. They do not specify colored or white as I recall. Therefore, any addition of an adjective to the word "members" would be a substantive change in the rules. . . . It seems to me that the only thing we could vote on without amending the by-laws would be the admission of these particular people. You would not have to amend the by-laws to vote on them, but if you vote to approve the admission of Negroes, or deny the admission of Negroes, you are putting an adjective in the by-laws that is not there.

Judge Grooms responded to this by saying: "Now we can do this: if it applies only to these two [Mrs. Bryant and Twila], we can take a vote on them tonight. . . . I think the thing turns on the question whether or not you are trying to settle this once and for all. If you are, then it is going to take a two-thirds vote to do it."

It is significant that Mr. Brown had stated pointedly in his previous comments that the purpose of this church conference was not to vote on any personalities, but to consider the basic question of whether or not Negroes would be accepted as members in the church. Responding to Judge Grooms, Mr. Easterwood said that his understanding was that this principle "would apply also to Dr. Gilmore's original motion to the deacons," because an adjective was applied there. As I have indicated, I did not ask for a vote when I made my recommendation to the deacons, and the subsequent amendment by the deacons to give a one week's notice was not in my original suggestion.

Judge Grooms summarized the situation: to exclude these two Negroes would require a one-third vote against them; to exclude all Negroes would require a two-thirds vote, because it would be amending the by-laws of the church.

Mr. Easterwood pursued his line of reasoning with the comment that Mr. Brown's motion of July 29 to rescind the church conference until August 26 had nothing in it that provided for a vote. He argued persuasively that we could not vote—without going through the regular procedure—to add an adjective—white or Negro—to the membership criteria. All that could be done according to Mr. Brown's motion was to consider. The congregation might turn Mrs. Bryant and Twila down, but not any future applicants without first amending the rules through the usual procedure.

The chair stated that "the two members who have made application for membership in the church, who were objected to and in turn referred to the deacons, are not under consideration tonight as personalities." Moreover, he said, the question is "whether Negroes, period, as a race, will be accepted."

After several others had spoken, including Mr. Brown again, the chair asked that I give the reason for my original recommendation. I began by indicating my concern with the fact that motives were being questioned at this meeting. I reviewed the provisions of the by-laws regarding membership, and appealed to them that we move together, not as opponents, questioning each other's motives, but as the church, seeking the mind of Christ:

> My purpose is not to win a battle. That is not my spirit. As I expressed to the deacons, and to all of those present, what I wanted to do and what I recommended to them, and they thought well of it, was in line with the Biblical instruction that the Apostle Paul used with several of his churches. I had hoped, and I still do have that hope, that a sufficient deposit of the mind of Christ is in us all. As I said that night, and I would say to you now, I believe that if we could study the scriptures regarding the nature of the church, the inclusive nature of the church, and if we could honestly come here Wednesday by Wednesday, earnestly praying together, talking with each other, studying the scriptures, and praying some more, and talking some more, and studying some more—I entertained the hope,

99

and I still do, that there is a sufficient deposit of Christ in us all that in due time, as the Quakers would say, we could have the mind of the Spirit.

This is the motivation of your pastor. In order that all of us could move together, not as warring parties, my recommendation to the deacons was that we do this for as long as was necessary. Mr. Brown is quite right. I was not thinking then, and I am not thinking now, about the Blue Book. I am thinking about a sufficient time of prayer and study and honest talking with one another that we might, in the grace of God, become more one than we have ever been, and that we, in the light of scripture, might do what we do. The subsequent amendment to my motion, that is, to give one week's notice before a vote, was made because it appeared that there were some who felt that something would be sprung on them. This concerns me greatly. I can tell you that this has been no part of your pastor's motivation to spring anything on anybody, nor have I seen evidence of it on the part of any of the deacons who support me in this struggle. In fact, just the opposite. The intent was that we would discuss as long as was necessary. Someone added to my recommendation that after we had talked and talked, and prayed and prayed, and studied and studied, then the congregation, out of fairness to all, would be given one week's notice before voting. . . .

When the time came for the congregation to consider Mr. Brown's appeal, however, the chair was overruled. The chair explained the result of this decision, and again stressed that the church was not voting on anything, but was in session to consider, to discuss, "to look at Christ carefully," and to have some searching of heart. The main motion before the church now was whether Negroes would be accepted into the membership of the First Baptist Church; and the moderator called for those who desired to discuss it. The discussion relative to receiving Negroes into the church began with Mr. W. B. Rogers, Sr.

It has been my privilege to be a part of this church and its ministry since 1947. It has been, most of the time, a very glorious experience for me. My wife and I feel that it has been our great privilege to have been a part of this fellowship. We have looked for some time on a fellowship, however, that has become more social, more pat-on-the-back, more come-to-my-party-and-I'll-come-to-yours. . . . The thing that I would like to say to you tonight is: what is it that we are afraid of with reference to colored people being a part of this group, this fellowship? I, for one, cannot understand this manner of thinking. It is beyond my comprehension. . . . This question that we are considering tonight is basic and fundamental, in my opinion, to Christ's church. . . . I said as far back as 1963, when the question came up as to whether or not Negroes were to be seated in our church, that if the fellowship could be torn apart by the admission of a few people to our congregation who are the wrong color, then the fellowship is not worth saving. I still say this. . . .

Dr. Harry Dickinson continued:

As I understand it, the objection of the group who has taken its stand against the admission of Negroes into this church may be stated thus: the members of this church are not yet ready to receive Negroes into this church. If that is true, I think that pretty clearly points out where the difficulty is, because the appeal is not whether Christ wanted Negroes into this church, it is rather whether the members of the church want to receive Negroes into the church. The pastor has said that what he wants to do is to go through a period of time, not finding out what the members of this church are ready for, but what Christ wants them to do. . . . If we act on where we are, is that sufficient to carry us on to meet his judgment?

Dr. Byrn Williamson spoke at some length, tracing past events. He then offered a resolution similar to the one he had presented to the deacons' meeting on August 26, 1969, pledging that the church would consider each individual applicant—black or white—for membership without regard for the color of his skin. (The text of this resolution is on p. 31). He pointed out that he did not think that this resolution should be voted on that evening, but that it should be discussed. To that end, he moved that his resolution be adopted.

Mr. Brown then challenged the validity of Dr. Williamson's motion because, he said, there was already a motion on the floor. The chair ruled that the previous discussion had been over the order of business, and reminded Mr. Brown that his earlier appeal had been on the order of business, and since the chair had been overruled, the main order of business was automatically adopted. Thus, he ruled, there was no motion before the body and Dr. Williamson's resolution was in order. Since it appeared that a real confrontation was in the offing, the chair called a five-minute recess, during which Mr. Brown, Dr. Williamson, and the chair reached an agreement. Mr. Brown explained their agreement to the congregation:

What we have agreed to do is that I am going to withdraw my motion—"Shall the church accept Negroes into the membership of the church?"—and I am going to yield the floor to Dr. Williamson to make a substitute motion, which to my way of thinking says the same thing, but he likes his motion better. And in that way we can get a motion on the floor which I concede gets to the same issue. Then that motion will be properly on the floor by all of us sitting right here, and will then be open for discussion, and then for debate, and, as I understand it, for a vote.

The chair quickly explained that it would be a vote on the resolution. Dr. Williamson then explained that his previous remarks were meant to give the full background and that his motion was as follows: "That all applicants for membership in the First Baptist Church will be considered, as in the past, on an individual basis, and will be neither accepted nor rejected because of race or color." Considerable discussion and debate followed, beginning with Mr. Brown:

> As I understand the sense of this motion, if you vote in favor of this motion you are saying that you will not vote against a person for membership solely because he or she is a Negro. If you vote *against* this motion, you in effect are saying that you will vote against, or that this church will not accept, a person solely because of his or her race. . . . I am one of those that believes that this church is really not ready to consider this question so far as its spiritual preparation is concerned, but I also firmly believe that we ought to go ahead and vote on the thing so far as the hereafter of this church is concerned.

He attempted to explain his position as to why the church was not ready and yet should vote on this issue. He sought to blame the pastor alone for having presented the two black people for membership and thereby having caused the difficulty that followed.

> When Mrs. Bryant presented herself for membership, it came as a total surprise to me, and I was chairman of the Membership Committee. We met with her and talked with her at length, and then we had a committee meeting. It was at that committee meeting that—and the pastor was present—he was told and the whole committee was told that this church was not spiritually ready to have her presented. [He was] told that there would be a division in the church when this matter was submitted for a vote, and the request was made at that time that the person not be submitted; that it be postponed, and that we go into a series of conferences of study, of prayer, of talking together to see if we could come to a spiritual union before the

102

actual submission to the church for membership of Mrs. Bryant. That request was refused by the pastor primarily, saying that he thought it should come to an issue at that time, and as you know, she was submitted the next Sunday morning and that precipitated deep division in the church.

This is a very curious and erroneous statement. How could the coming of Mrs. Bryant have been a surprise to him? I had told the entire committee of the possibility of her coming. When the matter of presenting Mrs. Bryant was discussed it was the feeling of the Membership Committee that she should be presented. It was the opinion only of the chairman that she should not be. It is rather curious that his reason for this was that the church was not spiritually ready. As I have indicated previously, I had tried to get the deacons to interpret the *Commitments* and prepare the church in August 1969. It was Mr. Brown who had spoken against taking any action on the ground that to do so would be only theoretical as long as we did not have any black people seeking membership.

Mr. Brown then went on to claim that some members of the staff agreed with him that the church was not spiritually ready, although he admitted that he had not learned this "directly from the staff . . . but in a roundabout way." In the light of the statements made by the staff at various church conferences, this was rumor, not fact. Mr. Brown went on:

> I am firmly of the opinion today that we are never going to come to any spiritual conclusion on this question by any sort of series of study conferences or prayer until Dr. Gilmore leaves the scene. I do not believe as long as he is here that we can come to any spiritual union on this particular question, and that is the reason why on the one hand I say we are not ready to vote on the question spiritually. We are not one on it. We have not been prepared for it. But on the other hand, I think as long as he is here we are not going to be. So I think we need to come to the point where we can go ahead and take a vote on it. If it causes a split in the church, then so be it.

He then stated his position regarding receiving blacks into the membership of the church. "I am in favor," he said, "of not denying membership to any person solely because of race . . . and I personally am going to vote in favor of the question."

Mr. Nash, who had sought to amend the motion so that Negroes would be refused membership, said heatedly that it was his conviction that if the deacons had faced up to the issue a

103

year before the church would not now have to face this situation. As far as discussion, prayer, and study periods, his response was:

> You could talk to me—you would say, "Well, he's an old hardhead"—but you're not going to change my thinking. You can't just pick out a little Scripture here and there and other places and say, "If you don't believe this, you're not a Christian." . . . I think if we deny someone membership in this congregation because he creates dissension, we have a perfect right to do that. You are not denying them salvation. If they are a true Christian, they don't want to create dissension. They don't want to disturb a congregation. Now, if we were the only church and it was a matter of their getting spiritual feeding, then I think every member in this church would say take them in. We would do it without hesitation. They have churches to go to. I imagine—I think that I can pretty well say—that if I went out to the colored church to join up with them, I wouldn't feel comfortable. I don't act the way they do. I don't believe the way they do. My morals are different from theirs. Now, why should we let down our bars? . . . I think this church has got to take a firm stand on this, or this bickering will go on and on and on. And until we make up our minds and let the outside people know—and it's for the pleasure of the outside world—let's not continue this dilly-dallying. . . . I think the time has come that unless we do take a stand, this congregation will continue to divide itself and we won't have peace.

An older member of the church now spoke forcefully against receiving black members:

> Friends, I have been a member of this church for forty-seven years. I have lived in Birmingham since 1902 when the population was 38,000 people. I was on the board of deacons in the latter part of 1940. Shortly after the end of World War II when Dr. Slaughter was here—one of the greatest preachers we have ever had in this church—Dr. Slaughter and the board of deacons at that time rejected the idea of integrating this church. That was brought about by a sailor coming back who had served on a submarine with some Negroes and his ideas had been precisely changed. The deacons and Dr. Slaughter were very much worried about this man, and they instructed the ushers what to do if any Negroes should approach the doors and try to enter this church.
>
> Now in recent times the entire northside of Birmingham has been almost completely occupied by Negroes. This church stands within five or six blocks distance of the border of that Negro settlement.

104

The value of this church and all its properties is somewhere around a million dollars, I've been told, or probably more. Now don't be fooled. The NAACP and other people are watching what we are going to do tonight. Let me tell you this. Nobody can see for a certainty what is in the future, but I believe with all my soul if we let down the bars to integrate this church, that within three years or less it will be better than ninety percent black, and I doubt if there will be very many of you people around here tonight who will be members of this church. Judge Grooms, whom I have a great deal of respect for, recently stated that he hoped his funeral would be conducted in this church. Well I hope, Judge, that you live for many years. But if we let down the bars and take in the Negroes, they will take control and they will monopolize this church. I don't think Judge Grooms would want to have his funeral conducted in this church. Now my friends, you had better take a long and hard look at this matter.

Dr. Gilmore has come here and has stirred up an awful stink, if you will excuse the expression. He has divided this church and has split us wide open. We are losing around $3,000-$4,000 each week in donations, in offerings. How long can that keep on and a church be able to function financially? There is a lot more to this thing than has been brought to light. So I urge you with all the emphasis at my command that you do not take in Negroes in this church as members. They have other places to go to, and let them go there and worship in their own way, which is certainly different from ours.

Now here is another thing. I don't believe that God Almighty ever intended to mix the different races socially, religiously, and otherwise. Now, what can integration of this church mean? How many young people meet at the church, fall in love with each other, and marry? And what would be the results? I wonder if Dr. Gilmore would want some of his boys to marry some Negro girls? I wonder if some of you people on his side who have children would want that same kind of thing to happen? I'd rather see my grandchildren in the grave today than see that happen.

And I'll tell you one more thing. I think integration is against the law of nature. I know of only one or two animals in all the kingdom of animals that I know anything about that mingle and mix with each other. That is true of all the fowls. They certainly do not inter-mate, inter-marriage, that kind of thing. As I said before, there is a lot more behind this matter than you might think, and you had better think long and hard before you vote to take Negroes into this church.

105

At this juncture, Mr. Hubert Caraway rose to speak. He had been a member of the church since 1962, and during the years his attitudes on race had changed radically. He said:

> I suppose there was no one more prejudiced toward the black race than Hubert Caraway. I travel quite a bit, and I would cringe when a person of another race was in the same restaurant or the same hotel, same airplane, but there has been a change in me and for the better. I have a feeling of release and relief within my soul that I haven't had for many years, and I attribute much of it to ... Herbert Gilmore. I don't have the prejudices at all that I once had. ...

> Now this is something that is soul-searching to me, and you can call it testimony or a confession, but I do not know when I have felt that I have been living better as a Christian than since this great man of ours has been pastor—and his staff. I stand behind them, because I think that if we will accept this leadership, First Baptist Church in Birmingham will be a great church.

My associate, Mack Goss, spoke to the issue against a broad background. "I see in our church here," he said, "maneuverings and attitudes that I think are rather a microcosm of what I see in the Southern Baptist Convention." He underscored how this was affecting our youth. One indication of this was the decline in the number of young men entering the Christian ministry. One of the major reasons for this, he said, is the way churches conduct themselves. He made an impassioned plea for the church to vote in favor of an open membership.

Mr. Porter, the two-time attender, replied:

> Last Wednesday and tonight we were told the eyes of the world were upon us, and they truly are. Gus Hall is looking right down on us. I am sure that all of you know who Gus Hall is. The Southern Baptist Convention is breaking up. I have relatives who work there, and they have told me what is happening. We have had many churches resign just because of actions like this. I have four Negroes that I work with all the time. One has been with my family fifty years. That doesn't mean that I want him in my church. This, tonight, is very obviously another attempt to continue this discussion on until many of our older members, and those who have to get up and go to work, must leave.

He then moved that the conference be adjourned until the following Wednesday, September 2, to continue the discussion. This motion was adopted at 10:20 p.m.

106

Something happened on Sunday, August 30, that indicated the extent to which the situation at First Baptist had deteriorated. The Rev. Joe Boone Abbott, Director of Clinical Pastoral Training at the Baptist Medical Center, and his wife and family presented themselves for membership in the church. One of the segregationist members objected. According to the by-laws, then, the Abbotts could not become members now until the objection had been heard by the pastor and deacons. It was ironic that the very people who were making much of the membership decline during the past year were responsible for lodging this objection. From this time on, no one was permitted to join the church. The segregationists were very explicit as to the reason: anyone asking to join the church at this time "would vote the way the preacher wanted them to vote." They were not going to take any chances in losing the upper hand. At the September deacons' meeting, Mr. Dunn, the former minister, explained the objections of the segregationists to receiving the Abbotts into the membership. He objected, he said, "to outsiders injecting themselves into a family quarrel; the Abbotts could not add harmony but further dissension in the church." He said that he "also objected to the motivation of the Abbott family in presenting themselves for membership."

Mr. Wallace Henley, the Religion Editor for the Birmingham *News*, attended the worship service at which the Abbotts were rejected for membership. He wrote of this tragic event in his column on the following Saturday, entitling the article "Distrust to Fear, Then Desperation."*

It was in an atmosphere of deep distrust that the church met for conference on September 2 to continue the discussion of the motion before the congregation: "That all applicants for membership in the First Baptist Church will be considered, as in the past, on an individual basis, and will be neither accepted nor rejected because of race or color."

The first to speak was Federal Judge H. H. Grooms, Sr. His statement is worthy of careful scrutiny by all churchmen seeking to understand the biblical witness regarding the church and racial brotherhood.† Judge Grooms recalled some of the history of the church since 1927, when he had joined. It was clear that

*The text of Mr. Henley's article appears as Appendix 10.

†The text of Judge Grooms' remarks appears as Appendix 11.

here was a man with a deep concern for the church. He then proceeded—in one of the most effective presentations on the topic I had ever heard—to bring to bear the biblical witness on the subject of race. Then he addressed himself to the practical consequences for First Baptist Church of what the Bible had to say: for its foreign mission outreach, for the church's own future, for the *Commitments* it had made in 1968.

I was moved deeply by the statement of Judge Grooms. However, the person who spoke next expressed the sentiment of the great host of the segregationist opposition. Obviously, what Judge Grooms had been seeking to convey escaped him entirely. To convey the tone and spirit of his response, I quote his statement in its entirety:

> Thank you very much, Judge, for what I would call a lengthy dissertation. This is my first appearance before a microphone in connection with these conferences which we have been having. When we go to consider this proposition of whether or not we should integrate this church, why should we depend on people who are more or less studying about the theoretical situation or some other kind of situation that really has but very little meaning. Here is an article that appeared in the Birmingham *News* about sixty days ago by Dr. David K. Grant, President of Daniel Payne College, a colored college out here adjacent to our airport. This property has been sold to the city of Birmingham and, according to the papers, the city of Birmingham paid the Daniel Payne College $800,000 for the property, and they are now seeking another location, which I hope they will soon be able to establish.
>
> Dr. Grant appeared in Boston, Massachusetts, before an assembly in which he said: "Integration, as the idea exists today, may spell almost immediate and catastrophic ruination for the United States." This was spoken by a Negro Birmingham man. Dr. David K. Grant, President of Daniel Payne College, in a speech in Boston, at the recent New England Rally for God and Family and Country said: "If this kind of integration we are experiencing continues, I predict that within another decade there will be stored in the hearts and minds of blacks pressures that will explode in such a way that no gun nor gas, nor any kind of bomb, will be able to stop one of the greatest catastrophes that this country has ever seen."
>
> Don't you think it's high time that we should pay considerable attention to what men like Dr. Grant have to say, instead of going off with a great many statements on the part of men and women who do not know specifically the real significance of what they are trying to get us to do? Dr. Grant said that the present concept is not

108

working. He said they want black teachers for black pupils. He said they don't want the white man's education because the white man's education is not the thing that will do the Negro the most good and, consequently, they want to use their own people in their own colleges or their own universities for the purpose of educating their people. I think sometimes we are more or less like the little boy going through the cemetery whistling to keep up courage. We have heard quite a number of people during these conferences speaking to us about love. Do you know who they were? You know most of them. I do. Did you see any expression of love on their faces when they were talking? I remember one of them we had here in Birmingham, an individual who had what I call a "million-dollar smile," one that you couldn't wear off, and one that was there professionally, and when they spoke of love, they manifested it in their own faces and expressions.

Allow me to digress for just a moment. It is my thought that if I were a young man and I were going to study for the ministry, I think about the first thing that I would want to do would be to join Barnum and Bailey Circus to become a clown, in order that I might learn something about the real facts of life, so that when I got out in my work I would be able, not only to explain it to myself, but to manifest it to other people as well. We are running a little short on time, and so, Brother Moderator, I want to say that he who laughs last, laughs best.

At this juncture, Mr. Findlay, one of the most vocal segregationists, said that he didn't see that any good would come from further talk and moved that debate be cut off and the vote be taken. This motion to cut off debate carried, and brought us to the moment of truth when the church would vote on the main motion—"All applicants for membership in the First Baptist Church will be considered, as in the past, on an individual basis and will be neither accepted nor rejected because of race or color." As I waited for the tabulation to be brought back to the church body, I prayed fervently that the discussion of the past few weeks—especially the statement Judge Grooms had made earlier in the meeting—would influence a sufficient number of people to carry the motion. My hopes crashed when the moderator announced the results: the motion was defeated 240-217.

At that moment I recognized the hopelessness of the church. Jesus' statement reverberated in my mind as I left the sanctuary—"If the light that is in thee be darkness, behold, how great is that darkness."

109

III

A special church conference was held the following Wednesday, September 9, to hear a supplemental report of the church Nominating Committee, whose responsibility it was to secure lay leadership for various positions in the church.

The session featured an attempt by the segregationists to seize control of the church by electing their candidates to the places of leadership. Having won the vote the preceding week not to accept Negroes, they moved on to seize the reins of power in order to control the future of the church. At the very beginning of the conference, a tip-off of things to come was given. After the Nominating Committee's report had been circulated, a leading member of the segregationist opposition, Mr. Dodd, amended the report. In an obvious power play, he offered a list of segregationist deacons to replace those suggested by the regular Nominating Committee. Should the segregationists succeed in securing the thirteen places open on the diaconate, they would gain control of the deacon body. The amendment passed easily—233-157. After a brief parliamentary hassle, a segregationist I will call Mr. Perry moved that the two lists of deacons be separated, and that they be voted on as separate groups. The chair ruled that this was in order and called for discussion.

A teen-ager, Mike Baker, took everyone aback by saying:

> While I was waiting on the tally, I noticed on the back of the page, Article 2, Section 2 of the *Manual of Rules*, the last sentence: "They shall be diligent in their attendance upon the services, and shall manifest at all times full cooperation with the church leadership and the entire program of the church."
>
> I would like to hear from these people who have been added to the report of the Nominating Committee verbally; that they fit these qualifications of "full cooperation with the church leadership and the entire program of the church," and that there be factual evidence that these people will attempt to be diligent in their attendance upon the services.

Mr. Nash violently disagreed with this request. This exchange prompted Dr. Tom Davis, a young deacon and a relatively new member, to confess that he was not acquainted with many of those suggested. At his request, the moderator had the candidates of both slates to come to the front of the church.

At this juncture I tried to prevent a take-over by the segregationists by speaking directly to the issue in the light of the requirements for a deacon as stated in the by-laws:

I could not possibly live with my conscience if I did not say something at this juncture. Surely all of us are aware that the kind of behavior that is going on here means *finis* for this church. I would point out to you one thing that is very significant. The last sentence of the by-laws which has been read is being violated at this very time. This body elected its Nominating Committee—all the body. The Nominating Committee has spent hours and hours studying carefully the various positions to be filled by various members of the church and yet, as was done on July 22, and now is being done again tonight, their work is thrown away. This is not in the spirit of following the leadership of the church—the lay leadership of the church.

Moreover, let everybody understand that most of the men who have been selected by Mr. Dodd and his group have done anything but cooperate with the pastor, the staff, and the leadership of this church. Instead of promoting peace, harmony, and a spirit of cooperation, they have sown the seeds of discord. They have been guilty of rumor-mongering—and I can cite you chapter and verse—and they have entered into league with those who would not only not cooperate with the pastor and staff, the leadership called by this church, but have done all in their power previously, and even at this moment have plans as soon as possible, to dismiss the pastor summarily.

I make no plea for myself, but I would lay it on your conscience, all of you, that if you vote to put this group in a place of spiritual leadership, then you have done that which drives the last nail in the casket of the church. Most of these men, according to the very by-laws which we are supposed to operate under, have violated everything that it says. I would urge their defeat.

Mr. Porter objected strongly to my remarks. Even though I had been careful to qualify my statement by saying that *most* of the men on the segregationist slate had not cooperated, Mr. Gates, one of the most thoroughgoing segregationists, who had been helpful, took offense to what I had said. "I dare you," he said, "in the last ten years to have been here on Saturday morning, and watched me clean up this church and repair your air conditioners. Your air conditioner wouldn't be working tonight if it weren't for my cooperation." Mike Baker responded to this statement:

111

When I asked the question that I did, it wasn't whether these people had given so much service to the church or been members for 52 years. It was whether these people are in accordance with the by-laws *that were not written by Dr. Gilmore.* My interpretation of leadership is the pastor and staff, and not the air conditioning system. I admire people who give this much time to the church. It shows they are really concerned in keeping it in running order. But I think that these people should, by order of the chair, state in accordance with the by-laws their cooperation with the pastor and the staff, and the leadership of the church, and also give their approval to all the programs and ministries that this church is at this time trying to fulfil through commitments that we accepted two years ago. And I think it would be in the best interest of all the people here if these people would do this, because right now I don't know where a lot of these people stand, but I would like to know. And if these people are delinquent with the qualifications as stated in the Blue Book, I would like to have them taken from the list.

Mr. W. B. Rogers, Sr., chairman of the church Nominating Committee, stated that at the July 22 meeting, even before his committee had submitted a list of deacons, another list of deacons was being circulated. He said the committee knew that this was coming. He spoke with urgency about this:

What you do with this report or what you do to it is strictly between you and your Lord. It is strictly between you and your best concept of the future of First Baptist Church. We have had high hopes and excited feelings about the ministries of the church under the leadership of the dedicated, committed staff that you have brought here. We are hopeful, and are still hopeful, that God has a use for this group here in this place; that he will bring about his purposes regardless of us who are weak, cynical, selfish, envious, greedy. All of us have these things in our hearts.

Mr. Long, who objected originally to the coming of the blacks for membership, said that he did not "want to feel like a sinner because nominations had been made from the floor," because the by-laws provided for that. (This provision of the by-laws was, indeed, being violated, because the nominations had not come from the floor, but through behind-the-scenes scheming.) He said that he was certain the men elected would cooperate "with the right leadership of the church. It could be that we've got the wrong leadership. Have you ever thought about that? A lot of people do think so. A lot of people are not convinced. But let the majority rule."

Judge Grooms challenged the amendment to vote by slates:

> I do not believe that we should vote on the deacons as a block. I have never heard of a Baptist church voting that way. The reason why you had a right to nominate from the floor was so that nominees could be voted on individually. Now, if you are going to vote on this thing on slates, then I don't have a right to vote. I think a Baptist ought to have the right to vote for whomever he wants to for deacon. I see some of my closest personal friends on this other side. There is no rule anywhere that requires that you vote on a slate. We are passing on individual deacons. This Nominating Committee report is not a slate because you have the right to nominate from the floor. I think we ought to vote on deacons individually. Let's put all the names up there and let the thirteen best men be the nominees here.

The chair ruled that individuals from both lists could be voted on if the amendment before the body was defeated, and the thirteen with the highest vote would be elected.

One of the very active men in the church, in evaluating both lists, said: "I can go up and down the list and I can say with no doubt in my mind whatsoever that the majority of deacons that have been selected by the Nominating Committee have been active on Sunday morning, Sunday night, in Training Union, and on Wednesday night. I, also, can say with no shadow of doubt in my mind whatsoever, that the majority of the others have not."

Judge Grooms noted that "on basic Baptist principles, this is out of order," and asked for the chair to so rule. He continued, "I think everybody ought to be able to vote for whomever he pleases. I think the results would be the same anyway, but everybody should be able to vote for the thirteen people best qualified in his opinion to serve as deacons. I have never heard of this happening in a Baptist church."

The reply of the chair was: "I agree with you. I have seen lots of things happen here in the last three or four weeks that have not happened in other Baptist churches." The chair then called for a one-minute recess to speak with Judge Grooms and Mr. Dodd, the sponsor of the segregationist slate. After the recess, the chair appealed to the congregation to express itself as to whether it felt that the amendment, calling for voting on separate slates, was out of order. The congregation voted 186 to 167 to continue the debate concerning the voting on deacons by slates rather than individually.

113

A relatively new member asked how the congregation, if it voted by slate, could know how the individual nominees felt about the program and leadership of the church. Mr. Dodd chose to ignore that question, and stated that he was only "a representative of a group" when he made the motion. He confessed that the group had spent many hours determining who should be nominated. His slate, he said, was composed of "men who have been put on the shelf in years gone by; who were never asked to serve again." This was a familiar refrain of the opposition: a common charge was that the church was being run by six families.

Mr. Nash picked up this theme of the control certain people had had in the church. "We've got to come to a screeching halt with some of these things that have been going on." Mrs. H. H. Grooms, Sr., asked him what he meant by "some of these things." He replied that everyone was "well aware of some of the programs that are going on in this church."

Mrs. Grooms responded, "I'm right in the middle of them."

"Okay," he said, "some of us don't approve of these programs."

Did he want to eliminate all of the programs?

"The point that I am trying to say is this: this church is split wide open over these programs . . . now what we are trying to do, we are trying to get this church back on the road, the road that God would have us travel."

With searching earnestness, Mrs. Grooms asked, "Does it come down to this—that we wipe out all the commitments, all of the things that we are doing that were started really before Dr. Gilmore came here—before Dr. Gilmore came, Mr. Nash? . . . I am very interested in what the WMU has been doing for the last few years. The WMU started these ministries. We started the internationals group, and we started these other things. Now, I want to know, before I vote on anybody, and I don't care whose slate they are—one slate or another—are you going to eliminate all of the programs?" She also responded to the charge that six families had been running the church: "I want you to know that I am proud to be one of the six families that Mr. Dodd and a few others could do without at the First Baptist Church, because we work too hard and have gotten too prominent in the work at First Baptist Church. Now, that came as a real shock to me because I felt like I was just one of the servants down here. Are you going to destroy the programs?"

114

Mr. Nash sidestepped her questions by saying that the deacons could not eliminate the programs that the church voted for; that the deacons were simply an advisory body.

In response to Mrs. Grooms' query regarding the programs, Dr. Williamson, a deacon, declared himself. When he stood to speak a chorus of boos greeted him. "I appreciate those boos," he said, "but if you don't mind, I'll go on and say my piece." He stated that he was for an open church and for the various programs, including the coffeehouse ministry, the international ministry, the tutoring program, and the *Commitments* the church had made. His concluding statement is worthy of the careful consideration of everyone who would wish to see his church be a dynamic one:

> This is an exciting time. It can be a tremendously exciting time for you and for me and for everybody here in this church to try. Now, I don't know whether we will win or lose. This coffeehouse is one of the examples. It may be the biggest flop First Baptist Church has ever had. We may get into the biggest mess. You may have hippies and all kinds of people who don't believe as we do, don't think as we do, don't act as we do. I don't know, but you don't know either. Unless you try something, you never get anywhere. . . . Now I know that you people who are on the opposite side think that you are protecting the church from us young radicals. The other side feels that they are protecting the church also. I have told you the things that I am for and I am for them 100 percent. If they don't work, they are new ideas—ideas that are interesting—we don't just sit and do nothing. We try. If we fail, we stop that and we try something else. But I think it is tremendously important to try something, and if we make a mistake, why let us make a mistake. Let's back off and try something else.

Judge Grooms moved "that this session be adjourned until Sunday morning, and that printed ballots be prepared for the whole congregation with the names of all twenty-six people on the ballot." Mr. Findlay amended the motion to adjourn until the following Wednesday, September 16. The chair made it plain that any adjournment would be a continuation of this meeting, with no debate cutoff, and the issue would be debated regarding voting on two separate slates of deacons. He further explained, in response to a question, that the twenty-six names would be on the ballot, but that they could be voted on with one "x" at the top of a given slate. The amendment to adjourn until the following Wednesday carried.

The monthly deacons' meeting was held on Monday, September 14. The action taken at this meeting was very significant for subsequent events in the life of the church. As indicated previously, an objection had been raised to the Abbott family's request for membership. The particulars of this objection were brought by Mr. Dunn, a former minister, to the deacons' meeting. Mr. Brown sought to defer any discussion about the Abbotts' request until the November deacons' meeting, but his motion failed to carry. Instead, Mr. W. B. Rogers, Sr., moved "that the deacons found the objection invalid and unscriptural, and that Mr. Joe Boone Abbott and family be recommended for membership in the church." This motion was adopted by a vote of 14-6, with 7 abstentions.

Chairman Marvin Prude then asked the deacons to make a recommendation to the church concerning action to be taken in receiving persons who present themselves for membership. This was urgently needed inasmuch as no one at the present time could join the church, because objections were being lodged against them automatically. Furthermore, the applications of the candidates who had been presented on July 5—the two blacks and four whites—were still in limbo, even though the deacons on July 6 had recommended them for membership. Mr. Brown now moved that "the deacons instruct the pastor not to present any candidates for membership for a vote by the church on their membership until after the quarterly conference in October 1970." This was an obvious attempt to stall. He knew that the segregationist slate of deacons would be elected before that time, and that they would not present the two blacks for membership. This motion failed, and the following motion was made by Mr. Billy Austin: "That the deacons recommend to the church at the special church conference on September 16, 1970, that the church accept members, and that no one object unless there are objections which are valid and scriptural." Mr. Brown amended the motion so that the pastor would give the church one week's notice before the vote was taken. To my surprise, the motion as amended passed unanimously.

At the beginning of the special conference on September 16, yet another parliamentary tug-of-war started. The chair explained that the motion before the house was to separate the two lists of deacons and vote on them as separate groups. He added that if the church wanted to discuss the qualifications of the deacons that that would come later.

Mr. Dodd argued that according to *Robert's Rules of Order* a motion related to methods of voting was not debatable. He then called for the question. The moderator replied that he did not recognize any motion before the body that was not debatable, unless there was a motion to cut off debate. A long and involved discussion ensued. Mr. Dodd interpreted the previous motion—which provided for the two slates of deacons—as a motion about a method of voting and therefore not debatable. The chair, however, ruled this out of order, as he felt it was a ruse by which to cut off debate. Immediately the decision of the chair was appealed. While the ballots were being passed out there were several questions from the segregationists that indicated a desire to cut off any further debate. The chair was overruled, and, declaring that there would be no further debate, Mr. Prude explained that the church was now voting on the motion to separate the two lists of deacons, one presented by the Nominating Committee, one submitted by Mr. Dodd. He was careful to point out that the body was voting on the motion, not on the deacons as such. The motion to separate the two lists carried.

The chair declared that the time had come for electing the deacons, and it was in order to raise questions or to discuss the election of these men who were to serve. Mr. Brown asked the chair to rule on "whether or not discussion as to the persons who have been nominated is in order." Mr. Prude responded by ruling that it was, since there were people who had questions in their minds.

Once again Mr. Dodd appealed the decision of the chair, even though Mr. Brown was still standing to continue his speech. The chair bristled, "I will not be intimidated here with this tonight, Mr. Dodd." After a brief recess, the chair asked Mr. Brown to continue, but he was prevented because Mr. Dodd continued his appeal. Mr. Nash joined forces with Mr. Dodd to remind the chair that an appeal had been made. The chair ruled him out of order, and Mr. Brown continued speaking. He sought to prevent any questioning of the deacon candidates, or discussion of their merits, by quoting a sentence from the church by-laws charging the deacons with "promoting peace, harmony, and the spirit of cooperation among the membership." It was his contention that none of the deacons of either slate could meet this test, and if

117

the church were to apply literally all the sentences of the by-laws, it was not possible for it to have any deacons at all. He summarized his position by saying:

> You've got one group that supports assumedly one philosophy. You've got another group that assumedly supports another philosophy. We might as well say that we are voting between the two philosophies. So, you might as well vote for one group or the other group on the basis of their philosophy, not on the individual qualifications since we are voting by slates.

A bitter exchange now ensued between Mr. Porter and the moderator, the essence of Mr. Porter's charge being that the chair was unfair in not permitting the appeal. The chair explained that a motion to cut off debate was in order and that he would recognize such a motion. The exchange became so bitter that a brief recess was called, during which Mr. Prude spoke to Mr. Dodd, who had made the appeal, Mr. Brown, Mr. Porter, Dr. Williamson, and Judge Grooms. After the recess, the chair explained his position as follows:

> The chair will look to the congregation for guidance in this matter . . . we are going to vote on sustaining the chair or overruling the chair in this matter of debate. The chair feels that this appeal is taken under the cloak of cutting off debate. I feel . . . it is absolutely wrong. I feel as if you are depriving some of the people here the opportunity to intelligently inquire as to the nominees' position on the various facets of the church's programs. I feel as if it is democracy at its best to let these discussions or questions be propounded. However, there seems to be concern for not getting this information across to the people, but in cutting off debate. Now this appeal has been made to virtually cut off debate. It could take a two-thirds ruling, but I am asking you to sustain the chair in this ruling and some guidance in this matter, so we are going to take a vote on this. What will it take to win this? On the appeal, on the guidance here, it will take a simple majority.

After some further wrangling and harassment of the chair by the segregationist opposition, the vote was taken. The chair was overruled. He explained in very careful detail the procedure for voting. Mr. Long and Mr. Nash now went to great pains, under the guise of speaking to the issue, to instruct the congregation how to vote. After the second effort by Mr. Nash, Dr. Thomas Davis spoke sharply: "Mr. Chairman, he is out of order. He is instructing these people in voting and he has been doing it all night."

118

As the congregation waited for the counting of the ballots, the chair asked all to engage in a period of silent prayer. When the results of the balloting were announced, it came as a surprise to no one that the entire segregationist slate was elected. These men were asked to come to the front. As I looked into the faces of these men I became sad, as I pondered the kind of church First Baptist would become under this kind of leadership.

5

*"We favor a membership which will be
open to any person who accepts Jesus
Christ as Savior and Lord, and who
desires to pattern his life after Christ's
teachings."* (Statement of Position,
The Company of the Committed)

The Company of the Committed

I

The church was now in the control of the segregationists. At
the July 22 church conference they had placed one of their
number as chairman of all the strategic committees. And at the
September 16 conference they had been able to fill all thirteen
deacon vacancies with their segregationist slate. I knew, and the
creative leadership knew, that there was no way now by which
to right the church.

In light of the resolution the deacons had made concerning
the receiving of members, it remained for Mrs. Bryant and Twila
to be presented to the church for membership. They had been
waiting since their first rejection on July 5. All of the other
candidates had agreed that they did not want to be presented
for membership at this time. Several of them said to me that
they "wanted to wait to see if the church accepted the blacks."
If it did not, they did not want to join either. In accordance
with the resolution to give the church one week's notice before
the vote, the congregation was informed through the church
paper that they would be presented on Sunday, September 27,

at the morning worship hour. According to the by-laws, a two-thirds majority was required for them to be received into the membership.

For several days prior to the presentation of Mrs. Bryant and Twila, I sought to prepare myself emotionally to resign in the event they were rejected. Once the resignation was written and I had prepared myself unequivocally for this act, I asked my staff to meet me at my home on Saturday night, September 26. I briefed them thoroughly as to what I was going to do in the event the blacks were rejected. I emphasized that they were free to do as they wished and that I was putting no pressure on them to resign. Miss Betty Bock, the Minister of Youth, indicated that she too felt she must resign in moral protest if the blacks were rejected. But when our meeting ended I did not know what action the other staff members would take.

When I walked into the pulpit on Sunday morning, September 27, the sanctuary was filled: the segregationists once again had succeeded in getting many members there who had not been in the church for years. It was the first time many of them had ever heard me preach.

I preached that morning on "The Meaning of Fellowship." In the sermon I tried to sound the biblical note that was relevant to this momentous decision. As I closed the sermon I said:

> Genuine fellowship unites men of differing backgrounds and outlook. John says it so well: "He who says he is in the light and hates his brother is in the darkness still. He who loves his brother abides in the light, and in it there is no cause for stumbling. But he who hates his brother is in the darkness and does not know where he is going, because the darkness has blinded his eyes" (1 John 2:9-11). How relevant this is for our modern scene! When Paul wrote his epistle to the Corinthians, he emphasized that "there are diversities of gifts, but the same spirit." We need to recapture the biblical idea that fellowship is sharing a common treasure, the fellowship of the Holy Spirit. This will correct the prevalent notion that fellowship is a back-slapping, happy association of like-minded people. When we ground the fellowship in something beyond itself, pointing it to its source of power for the doing of its work, we are not concerned to make every individual conform to a set pattern. With Christ in the center, there is ample room for many ministries. The uniqueness of each personality can be utilized. The diversities in cultural, national, and racial backgrounds can be brought to the service of the Christian fellowship.

121

Indeed, the fellowship of the Holy Spirit, which is the church, is God's instrument for achieving his purpose in history, which is to bring all peoples and nations to the worship of Jesus Christ. It is commissioned to "sum up all things in Christ." The church, as the "New Israel," must be an all-inclusive fellowship. Nothing is to keep men out of it except their failure to hear and answer the call of the love of God. This beloved fellowship of the church is to transcend all barriers which men artificially erect. In a daring image, Paul insists that so long as any race remains outside the society of the church, the fellowship is in that measure defective and is missing one of its limbs or members (Ephesians 2:11-22). The church is to win all nations that they in turn may contribute to it. Then, and then only, shall we see the fulness of the Christ—when we are all become a full-grown man, the one man in Christ Jesus, grown to the fullness of his stature.

I preached earnestly, hoping that a miracle of grace might take place in the hearts of the hearers so that, obeying the gospel, they would vote to accept these black people into the membership.

I shall always treasure the compassionate concern expressed by Katherine Goss, my associate's wife, who volunteered to stand next to Mrs. Bryant and Twila when they were presented to the congregation. She had been Mrs. Bryant's Sunday School teacher, and a genuine bond of love had been forged between them. Katherine, like many of us, could never forget the tear-stained face of Mrs. Bryant that mirrored her spiritual desolation when she was rejected in July. She wanted to identify with her in utter commitment.

Mrs. Bryant and Twila were presented to the congregation without any fanfare or cajoling. When the vote was taken, the majority voted to receive them, as they had done previously on July 5, but a two-thirds majority was required. I went to the pulpit and apologized to the two of them, because the church had refused to receive them into the membership, and then I read my resignation:

Two years ago I began my ministry among you. At that time I was convinced that God had led me here. The *Commitments* which the church had made in July 1968 awakened in me a deep desire to help you accomplish these goals. My whole being responded to the fashioning of a church that was truly a church. In the light of the *Commitments* I envisioned a church that:

— Was concerned to meet human need in as many ways as possible.

— Was concerned to preach the gospel of Christ by word and deed, with the hope of relating men and women of our community to Christ as Savior and Lord.

— Was open to anyone on one basis only: that he was a disciple of Jesus Christ.

My understanding of the Christian faith compels me to believe that:

— God is the Father of us all; therefore, "he is no respecter of persons."

— Christ died for all; all persons, therefore, are of infinite worth.

— In Christ neither color, condition, race, or sex is significant.

— The church is the Body of Christ commissioned to reconcile all men to God, because it is a group of men who are already at one with God and with each other.

This morning, by your action in rejecting these two people, because they are black, you have denied these fundamental truths of the Christian Faith. I have said that I would not be the pastor of a racist church. I meant what I said! So this morning I respectfully request that you accept my resignation, effective November 1, 1970.*

I grieve in my heart that it could not have been different. I ask God and you to forgive me wherein I have erred. Keenly conscious of my shortcomings, yet I must say to you that my motivation has been right, that I have worked hard, and done the best I could.

With love in my heart for you all, I pray that God may guide you in the days ahead.

In that emotional moment I saw men and women weeping openly in bitter disappointment.

Miss Bock, as a matter of personal commitment and Christian conviction, then read her resignation:

Dear Members of the First Baptist Church:

The experiences which I have been permitted to have as a member of First Baptist Church during the past four years have had a life-changing impact on my life. The past twelve months in which I have

*This date was later changed to October 31, since November 1 was Sunday, and there was a concern among some of the segregationists that if I preached on November 1 they would be legally responsible for my salary for all of November. Had I thought of it earlier I would indeed have resigned as of October 31.

served as Minister of Youth have provided a challenge to which I have sought to give every ounce of my energy. I am very grateful for the privilege of having served in this position.

With deep regret I feel that I must submit to you my resignation effective November 1.

The action taken here this morning makes it impossible for me to continue my ministry. I cannot lead in ministries in which evangelism and ministry must be separated. To minister to any individual in the name of God and to be unable to share with them the Good News for fear that they will respond, contradicts the most basic concept of the Christian faith. Twila was one of the first students to participate in our tutoring program. We have sought to communicate God's love for her and she responded. Now she is unacceptable for church membership.

I came on the staff because of the *Commitments* which were voted by the church. The ministries in which I have been involved came about because a group of people took seriously the *Commitments*. My understanding and interpretation of these *Commitments* is based on what was communicated to me as a member of the church *prior* to the adoption of it, not as I was interviewed for the staff. If I have misunderstood the *Commitments* or the church is no longer committed to the concepts expressed in it, there is no way for me to continue my ministry.

The racial issue is the basic issue in our struggle. This has been pointed out clearly in the events which led up to this moment. For example, the exodus of members after the Negro children began coming to Sunday School on a regular basis; the deacons' meeting in May at which time several deacons stated, "The basic reason for this meeting is the question of race"; the vote of the church on July 5; the vote of the deacons on July 6. The terms racist and Christian cannot be used to describe the same church.

In closing I can only say that I have done the best that I have known to do in each situation. God knows my heart and my motivation, and one day I will have to give account to him.

I am deeply grateful to each young person who has responded to my leadership. The youth of this church have had a profound effect on my life the past months. I am also grateful to each parent who has allowed me the sacred privilege of having a small part in the pilgrimage of his child. To the church I am grateful for the privilege of these past twelve months. I am as certain now as I was last September that the Lord led me here. I will wait for his leadership concerning where he would have me to serve now.

When Miss Bock finished an event took place that I shall always cherish as one of the high moments of my ministry. Dr. Byrn Williamson stood and asked to speak. As he made his way to the microphone at the front of the sanctuary, all eyes were directed to him. His first remark was to me: "Dr. Gilmore, many of the church members feel as you do that we have no moral right to deny membership to these Christians solely because they are black." Then he turned and spoke to the congregation: "We would like to show our disapproval of this action the church has taken now by standing and leaving this service immediately to assemble in room 100 of the education building for prayer." All over the sanctuary people stood and began to file out. My emotions were scrambled. On the one hand, there was a deep sadness, and on the other hand, great joy. I thought that my associate pastor, Mack Goss, who was sitting to my left, was going to faint. He kept saying, "Oh, my God!" A news reporter who was present estimated that some 300 people left the sanctuary. I remember looking behind me in the choir loft. There had been approximately sixty voices in the choir that morning and all but two—other than wives of the staff—had gone.

When those who were protesting had left, I looked at those who remained, and a sense of desolation came over me. At least eighty percent of them were sixty-five years of age or older. Oppressive thoughts surged through my mind. I was acutely aware that unless the grace of God changed the thinking of these who remained there was no future for the church. I loved these people, as I pitied them, because they had been victimized by a religion that had sold out to its culture. Families had divided over this issue. Those who remained sat in a trancelike, shocked state as they watched their fellow members leave the sanctuary. Some of them wept; others became exceedingly angry.

After I had pronounced the benediction, several of the segregationists gathered around me and expressed themselves in an ugly way. There were others, however, who spoke very kindly. They admitted that they thought the other group was right, but that they could not bring themselves to break ties of family or friendship or to create disunity in the church.

When I joined the group that had left I found a sense of quiet elation and joy, even though it was expressed frequently

125

through tears and sobs. Several of them said to me: "This is the greatest day of my life; I have never felt so free."

The exodus from the sanctuary was picked up by the news media and sent around the world. This further incensed the segregationists because, from the very beginning, they had resented any news of our struggle being known by the general public.

The group that had left the sanctuary decided they would meet again the following Sunday to talk about the possibility of establishing a new church. From the very beginning this was a lay movement. These men and women had seen a better way and they wanted to express it if at all possible in a new fellowship.

The following Sunday, October 4, the group decided to pursue in earnest the possibility of establishing a new church. They had been meeting together weekly since September 6. The calculated efforts of the segregationists to seize control of the church made them aware that they had no future in the First Baptist Church. At the September 6 meeting, Dr. Williamson, who was later elected chairman of the group, made this observation:

> It is apparent that the *Commitments* adopted by First Baptist Church of Birmingham in 1968 were not understood or accepted by a number of the members. This meeting is to afford a representative number of those devoted to the *Commitments* an opportunity to talk together.

His suggestion that the group call themselves "The Company of the Committed" (the title of Elton Trueblood's book) was adopted enthusiastically. Mrs. H. H. Grooms, Sr., seemed to express the sentiments of the group when she said: "We need to be aware that this is a parting of the ways . . . that we are the radicals . . . that we have to be able to take what is coming."

On September 13 they had adopted a "Statement of Position" that everyone who wanted to be a part of the group was asked to sign.

> Resolving to recommit ourselves individually and as a church we, the members of First Baptist Church of Birmingham, Alabama, reaffirm our position as follows:

> We support the 1968 *Commitments* of First Baptist Church, and support our present staff in the enthusiastic and determined fulfillment of these *Commitments*.

126

We favor a membership which will be open to any person who accepts Jesus Christ as Savior and Lord, and who desires to pattern his life after Christ's teachings.

We favor an innovative program that will enable us to express our commitment to a risen Lord in a free, creative, and flexible manner in ministering to the needs of our community.

The group was asked, in the light of these intentions, to continue to designate their financial contributions through the First Baptist Church during the month of October to "The Company of the Committed."

This action drew the wrath of the segregationist deacons at their monthly meeting on October 5. A motion was made by Mr. Adams that the funds designated for "The Company of the Committed" be held, until a study could be made and a recommendation be brought to the deacons. When it was reported that the funds given up to this time had already been turned over to the treasurer of the group, it was agreed to acknowledge that the transaction had been made. Mr. Dodd, the newly elected chairman, suggested, however, that the chairman of the Finance Committee secure legal advice on the future handling of designated funds for "The Company of the Committed." There was also an attempt to charge the pastor, by implication, with spending money not approved by the deacons for the renovation of the church offices. This completely false charge was rebutted by the chairman of the renovation committee.

One of the actions taken by this segregationist diaconate was especially revealing. All during my ministry I had encouraged the fullest possible use of the facilities of the church, not only for our own program of religious education, but for outside groups, both religious and secular, whose programs benefited the city. The location of the church made it ideal as a meeting place. It was the conviction of the creative group of the church that this was a ministry the church ought to perform. This idea was not, however, shared by the segregationists. The chairman of the Property Committee was instructed to investigate to ascertain if those using the building were reimbursing the church for its use. In other words, their philosophy was inimical to the church's having a concern for every dimension of life that would benefit the city. With this outlook the church could never be helpful to other groups working for the common good. There was another action that foretold a radical change. The

127

deacons referred the study of the *Commitments* adopted in 1968 to the Planning Committee. It was these *Commitments*, adopted unanimously more than two years before, that launched the ministries that resulted in the coming of the blacks. They were concerned to do something about these *Commitments* so that this could not possibly happen again.

For several months, we had been pointing toward the opening—on October 1—of a coffeehouse in one of the buildings owned by the church. Since a great deal of effort had gone into its formation, and considerable publicity had been given to it, the creative leadership decided to proceed as planned. If it were closed, it would be closed by the segregationists. The ministry through the coffeehouse to the inner city teen-agers during the month of October was effective—so effective that "The Company of the Committed" offered to pay the First Baptist Church the commercial rate to rent the building so that the ministry might be continued. The offer, however, was summarily denied, and the coffeehouse was closed on October 31—the day of separation—because, as one of the segregationist deacons explained to a reporter, "it drew too many 'niggers.' "

All during October "The Company of the Committed" met in separate meetings to chart its course for the future. They instructed their treasurer to send a letter to those who had indicated a desire to be a part of the group. Each person was asked if he thought that "The Company of the Committed" should be constituted into a church, and, if he answered yes, how much money he would give to the church annually. Within ten days, the financial pledge was in excess of $97,000, and an overwhelming number expressed the desire to form a new church. It was apparent to the leaders of the group that there was sufficient financial strength and personal commitment to proceed with the planning for a new congregation. On October 25 the group formally decided to organize a church as soon as satisfactory arrangements for worship and ministries could be made.

Since my resignation date had been changed at the October 21 church conference from November 1 to "11:59 p.m., October 31," as a segregationist put it, the group did not know where it would worship on November 1. On Wednesday, October 28, however, they were granted permission to worship at the Baptist Building Chapel on November 1 and subsequent Sundays. I was asked to serve as their "spiritual advisor."

128

At the quarterly church conference in October, all the other staff members had resigned—Associate Pastor Mack M. Goss, Minister of Education Carlisle Driggers, and Associate Pastor — Minister of Music John N. Sims. In addition, four secretaries, the organist, assistant organist, pianist, and assistant pianist resigned. The Financial Secretary, who sided with the segregationists, remained. Members of "The Company of the Committed," who held ninety percent of the places of leadership in First Baptist Church, also resigned. The separation was now final and complete. It only remained for all of us to fulfil our obligations through October 31.

II

I wrestled in my soul as to what I should say to the congregation of the First Baptist Church in my last sermon. It was not to be perfunctory to me; I was very eager that it be meaningful and redemptive, and I wanted to end on a positive note. The sermon was entitled "Finally. . . ," the title taken from Paul's statement to the church at Philippi in Philippians 4:8, 9.

"My pilgrimage of two years has left some indelible impressions on my mind. I mention these not to fault but to assist us all in grappling with the present and future demands of Christian discipleship. For one thing, I have been confirmed in my suspicion that time does not necessarily aid the good. This myth of time, as I call it, is often appealed to as a refuge from facing the harsh demands for change that is needed *now*. It is used as an argument to buttress the status quo. It is appealed to when we do not want to change our fundamental habits and practices. Time, however, is morally neutral. The actions of men determine the moral content of time.

"Christ demands that we live up to the limit of our vision and do all we can to correct the injustice and wrongs we see. If a thing is wrong, it is mandatory for the Christian to set about righting it—*now!* Anything that is wrong, whether it be adultery or racial injustice, must be corrected with all haste, to the limit of our ability.

"Recent events in our church have forced upon my mind the reality of the mystery of response to the gospel. Some of you here today have worshipped in this church twenty, thirty, or forty years. You have heard the same preachments and yet—how mysterious and mystifying—you have responded in totally different ways. Some of you have responded by opening your lives to love all men and to desire fellowship with them in the church. Others of you have responded to the same preachments by limiting your fellowship in the church to white people only. This, indeed, is a great mystery!

"Our struggle together has underscored for me the importance of what happens at the local church level in Baptist life and in the work of the Kingdom of God. What happens in the local church is of ultimate significance because this is where the gospel must take root in the world. Baptists cannot pass their problems on to a higher body for resolution or solution. So, what happens at the First Baptist Church, Birmingham, affects every Baptist church in the world; indeed, it affects the total Kingdom enterprise. It is for this reason that recent actions of our church are the occasion of great sadness and great joy. It is tragic that our church voted to exclude the blacks for membership. It is very encouraging that three hundred people put their lives on the line to receive any person who is a follower of Christ.

"As with a hot iron my mind has been branded with this fundamental affirmation: the church must recognize the priority of truth, as revealed in Christ, above all other considerations. Let me be specific! A positive stand by the pastor and many members on the matter of integration has split the church. But is it more fearful to be split now by the weakness of man or to be sifted for eternity by the judgments of God? I have been concerned as to what will happen at the day of judgment if we do not the truth.

"Our experience here reveals clearly that the truth of Christ is not determined by the counting of noses. This should be a warning and a demonstration to all Baptist churches everywhere that the democratic process is no guarantee for the triumph of the truth of Christ. The democratic process offers the best hope for orderly consideration of issues *only* when those involved in it have a prior loyalty to the truth of Christ and desire, above all else, that Christ's will be done.

"Our debacle reveals the sad state of the church and the ministry everywhere. Most churches have long since ceased to be scrupulous in their membership demands. A Baptist church is the easiest group to get into and the hardest group to get out of in the world. Great hosts of people have their names on our church rolls who neither understand nor care about the mission

130

and message of the church, or the things of Christ. But, as in our case, these people in a time of crisis vote their prejudices and determine the future of the church for which they have no concern. No single condition in our churches is in greater need of change than this one, for it makes churchmanship a travesty and mockery.

"This condition of the church has a profound bearing on the minister's relation to the church. I am convinced that in most churches it is impossible to preach the gospel of Christ in its fullness without violent controversy resulting. Instead of the churches being peopled with those who desire earnestly the gospel, there are multitudes in the church who find the gospel a scandal and offense. Instead of finding delight in the minister's opening up new vistas of the gospel, they are incensed and make him a scapegoat of their hostility.

"The reality of the demonic has become real to me. There are powers in the soul, in the church, and in society against which the mere goodwill of the best of us is powerless. I have seen people who are well-meaning, decent people become vicious in their actions. Their prejudices were touched and their actions became irrational.

"Just a few weeks ago, before the racial crisis in our church, I had dinner in the home of one of our members. Some of their neighbors were invited. I was praised to the point of my embarrassment to their neighbors. They stated then that I was 'the finest pastor and greatest preacher the church had ever had.' Nothing has happened in my relationship to this couple since then—except that two black people came for membership in this church. I became for them the scapegoat on which their hostility has been vented. . . .

"I have learned in our travail that every man must take a stand. On great moral issues such as we have confronted, no man can straddle the fence. He must take sides decisively, or in his cowardice or indecision he *has* taken sides—against the right. As Fosdick once said, 'Every man is either part of the problem or part of the answer.' Every man must decide whether his life will count for justice or injustice, for reconciliation or separation, for an inclusive church or an exclusive church.

"Lest anyone think that, in my expression of sober realism about the church I have lost faith in her, let me state categorically that I believe that the best hope for the world lies in the Christian church. I have seen this validated here. The

131

church, true to the Master's intent, is a fellowship that transcends race, nation, and class, and Jesus Christ is her chief cornerstone. Such a fellowship, uniting all men in love for each other because of their love for Christ, is the most desperate need of our world. . . .

" 'Finally, brethren, whatever is true, whatever is honorable, whatever is just, whatever is pure, whatever is lovely, whatever is gracious, if there is any excellence, if there is anything worthy of praise, think about these things . . . and the God of peace will be with you.' "

Following the benediction, the two groups of the church mingled very little. There were a few, however, who expressed to me with choked emotion that they wished they could go with our group. Several embraced me and expressed appreciation for my ministry to them and to the church. As I walked from that pulpit for the last time my only solace was that I had honestly tried to be a faithful minister of Christ. But there was a dull ache in my heart because I had not been able to commend the inclusive gospel to all the people.

III

Church people can be the most vindictive and vicious people in the world—that is, those who are *just church people*. Their cause is sacrosanct and they do their malicious work in the name of God. Their tongues are venomous and their consciences infinitesimal. They call bigotry common sense and moral courage stupidity.

Four months after I had left, the First Baptist Church finally released a statement to the press.* It appeared in the Birmingham *News* on February 26, 1971, and the Birmingham *Post-Herald* the next day. The church's officials used a denominational executive to forward this statement to the Baptist Press, and subsequently it was sent to all the Baptist state papers in the Southern Baptist Convention.

Though the statement was compounded with error, misrepresentation, and false implications, I chose not to answer its false allegations, but to respond only to the basic charge that the issue that led to my resignation was not race.

When the Baptist Press staff saw the statement released by

*The statement and my response to it appear as Appendix 12.

First Baptist, they called to ask if I had responded to their charges. A copy of my statement was sent to them. Subsequently they sent my statement, along with the First Baptist statement, to all of the Baptist state papers within the Southern Baptist Convention. Several state papers, strangely enough, chose to print only the First Baptist statement and to ignore my response altogether.

The Washington *Post* had sent Miss Betty Medsger to Birmingham in October 1970. She spent four days interviewing both my friends and foes and various community leaders—political and religious. (Her story is printed as Appendix 13. The reader can judge for himself if race was the main issue.)

The lengthy struggle, lasting several months, and sent around the world by the news media, brought more than 5,000 letters and telephone calls from around the world. Various religious groups and denominations sent copies of resolutions commending those of us who had formed the new church. Special prayers were offered by groups as diverse as Roman Catholics and Jews. Here was expressed real ecumenism, a common concern for human justice in the name of God. This is the other side of "church." These expressions of concern meant much to me; indeed, they strengthened me during critical times. I shall always be grateful for the great host of nameless friends who prayed for me and the new church. Throughout the struggle my family supported me with unswerving devotion. My wife encouraged me time and again to be true to my convictions and assured me that she was willing to pay whatever price was necessary. Even when the conflict was the most intense, her sense of humor was always present.

Many people have asked if I would do the same thing if I had to do it over. My answer is an unequivocal yes. I would try even harder to be fair and right, conciliatory and redemptive, but I would champion even more vigorously the universal love of Christ, and the inclusive nature of the Christian church. This racial struggle has greatly affected me and my family. But if I had run from it I would have become nothing more than a religious functionary, mouthing meaningless clichés, manning the religious store so as to preserve the status quo. I would have died emotionally, intellectually, and spiritually. I could not have lived with myself, knowing that I was a common coward, unworthy to wear the prophetic mantle of Christ's minister.

What has this struggle done to me? For one thing, I have been

133

dubbed a "liberal" by many of my peers and disowned by them in various ways. This saddens me, for I am a loyal Baptist, and I desire the friendship of my brethren. I am not a doctrinaire liberal and I dislike theological labels—I simply try to tell the truth as I see it. Nothing is more gratifying to me in my entire Christian experience than the genuine Christian discipleship I have witnessed in the lives of the members of The Baptist Church of the Covenant (the name adopted by The Company of the Committed). For their authenticity, their daring, their confidence and love, I shall be forever grateful.

The experience has confirmed my conviction that my highest loyalty is not to the church, but to the Lord of the church. The unity of the church is secondary to the truth of the gospel, which the church is commissioned to proclaim. To withhold the truth in order to preserve the unity of a racist church is to preserve something that is not worth preserving. A church that does not lead but allows itself to be led, a church that does not trumpet the call for racial justice, is not indispensable; Christ is! I am intrigued by and more enamored than ever of the church as Christ intends it—not as it now is. I am not disillusioned, but realistic. I cannot conceive of a Christianity apart from the church; but the church as it is causes my greatest difficulty.

The church as an institution has been very hard on me. My family has been displaced and caused to suffer greatly because of the blindness, smallness, bigotry, and prejudice of the institutional church. Nevertheless, the best people I know, the finest dreams of my experience, the most challenging goals of my existence, have come from the church. True to her Lord, creating a fellowship of the Spirit that transcends race, color, nation, condition, sex, and class, the church is the most desperate need of mankind. I intend to stay with the church and to add my feeble efforts to make it what Christ intends, in order that "justice may roll down as waters, and righteousness as a mighty stream."

The struggle has brought rich friendships with my black friends. My black friends across America have stood by me. I have preached in many of their churches and they have honored me in various ways. I have come to a better understanding of the awful, inexcusable way most of them have to live. Knowing their lot first-hand, I resolve anew to do all I can to remove their oppressive chains, forged by hate, prejudice, and injustice.

For the opportunity that has come for an enlarged ministry to the total Christian community, I am deeply grateful. The struggle has made possible my being invited to several universities, colleges, and divinity schools. The common concern of all denominations to recover the essential nature of the church and to establish racial justice has given me the high privilege of sharing in the life of the various Christian denominations. In these associations I have made new friends for which I am grateful.

Best of all, through this struggle I know afresh the reality of the presence of God—sustaining when worn out, encouraging when downhearted, instilling fire when the heart is cold, preventing the wrong word from being spoken when the tongue is hot with anger, refreshing when utterly drained. The grace of the Lord Jesus Christ is the greatest of realities to me. I thank God for the struggle and take heart!

Epilogue

The most significant thing in the struggle of the First Baptist Church of Birmingham, Alabama, is not that the segregationist opposition, by the counting of noses, had their way. Rather, it is that two hundred fifty-five people in Birmingham disavowed such a racist position and committed themselves to build an interracial, intercultural, and international fellowship. This is nothing short of a miracle in a city that only a few years before had earned itself the contempt of the world for its racial tactics. This is the city where four little girls were murdered by a cowardly bombing of the Sixteenth Street Baptist Church in 1963. John Beecher, a son of Birmingham, whose boyhood home was burned during the racial turmoil, wrote this angry and prophetic poem about Birmingham:

If I Forget Thee, O Birmingham!*

I

Like Florence from your mountain.
Both cast your poets out
for speaking plain.

II

You bowl your bombs down aisles
where black folks kneel
to pray for your blacker souls.

III

Dog-torn children bled
A, B, O, AB as you.
Christ's blood not more red.

*Robert McNeill, *God Wills Us Free* (New York: Hill and Wang, 1965), p. 200.

IV

Burning my house to keep
them out, you sowed wind. Hear it blow!
Soon you reap.

Now, however, there was to be a redemptive reaping and sow-
ing, and a portent of the birth of a new Birmingham.

"The Company of the Committed" met for the first time as a
church on November 1 at the Baptist Building Chapel (to the
dismay of some Baptists in the community). All of us were
deeply grateful to the Rev. Oley Kidd, Superintendent of
Missions for the Birmingham Baptist Association, for his kindness in urging us to use the facility. The following Sunday, "The
Company of the Committed" incorporated itself, in order that
it might be a legal entity before the law. After considerable
discussion, it chose its name—The Baptist Church of the Covenant.

The forming of the Baptist Church of the Covenant has not
been without agony and sorrow. It has divided families. Jesus
said, "Think not that I am come to send peace on earth: I came
not to send peace, but a sword. For I am come to set a man at
variance against his father, and the daughter against her mother,
and the daughter-in-law against her mother-in-law. And a man's
foes shall be they of his own household." Those words are stark
reality to many of these people. Forming a new church has
meant leaving old friends. In the case of one woman, it meant
severing a church affiliation of sixty years. Judge Grooms expressed the sentiment of many in the new church by his
statement: "Fellowship is great but is not the ultimate thing.
When unity and principle are opposed, there is no question as to
one's choice." These people are determined to be the church.

There was a marvelous enthusiasm and verve among the
people, even though the facility was much too small for the
number attending. "The Company of the Committed" had
faced up to the fact that it was impossible for all of the staff to
be kept, but it assured every staff member that he would be
taken care of financially until he could secure another place of
service.

On December 20, 1970, The Baptist Church of the Covenant
was chartered with 306 charter members, 255 of whom had
come from the First Baptist Church. Significantly, at the

chartering service, representatives from every level of Southern Baptist life were present.

The members of The Baptist Church of the Covenant have turned their faces in the right direction and felt the fresh breeze of God's truth anew. This does not mean in any sense, however, that the church has arrived. Indeed, because of the decision that was made, the struggle to be true to this vision, as it expands, will be even more intense. Having made our witness before the court of the world, it is now imperative that we not compromise our mission, but remain faithful to what we have begun. This much can be said with certainty for this company of Christians—at a critical moment in their pilgrimage *they chose to live!*

Appendices

APPENDIX 1

Statement by Dr. Gilmore in the special deacons' meeting, August 26, 1969, called in response to charges growing out of the attendance of Negroes at the August 17 worship service.

I take very seriously the Christian faith, which affirms that Christ is Lord of all. I believe that Christ taught that every person is of equal worth to God, and therefore should be to us. If I spent my time trying to answer my critics, I would not have time for anything else. Your friends don't need an explanation and your enemies won't believe it.

I do want to state clearly to you, however, what my feelings are in this matter. The charges that I came to integrate the church, that I have sent Miss Bock out to enlist the Negroes, are false. In the spirit of the *Commitments* made by the church, I have sought to lead the church to minister to human need wherever it is found, no matter the color of the person who had the need. If our ministry is of such authenticity that it draws forth a response from our black friends to desire membership, I believe they should be received. I am not interested in being the pastor of a racist-oriented church, indeed, I will not be. I made this very plain to the Pulpit Committee when I came. The only reason I came to Birmingham was the challenge of the commitment of this church to remain downtown and minister to human need.

As to the charge that I have preached too much on social issues, I feel if anything, that I have not preached enough on these matters. This church, located where it is, cannot avoid the racial issue, even if it desired to do so. We cannot go to Central City, an integrated community right across the street from this church, and recruit white children only for our Sunday School and other church activities. If someone goes out in the name of the church and knocks on the door of a home where a black mother answers, what is he going to say? Are we going to have him mumble, "Sorry, I got the wrong address?" That would be a mockery of the Christian gospel.

My first responsibility is to God; the second responsibility is to be faithful to my own conscience. I have tried to commend myself to the membership and I regret that, apparently, I have failed in this effort with many. I cannot escape the haunting suspicion, however, that this is not the real issue. It is not a matter of my person, but the ideas I hold relative to the application of the gospel to embrace all men, that is the occasion of rejection. I grieve that this is so.

APPENDIX 2

Sermon, "Christ and Conflict," preached in First Baptist Church, July 5, 1970, the date of the presentation for membership of Mrs. Winifred Bryant and her daughter Twila.

"Do not think that I have come to bring peace on earth; I have not come to bring peace, but a sword."

Matthew 10:34

The title of my sermon may seem strange to the ears of many of you. For a long time we have so domesticated Christ that we are not aware that Christ himself said that he "came not to bring peace, but a sword." We do not understand that to follow Jesus Christ is to be inescapably involved in conflict.

We cannot read the life of Jesus, however, without becoming increasingly aware that the more he performed his ministry of love, the more bitter was the hostility and conflict which raged about him. One of the most disconcerting questions we can raise is why this was so. And yet, careful reflection will make us aware that to teach and to live the truth in the presence of error and falsehood always brings conflict and misunderstanding.

The modern church is not sufficiently aware of this dimension of Christian reality. Many a church affirms by its actions that the ultimate standard for its existence is the maintenance of pseudo-harmony and peace. When this is the basic attitude of a church, it has surrendered genuine creativity and lost authentic discipleship.

There is ample biblical testimony to the inevitability of conflict for anyone who truly follows Jesus Christ. The central tenet of the Christian faith is the Lordship of Christ. Christians are to follow Christ up to the limit of their vision, regardless of the consequences. This means that there is always a radical tension between people who are joyful disciples of Christ, seeking to live up to his demands, and the actualities and practices of human society. In this sense Christians always work in a hostile environment. The first letter of Peter reminds us that while Christians are not to suffer as murderers or thieves who fall below the level of prevailing morality, they are "not to be surprised at the fiery ordeal that comes upon" those who answer the calling of Jesus Christ by rising above customary standards (I Pet. 4:12-19).

142

The church cannot live apart from the world in insulated isolation. It is to permeate the world and to be thoroughly pervasive in the world. Taking seriously the Lordship of Christ, Christians are to carry his standards with them wherever they are. The businessman, the worker, the teacher, the athlete—all must live in obedience to Christ's command. This means that the Christian is frequently pulling in a different direction than the crowd. And this is an altogether different picture than the smooth, affable, gentle manner that is popularly associated with religion. When we see Christ as he really is, we become aware of that aspect of the gospel he enunciated: "I have not come to bring peace, but a sword."

When Paul writes to the Ephesians, he describes the work of Christ in this way: "For he is our peace, who has made us both one, and has broken down the dividing wall of hostility . . . " (Eph. 2:14). This is the picture of peaceful harmony and undisturbed love. But to accomplish this work among sinful men, quite a different kind of relationship was necessary. In the garden, Judas came with "a great crowd with swords and clubs" (Matt. 26:47). Taken into custody, it is said of Jesus that "they spat in his face, and struck him; and some slapped him" (Matt. 26:67). Before Pilate, the crowd "shouted all the more, 'Let him be crucified' " (Matt. 27:23). The peace that breaks down the dividing walls of hostility comes to us by way of the conflict and turbulence of Jerusalem streets and the hideous violence perpetrated on Calvary.

How is it that we have come to associate Christian discipleship with that which is removed from the demanding, the desperate, and the dangerous? . . .

Not only is there solid biblical and theological grounding for the inevitability of conflict, but there are also sound sociological principles reminding us that every time we take a stand for authentic Christian values, there will emerge conflict and opposition. Sociologists tell us that conflict is inevitable in social change; that conflict opens up great opportunities for creative advance if we understand the issues involved.

One of the tragedies of modern Christians, both individually and collectively, is that they are often unwilling to enter the fray and to fight for justice, for right, for fair treatment, for honest government, for good politics. Conflict is thought of by too many Christians as something to be feared like the plague and to be avoided at all costs. Sociologists remind us that in recognizing the dangers in social expressions of hostility, we must also see the potentialities for important gains. Sharp disagreements are inevitable. There is no human development without facing challenge, difficulty, or opposition. If social progress is to be made on fundamental matters, existing structures of power and privilege must be challenged. Such deeply rooted interests never yield gracefully nor easily.

Many Christians today think of the church as the great ark of safety from which they may be spared the dangers and the conflicts of our age. Or, to use a more familiar metaphor, they think of the church as a quiet haven from the storm. They need to learn the lesson Phillips Brooks learned from a little urchin who played on the wharf in Boston Harbor. The renowned preacher had described a port as a place to which ships come for safety. The little boy said to him: "Sir, you don't know anything at all about ports. A port is not a place where ships come for safety; it's a place where ships go from into danger." Would to God that we understood the church like that! It is not primarily a place where we come for safety. It is a place from which we go into danger, empowered by the presence of the living Christ.

In any major social change, there is involved a spectrum of public opinion ranging from a few extremists at one end, through the comparatively less committed mass of the citizenry in the middle, to the extremists at the other end. The people in the center, by the swinging of their allegiance, determine the final decision. When the individual Christian or a Christian church refuses to disagree sharply with the extremists at either end, we have little hope of exerting influence on those in the middle who will shape the future. The more we shy away from controversy, and our utterances are muffled or mild, or we are silent, the more likely it is that we will stay on friendly terms with our extreme opposition either to the left or to the right. If we do not enter the fray, there is little likelihood of guiding the conflict in the proper direction.

We cannot simultaneously witness to the gospel and retain a genial, cooperative relationship with *all* people. We are men of truth, and the truth divides as well as heals. The modern church, in its feverish search for pseudo-harmony and for isolation from conflict, has crucified Christ afresh. In recent years there have been several instances in which a lonely minister has taken a prophetic stand leading to widespread opposition in the community, only to find his own congregation also turning against him. Even when members might themselves tolerate his position, they cannot stomach such unfavorable publicity for their church. Community censure seems particularly shocking to them because they have never before experienced such widespread hostility. But why should this come as so great a novelty? Should not a genuinely Christian church become accustomed to serious periodical opposition from the rest of the community? . . .

What a great time to be alive! I think that I am aware of the high stakes for which we are playing, but I repeat, what a great time to be alive! And what a great time for the church to be the church! Did not our Lord say that Christians were blessed when in conflict and facing danger? "Blessed are you when men revile you and persecute you and utter all kinds of evil against you falsely on my account. Rejoice and be glad, for your reward is great in heaven, for so men persecuted the prophets who were before you" (Matt. 5:11).

The forces of wickedness in a community do not usually expect, when they challenge the church, to take on a formidable opponent. It has been suggested that those perpetrating evil in American communities sleep more soundly at eleven o'clock on Sunday morning than at any other time in

144

the week. They ought to be trembling during the hour of worship lest "those Christians" emerge from the churches to destroy all nefarious plans and practices. On the contrary, those who profit from evil are not trembling on Sundays—they are sleeping. They have learned from long experience that usually when Christians come out of their church nothing happens. This, of course, is a slight exaggeration; a few things will happen. Some husbands will treat their wives with greater appreciation, contributions to the Community Chest may increase somewhat, but with respect to the basic evils of contemporary society very little is likely to happen. Racism will continue. Smut will continue. Political intrigue and dishonesty will continue. Injustice and inequity will continue—unless the church of Jesus Christ recognizes that the place where it is to do its work will call for radical confrontation and conflict.

There is something about the Gospel that calls for the decisive rejection of many common practices. There ought to be a stalwart, robust quality about the reaction of the church—a whole-hearted devotion that refuses to settle for speaking "smooth things." We can find the full resources of the Christian Faith only when we remain loyal through great difficulty. The most glorious hours of the church have been those in which she was in radical conflict. We experience the richest fellowship with God only when we are utterly committed.

It is imperative that the church not be silent and seek for peace when injustice is all around it. The words of George Russell to Rudyard Kipling are among the most incriminating I have ever read. He wrote:

> You had the ear of the world, and you poisoned it with bigotry and prejudice. You had the power of song, and you have always used it on behalf of the strong against the weak.

My soul, what an indictment! And to anyone who is aware, it is quite possible that unless we change, the historians will have to write that this is precisely what Christians and the church have done in our time.

The church is in the business of making "saints." The church is to be true to her Lord, no matter what conflict or difficulty may come. When the church is true to Christ and fights for him in the midst of the real issues of its own locality and age, then Christ is honored, and the "saints" who fight for him make it easier for others to believe in God. This is no time for timid Christians nor timid churches. This is a time for men and women who possess genuine faith in Jesus Christ, who is Lord of all. If we believe that he holds the future, let us conduct ourselves manfully as we follow him.

The late C. S. Lewis carried on a lengthy correspondence with a friend in America. The letters were subsequently published under the title *Letters to an American Lady*. He was aware that one of the reasons this woman was desperately ill was her attitude. In one of the letters, he wrote to her:

> Notice in Dante that the lost souls are entirely concerned with their past! Not so the saved (p. 96).

145

How profound! The church that is concerned to hold on to the past and to keep things the way they have been shall be damned and lost. But the church that faces the future unafraid with her Lord shall be saved, and will make all things praise him.

APPENDIX 3

Speech by Federal Judge H. H. Grooms, Sr., at the quarterly church conference, July 22, 1970, to the motion that the positions of Pastor and Youth Director be declared vacant as of September 30.

This is the most serious motion that has ever been brought before this church. In the 98-year history of this church, we have never asked a pastor to resign. We have now had six pastors in sixteen years, and you are asking the sixth to resign.

It is important what is going to happen to the pastor. But what will happen to the church? The passing of this motion will advise every pastor in the Southern Baptist Convention, even in the whole country—and every Education, Youth, and Music Director will know about it—and he may just ask to hear this record that we are making out here. The effect of this can be catastrophic in this church. I think we ought to drop it. There are other ways of handling it. The future of this church cannot be measured in this situation.

I have always found this church to be reasonably fair. In every proceeding I have ever had I have never tried anybody in absentia. It isn't the American way or the Christian way. He has been condemned without a hearing. Is that really fair? Is that the Christian way to handle this matter?

We say "my" church and "our" church as though we own the church. I do not own a brick in this church and I have contributed thousands of dollars. This is Christ's church! Would he be pleased with what we are doing here tonight? If you think he would be, vote your conscience on this matter and sustain this motion.

We called this preacher after we gave notice to all members of the church, and now you propose to discharge him without advising all the church about this matter. This, in my judgment, will wound this church for all future times. He has come here, and he has a reasonable chance to relocate himself if he resigns from this church, but this is more or less a summary disposition you are making of the matter. Ordinarily, we do not handle matters on this basis.

Now, it seems as though we do not have enough trouble with the black issue which has split the church—but I think the church can be rehealed over that—we now propose to drive another wedge in the membership of this church. There are people who will vote to receive the colored people and, [even] if they are dissatisfied, will go along with the church program.

But there are people who have been so close to this church for so long that this wound will be mighty hard to heal, and I do not want to see the wound inflicted upon the church. The last thing he [the pastor] told us was for us to decide this question about the Negro, and then he will know where he stands, and the church will know where the church stands. I believe that this action here may be entirely premature. . . .

For the future interest of this church—and I say this in all sincerity, as I do not believe anybody loves this church more than I do; I have been here 43 years, married here, and I hope to have my funeral here—I do not believe we should inflict wounds upon people when they can be avoided, and I think this one can be avoided. Here we are rushing in to determine a matter, I think, entirely prematurely and without further ado. I think it is the Christian thing for us to lay this aside to a definite date to give the pastor a chance to answer, and if he is in the wrong and guilty, he can come and answer if he wishes to do so, and we will not inflict the wounds that are about to be inflicted.

I am not questioning [Mr. Adams'] sincerity, but the wisdom of driving another spike into the coffin of the First Baptist Church. . . .

Sermon, "With Christ at the Crossroads," preached in First Baptist Church, August 16, 1970, the Sunday before the special church conference at which the motion of July 22 to fire Dr. Gilmore would be discussed.

"For he has made known to us in all wisdom and insight the mystery of his will, according to his purpose which he set forth in Christ as a plan for the fullness of time, to unite all things in him, things in heaven and things on earth."

Ephesians 1:9-10

Twenty-three months ago I was called by this great church to be its pastor. I came with high hopes and great ambition. I want to express my gratitude for the privilege of serving as your pastor. Some of the finest people I have ever known constitute this congregation. During these twenty-three months I have sought, under God, to be the pastor of all the people. My conscience is clear before our heavenly Father. I have played no favorites. I have been pastor to those who have disagreed with me. I have sought to be the pastor of both the integrationists and the segregationists, of the liberal and the conservative. I have tried to represent Christ through this church, in this city, to the best of my ability. I have tried to speak and live the truth of Christ up to the limit of my vision. No man is more conscious than I that this vision is not all it ought to be, but I can honestly say that at no time in my ministry have I cut corners, and I never will. It grieves me that what I have said and done apparently has greatly offended many of you. It has been my intention to bring both the comfortable word and the uncomfortable word, knowing that ultimately my conscience before the Lord God takes priority above everything else.

When I came as your pastor I took very seriously the *Commitments* you had made. Indeed, as I have said to many small groups, I would not have come the first mile toward Birmingham if it had not been for those *Commitments*. It was my conviction that here was a congregation trying to be the church that caught hold of my imagination and brought me here. In the light of those *Commitments* I have sought to build a bridge between proclamation and practice. If anyone could say after these twenty-three months that the First Baptist Church was the same as it had always been, as some apparently would like to be able to say, that would not be a eulogy, it would be an epitaph.

149

It is my conviction that the true minister of Christ, who preaches without fear or favor, and cuts no corners, will get the same response that the Lord himself got. There will be those who love him devotedly, and there will be those who hate him with a passion. I regret that this is so. I take great comfort, however, in one thing—and you share in it and all of us ought to rejoice in it—that in the city of Birmingham and the State of Alabama, and in ever-enlarging ripples of influence, the First Baptist Church of Birmingham, true to that which it has set out to do, has made a mighty impact for Christian justice. I rejoice in that!

I would be the first to admit to you, my dear people, that I have clay feet. I am aware of some of my failures and shortcomings. I wish they were not present. But you also have clay feet, and I could hope that, in the grace of God, we would find that same charitableness of spirit that marked our Lord, so that we did not dwell on the flaws, but on the good things.

It may seem strange to some of you that I talk about progress. Strange, because I'm aware that the Sunday School is down, that the Training Union is down, and that we are not reaching our budget, even though we have given more than at any other time in our history. Strange, then, it may seem to you, that I would talk about progress, but I dare to do it because it is your progress. For the first time in the history of Alabama, there has been a church that has set out consciously, deliberately, to try to build a church wherein black and white does not matter. I glory in that!

We have made progress in that I have sensed that God is in our midst. I have never felt such freedom in all my life. I have never had such abandon. My work has not been work to me; it has been sheer joy. To study, to do research, and to work pastorally has had a pulsating quality to it because I have sensed that God is in our midst. There has been an excitement, there has been a ministry, there has been a penetration into the community. Notwithstanding that it is not all that it should be; yet, it is laudable.

I want to share with you the motives that have marked your pastor. I regret exceedingly that some of you apparently think that these motives have been mixed. Let me say before God that whatever mistakes have been made, and whatever shortcomings are evident, one thing is sure: Your pastor has tried by word and deed to speak and to do what he considered it right to speak and do under God. I have done what I have done before God and not in a corner. I want no man to be able to say of me after two years that they don't know that this minister is anywhere around.

The basic assumption of your pastor is expressed by Paul as he writes to the Ephesians. I believe with all my soul, and am prepared to act on it, that in Christ Jesus "all things are to be summed up." He is the Lord of all—all men, all nations, all institutions. He is just as much the Lord of General Motors as of the church; just as much the Lord of politics as of prayer. It is out of this basic understanding that I have preached and lived these twenty-three months with you. Now, let me give you the particulars of my faith.

In the first place, I have lived among you out of the reality of the

150

American hope and dream. Those immortal words, "We hold these truths to be self-evident, that all men are created equal"—they are not tarnished for me. I believe them! Just a few days ago . . . I visited with a young man who is a professor of art at Tokyo University. We had been in each other's company only a brief time when he said, "You are from Birmingham, Alabama?" I nodded yes. "You have a real racial problem there, don't you?" I said, "Yes, sir, we do." That was before I knew how deep was the problem in my own pastorate. And then he said, as he turned and looked me squarely in the eye: "What is your church doing about it?" At that moment I was happy to tell him what we were trying to do. Then we enlarged the scope of our conversation. He said: "Dr. Gilmore," and I'm repeating his statement almost verbatim, "the Communists are kicking the teeth in of America because you have not solved your racial problem."

Now, my dear people, like it or not, this is the way other peoples of the world look upon us. For several days running I looked into the faces of millions of people who were not white. Seas of people! Brown and yellow! And this great statement of the founding fathers of this nation burned in my soul—"All men are created equal." . . .

One of the things that has marked my action and my preaching is that I take very seriously this American hope and dream. Worship is no substitute for obedience. High-sounding phrases and empty words will not do the job. Some of you have been offended by the coming of Negro children to our Sunday School, and several of our families have left since February. But let me tell you what burns bright in my heart. I believe that the greatest gift that a parent can give to his children is a conscience free of prejudice. I want my children to rub shoulders with yellow men, and black men, and brown men, because this is the world. The hypocrisy of the American stance cannot go on if our performance does not match our proclamation: "As he died to make men holy let us die to make men free."

There is a second thing that has marked my living and my preaching: I live by and preach by the reality of conscience and judgment. There is nothing more precious to me than this basic reality. If all the men of earth could be screened from what I say and do, there still would be two who would know it. I would know it and God would know it. My dear mother was always saying to me: "Remember, son, if you do wrong you will know it." That has been one of the great legacies of my parents to me. I take seriously the fact that one of these days I will appear in judgment, and I shall give an account of what I have said and what I have done, and so will you. The twenty-fifth chapter of Matthew's Gospel is not mere poetry. It is sober truth! "As you did it to one of the least of these, my brethren, you did it to me. . . . As you did it not to one of the least of these, you did it not to me. . . . Depart you into. . . ."—which? Oh, this fact of judgment! The fact and reality of conscience! Dear friends, do we want to go on with a conscience marked by hate and prejudice? Heaven is not segregated. We are held responsible for what we do.

151

This past week I was reading the book *Southern Churches in Crisis*, by my friend Dr. Samuel S. Hill, Jr. If you haven't read this book, sell your shoes, if necessary, and get a copy. Dr. Hill documents the fact that in Alabama Baptists and Methodists constitute 86.7 per cent of the Protestant population (p. 39). Since Protestantism is virtually dominant, the basic responsibility for the behavior of the South, therefore, is in the hands of two religious groups—the Baptists and the Methodists. Moreover, since Baptists are numerically so predominant in Alabama, and indeed throughout the South, the behavior of our region is in large measure our responsibility.

Finally, let me give you the third, and most important, conviction behind my preaching and living: I believe in the reality and the integrity of the gospel. I have several questions to ask. Shall it be our culture that determines what we think in the area of race? Or shall it be Christianity? Is there anyone present who, having read the New Testament, honestly believes that if the Lord Christ were to walk the streets of Birmingham today he would classify men in terms of black and white?

Christians are supposed to be different. That prejudiced hatemonger, Saul of Tarsus, after he was genuinely converted by the Christ, could go into the Graeco-Roman world that was split asunder by hate and prejudice and say: "There is neither Jew nor Greek, there is neither slave nor free, there is neither male nor female; for you are all one in Christ Jesus." It was a universal gospel that did not mark people off because of their race or their condition or their sex. And the Christian gospel still does not.

Other questions persist: Shall we be content with the brokenness of our society or shall we become agents of reconciliation? Are we prepared to go on fighting the Civil War indefinitely? Are we going to go on as Southerners nursing our wounds, or shall we become, indeed, a part of the Union? Shall we bear a faithful witness that includes all men or shall we practice an exclusivism like a country club? It was inevitable, dear friends, that this reality should be faced. You should have known this when you committed yourselves to stay on the corner of 22nd Street and 6th Avenue to minister to this community. Any reflection at all should have made every one of us aware that the posture of our mission, if we did our work well and authentically, would call forth a response from our Negro friends. We have been highly naive. It was inevitable, if we did Christ's work well, that we should penetrate ever more deeply into the community. Shall we delude ourselves by talking about meeting the spiritual needs of men as over against the needs of the whole man? This is the issue: Shall we have Christ's spirit or the spirit of the world? Shall we mark people off in terms of things over which they have no control, or shall we see them as persons for whom Christ died?

How long is it going to take us to recognize the elementary truth that the color of a man's skin is a superficial thing? That is the gospel! Can we love God without loving all of his children? This is the South's great problem. Indeed, it is the greatest problem confronting our nation. We say

152

we love the Negro. I have heard men who are racists say: "Why, I love the Negro." Listen to me now! Don't turn me off, because I'm going to zero in on something that is very, very important. Love that is paternalistic, that looks with condescension, is not love. The worst thing I could ever do to any one of you is to say to you: "I'm willing for you to have just as good a home, just as good a school, just as good a car, food, and clothes—but I don't want to have anything to do with you as a person." That is the worst thing I could do to you.

I read of a Southern city nestled in the mountains. Entrance into the city was by a winding road without guard rails. There were many accidents. Cars would come over the cliff and end up in utter tragedy at the bottom. So the town decided that they would put an ambulance down there. Someone suggested that it might be better if they put a guard rail up there. The city fathers were infuriated because they said they were ministering to people who were hurt. I see a parable in this. We have given little handouts to our Negro friends, and we take pride because we have done our bit. But we have done very little in terms of correcting those basic institutions that continue to destroy the Negro, and put the foot on the neck of those who have no chance. I, for one, am prepared both personally and institutionally to hit at injustice wherever it is.

Shall we make the truth of Christ the rule of our life together? Or shall it be congregational prejudice? Let everyone understand this fact: You don't settle the matter of truth by counting noses. An American poet says that there are two kinds of people: there are anvils and there are hammers. That is to say, there are people who are willing to be acted upon and there are people who are willing to act. I want to be God's hammer! I would love for this congregation to be God's hammer, changing society according to the pattern of the Lord Christ, issuing in justice and equity.

Permit me a very personal word. I count not my life dear to myself. I come to you not in weakness but in great strength. I come to you not in the posture of begging but in the posture of affirmation. And I want to say to you that so long as the Lord God gives me breath I shall protest, by word and deed, injustice wherever I find it. I want to be among those who drive nails in the coffin of prejudice and hate. We have just begun as a pastor and people. I cannot help but identify with Christ as he stands looking over Jerusalem. What an opportunity we have! I make no plea for myself. My plea is for you to be the people of God. . . .

APPENDIX 5

Speech by Mr. "Brown," the Birmingham attorney, at the church conference, August 19, 1970, in response to the request for specific charges against Dr. Gilmore.

I want to speak to you tonight in favor of this motion. I'm sorry that we had to go through some parliamentary procedure before we could get to the point of considering this motion tonight—before we could get to the point where somebody in favor of the motion could speak to it. I heard someone say a short while ago that when we come to a consideration of this matter, we tread on holy ground. I believe that and I feel that way tonight, and I hope that what I say and what I do is in that spirit, and I hope that everything that proceeds from this time on is in that spirit.

I want to say at the very outset, if there are going to be any tags made, any labels put on, or people put in categories tonight, I want you to know now and at the end of what I have to say that I am fully in favor of all of the programs of this church. I have voted for every ministry that has been instituted in this church. I have also voted in favor of the membership of the persons who had been presented in candidacy for this church. I am in favor of the program of this church being continued. What I say here tonight is out of my, conscience, based on what I firmly believe to be the leadership of the Holy Spirit.

I prefer not to be here, but I feel that the time has come to talk to this question tonight. And I think the time has come to take a stand. I am here to do that. I want to say also that what I am going to say to you tonight is not based on rumor, and is not based on hearsay. Much of what I have to say, the great majority of it, is based on personal information that I am going to give to you. It's not a judgment that I have come to within the last two or three months. It is something that has been progressively growing in my heart, in my spirit, over a period of about a year and a half. I came to the point last summer where I wondered if I could continue to work here in this church even though I agreed with the program of the church.

I went to Arkansas last summer and talked to a pastor who is a very close friend of mine and I put this in front of him. I said, "What am I to do?" He said: "My advice to you is that you go ahead and work whenever you can. If you oppose something, you speak against it, but you say nothing against the pastor until such time when a question comes up in a Church Conference." And we are here tonight.

154

And I want to say also that I feel perfectly free in what I am going to say tonight because I have gone to Dr. Gilmore in individual conference on two occasions, and I have told him everything that I'm going to tell you tonight. This is consistent with the Scriptures, and is consistent with the Blue Book of the Church [the official constitution and by-laws of First Baptist Church]. I want to read to you from Matthew 18: "If your brother sins against you, go and tell him alone. If he listens to you, you have gained your brother. But if he does not listen, take one or two others along with you, that every word may be confirmed by the evidence of two or three witnesses. If he refuses to listen to them, tell it to the church; and if he refuses to listen even to the church, let him be to you as a Gentile and a tax collector."

Over a period of about two years since Dr. Gilmore has been here I have had a very peculiar, close working relationship with him. I say peculiar, because I was put on two or three committees prior to the time he came here; I was put in a position of responsibility as Chairman of the Staff Committee and Chairman of the New Members Committee. Through these committees and working in the body of the deacons, I have had opportunity many times to sit down with him in close committee meetings, and many times he and I have gathered for lunch together and talked in individual conversations. Therefore, what I am saying to you tonight, as I have said before, is based on my own personal, first-hand information.

My bases for being in favor of this motion are two: first of all, I think Dr. Gilmore is scripturally unsound; secondly, I think he has been responsible for much of the disunity and disharmony in this church. It became very apparent after a period of several weeks and months of discussions that he and I did not see eye to eye theologically, doctrinally speaking. This didn't come to me all at once. It took me several months before I began to question some of the things he said. It took us several meetings also before I began to understand what I believe to be his beliefs, and his position on various doctrinal grounds.

He told me in some of those meetings that I didn't quite understand the modern approach to the Bible. He suggested that I read certain books. One of the ones he suggested that I read was *A Guide to Understanding the Bible*, by Harry Emerson Fosdick. Well, I read that book and, frankly, it almost made me sick to my stomach. Harry Emerson Fosdick died just about a year ago, and he was characterized like this in the AP report out of New York. It says that "the Rev. Harry Emerson Fosdick, whose liberal voice has been stilled." It mentions in this clipping that he preached a sermon in 1922 that was the foundation of his belief. In this sermon—and I'm quoting here—his sermon also questioned the doctrine of the Virgin Birth, the inspiration of the Scriptures, the atonement of Jesus, and the second coming of Christ.

Now, I want to put to you tonight certain beliefs which Dr. Gilmore has expressed to me both individually and from the pulpit, and I want you to test them in the light of the Scriptures. Now, some of you are going to

155

immediately jump and say we cannot test him; we cannot judge him. Well, let's see what the Scriptures have to say about this—"Do not quench the Spirit, do not despise prophesying, but test everything; hold fast what is good, abstain from every form of evil" (I Thessalonians 5:19-22). First John: "Beloved, do not believe every spirit, but test the spirits to see whether they are of God; for many false prophets have gone out into the world."

There are two main methods of testing that I want to bring before you tonight. One is the Scriptures, the second is the historic traditions of the Baptist people. You say: "Well, how can you do that?" Listen to what Paul wrote to Timothy: "But as for you, continue in what you have learned and have firmly believed, knowing from whom you learned it and how from childhood you have been acquainted with the sacred writings which are able to instruct you for salvation through faith in Christ Jesus" (II Timothy 3:14-15). Now, let's see what the scriptural tests are before we can get to his beliefs. This is what Paul says to the church at Colossae: "See to it that no one makes a prey of you by philosophy and empty deceit, according to human tradition, according to the elemental spirits of the universe, and not according to Christ" (Colossians 2:8). Test a person to see what he says, to see whether his philosophy is based on human tradition, or elementary spirits of the universe, science, or whether it's based on Christ.

Here's another test: the wisdom and knowledge of man. Paul, writing to the church at Corinth, says: "When I came to you, brethren, I did not come proclaiming to you the testimony of God in lofty words or wisdom. For I decided to know nothing among you except Jesus Christ and him crucified. And I was with you in weakness and in much fear and trembling; and my speech and my message were not in plausible words of wisdom, but in demonstration of the Spirit and power, that your faith might not rest in the wisdom of men but in the power of God" (I Corinthians 2:1-5).

Another test—myths and fables. Paul again, writing to Timothy: "Have nothing to do with godless and silly myths" (I Timothy 4:7). Peter wrote: "For we did not follow cleverly devised myths when we made known to you the power and coming of our Lord Jesus Christ, but we were eye witnesses of his majesty" (II Peter 1:16). And then he goes ahead and he says that these eyewitnesses have made the prophetic Word more sure. Concerning false prophets and teachers: "But false prophets also arose among the people, just as there will be false teachers among you, who will secretly bring in destructive heresies, even denying the Master who bought them, bringing upon themselves swift destruction. And many will follow their licentiousness, and because of them the way of truth will be reviled" (II Peter 2:1-2). Paul, writing to the church at Corinth, says: "And what I do I will continue to do, in order to undermine the claim of those who would like to claim that in their boasted mission they work on the same terms as we do. For such men are false apostles, deceitful workmen, disguising themselves as apostles of Christ" (II Corinthians 11:12-13). Now

156

those are the tests, ladies and gentlemen, from the Scriptures that I want you to keep in mind.

Now, what does Dr. Gilmore believe? Dr. Gilmore does not believe that the Bible is the infallible Word of God. He does not believe that the Bible is free from error. On the other hand, he believes that the Bible contains errors. He believes that the Bible is authoritative in part, but not totally. He believes that each person has the right to decide which part of the Bible he will accept as complete authority and what part he will reject. I ran across my notes last night on a sermon he spoke, in which he discussed the Bible, and he said the Bible must be relevant to modern day scientific knowledge. If it's relevant today, will it be relevant tomorrow when that scientific knowledge changes? Dr. Gilmore believes that parts of the Bible are more inspired than other parts of the Bible. Dr. Gilmore believes that the Bible contains myths and fables.

Now, what are specific examples? The first three or four chapters of Genesis that contain the teaching of the creation of the world, the creation of Adam and Eve, the establishment of the Garden of Eden, the fall of man, the introduction of sin into the world. Dr. Gilmore says that these chapters and these teachings are not intended to be a true account; they are not intended to tell you how God created the world. Dr. Gilmore does not believe that Adam and Eve ever lived. Dr. Gilmore believes that the only purpose of these chapters being in the Bible is to present to you the truth that God created the world and everything in it. He believes that this is a fable, like the fable of other nations.

Another example: Dr. Gilmore does not believe in the description in the Bible of Noah and the Flood. He does not believe that the Flood as described in the Bible ever happened. It's only a myth and a fable. The only purpose for that being in the Bible is to teach that God will punish sin. Another example: Dr. Gilmore does not believe in the description in the Bible of Jonah and the whale. He does not believe that that ever happened. He believes that to be a myth or a fable; that the only purpose for that being in the Bible is to teach that God chastises his people.

Now, why is this important? Let's take Genesis—why is it important that it be authoritative, that it be accurate, that it be inspired? Most major doctrines of the Bible have their origin in Genesis. You have here the origin of the teaching that God created the world in an orderly fashion, that God created man, that God created man in his own image, that man is the highest form of creation, that Satan tempts man to disobey God, that man sinned and fell from God's fellowship, that man is now under the condemnation of sin, the promise of the restoration of man to God, the promise of a Savior is found in Genesis. The scarlet thread of redemption runs from Genesis clear through to Revelation in the Bible. You take out Genesis, you take out the beginning of that scarlet thread of man's need for redemption. Now, what do you do if you take Genesis out of the Bible? Then it gives you and me and anybody else the right to believe any method we want to about how the world was created, how man was

157

created. We do not have any teaching of how man had a peculiar fellowship with God and has the hope of that once again. We do not have any teaching of how man was created in the image of God, we do not have any teaching, or the origin of teaching, of the fall of man, how man sinned, and is under the condemnation of sin. We have no reason for the covenant promises that God made to the Jewish people, if you take out Genesis. We have no authority for the fact that marriage is ordained by God, because that is in Genesis, first three chapters.

Now, there are larger results to this, people. It gives the right for each person to decide what part of the Bible he wants to believe as authority and what part he wants to reject. If you cannot understand and prove a portion of the Bible based on today's knowledge, you have a right to call it a myth and not to accept it. Each person, in effect, has to be inspired himself to decide what part of the Bible is authority for him. We have no common basis for our faith. Because while I may say, this part is authority, you may say that's not authority for me, and that's true. We feel that each person interprets the Bible in the leadership of the Holy Spirit and we may disagree on the interpretation of the passage but, ladies and gentlemen, we have never disagreed on the fact, as Baptists, that the Bible is the sole authority, and you go there to determine how the Holy Spirit will interpret that portion to you. It means also that God made errors in the giving of the Holy Scriptures and the preservation of the Scriptures. Is God subject to error in giving us the Bible? The Bible says that all Scripture is inspired by God. *All Scripture!* And is profitable for teaching, for reproof, for correction and for training in righteousness.

Now Dr. Gilmore will tell you, as he has told me, and as he told us before, that he has a high view of Jesus Christ. Jesus Christ is his Lord. What does Jesus Christ say about the Scriptures? Jesus believed in Adam and Eve. He believed in the inauguration of marriage by God, as given in Genesis. "The Pharisees came to Jesus, and they tested him by asking, 'Is it lawful for a man to divorce his wife for any cause?' He answered, 'Have you not read that he who made them from the beginning made them male and female, and said, "For this reason a man shall leave his father and mother and be joined to his wife, and the two shall become one?" ' " In Matthew 19 and Genesis 2. Jesus believed in the account of the Flood and Noah. Luke 17: "As it was in the days of Noah"—this is Jesus speaking—"so will it be in the days of the Son of man. They ate, they drank, they married, they were given in marriage, until the day Noah entered the Ark, and the Flood came and destroyed them all." Jesus believed in the account of Jonah and the whale. Matthew 12, Jesus speaking: "For as Jonah was three days and three nights in the belly of the whale, so will the Son of man be three days and three nights in the heart of the earth." Now Jesus was saying: even as I am to die and be buried, just in the same way that Jonah was in the belly of the whale. Now—if that is a fable, is Jesus' death and burial a fable, also? Jesus did not believe that these were fables. Jesus believed that the Scriptures were true and authoritative. Why do

158

these people proclaim that Jesus is Lord of their lives and not believe the Scriptures as Jesus did?

Now let me tell you one more specific example of Dr. Gilmore's beliefs. And this comes out of his belief as to Genesis being a fable. Dr. Gilmore told me one day in his office that he did not believe that man was born a sinner, that he believed that man became a sinner because he was influenced by the sinful culture in which he lived. Now this is contrary to the teachings of the Bible. Paul spoke very clearly in Romans that as by one man sin entered into the world, "and death through sin, and so death spread to all men because all men sinned." He then talks about Adam. This is Romans 5:18: "Then as one man's trespass led to condemnation for all men, so one man's act of righteousness leads to acquittal and life for all men." Now what this means, and what it means if it's carried to its ultimate conclusion, is that if man was not in a sinful culture, he would not be a sinful person, because we were not born that way. So, if you took all sin out of culture, then according to his beliefs, man would not be a sinful person. If he was not a sinful person, he would not need a Savior. That is contrary to the teaching of the Scriptures.

Now, let me speak just a little bit more. I know I am taking a long time. I've written this out, because I have tried to be brief, but I want to be correct, and I think the church ought to know these things. . . . Jesus said that "heaven and earth will pass away, but my words will never pass away" (Matthew 24:35). Jesus said: "Till heaven and earth pass away, not an iota, not a dot, will pass from the law until all is accomplished" (Matthew 5:18). Jesus, after his resurrection, did say that he began at Moses and the prophets and "he interpreted to them in all the scriptures the things concerning himself" (Luke 24:27). Test his teachings by the Scriptures to see whether or not he is doctrinally correct.

Now, just test him by reference to the historic Baptist traditions. I've heard him say on many occasions, and this is true, that the Baptists are not a creedal group. We do not have a creed which everybody has to agree to, but we have a Statement of Baptist Faith and Message, which was adopted by the Southern Baptist Convention. In 1925 it was adopted first, prepared by a man named E. Y. Mullins. It was reaffirmed with a slight amendment in 1963 by the Convention. Herschel Hobbs was in charge of the committee who prepared the draft that was adopted in the 1963 Convention. Herschel Hobbs wrote an introduction to it, and this is what he said: "Baptists emphasize the soul competency before God, freedom of religion and the priesthood of the believers; however, this emphasis should not be interpreted to mean that there is an absence of certain definite doctrines that Baptists believe, cherish, and with which they have been, and are now closely identified. And here they are."

Now Dr. Gilmore stated in a small committee meeting one night that he could not accept this Statement of Baptist Faith and Message; in particular, we were talking about the first paragraph on Scriptures. He said that night that he could not accept that paragraph. In deacons' meeting some

159

two or three months ago, he said, on the other hand, that he could accept that paragraph. In 1969 at the Convention in New Orleans, the Convention directed all the agencies of the Convention to adhere to that Statement of Baptist Faith and Message. At the Convention this year, an amendment was proposed to the statement of Scripture. And this is the amendment: "The entire Bible is the inspired, authentic, and authoritative Word of God: that it is both doctrinally and historically reliable." That amendment was defeated, but in speaking to that amendment, Dr. Herschel Hobbs said—and I've got the tapes of the Convention at home—that he believed that everything that is said in that amendment is incorporated in the original statement, that he intended for it to be in there, that he believed it as it was written, and that he did not see any need to amend it to put it in there because it meant the same thing. E. Y. Mullins was the author of the 1929 Statement of Faith.

Last year a small group of people formed a group called the "E. Y. Mullins Fellowship." I remember last year when Dr. Gilmore gave his report when he came back, that he said that he had gone down with others and attended the meeting of the E. Y. Mullins Fellowship. *Newsweek* magazine, on April 20, 1970, said that this was a group of about 250 teachers, pastors, and laymen. It calls them the liberal group of the Southern Baptist Convention. They put up a person to run against Dr. Criswell last year. He was soundly defeated. Since that time some of those members have left the Southern Baptist Convention because the Southern Baptist Convention reaffirmed its position on the Scriptures and other statements of faith. Dr. Gilmore was a member of the E. Y. Mullins Fellowship.

One other example. You heard the controversy about the Broadman Bible Commentary. Here it is right here, beginning with Genesis and Exodus. I bought it because I wanted to read it and to be able to say to you that I had read it. As you know, the Convention voted this year to withdraw that, and direct that it be redrafted and re-published in a form consistent with traditional Baptist beliefs. That vote was passed by 5,394 to 2,107. Dr. Gilmore stated when he came back here in June of this year that he had read that Broadman Commentary, that volume, and that he found nothing whatsoever objectionable in it. But I say to you that Dr. Gilmore's beliefs do not agree with the historic positions of the Baptists of the Southern Baptist Convention, which have been reaffirmed consistently.

I want to speak very briefly on my second point. We are a disharmonious church. We are not unified. We are not together. It is said that we ought to have the mind of Christ, but we do not have the mind of Christ. What does the Bible say about divisions and dissensions within the church? Paul, writing to the Romans, says: "I appeal to you, brethren, to take note of those who create dissensions and difficulties, in opposition to the doctrine which you have been taught; avoid them. For such persons do not serve our Lord Christ, but their own appetites, and by fair and flattering words they deceive the hearts of the simple-minded," the innocent. We have divisions within families in this church. We have divisions between the young and the old. We have divisions between friend and friend. We have division between members and the staff. We have a division between pastor and people.

Now, have all these divisions existed for 17 years? I have not seen them and I've been here 10 years. Have you known during the time that you've been here of a time when this church was as divided as we are tonight? It has been said that there is only one division in this church, only two groups, but that's not so, people. I can stand up here and tell you of group, group, group and group that is divided on a number of questions. It is not one question that divides us. In the last year and a half or two years we have been growing in numbers of division. We have been growing in the gulf that separates us within this church until we come to tonight. In April of this year we had a special deacons' meeting that lasted about three hours. Some deacons called that meeting because they were aware of the divisions that existed in this church. We spent about three hours that night in which we laid before the deacon body and the pastor and the staff the divisions that existed in this church—not one division but the number of divisions that existed. A motion was ready at that time, ladies and gentlemen, for the April quarterly conference, to ask for the resignation of the pastor. That motion was not presented at that time. It was hoped that because we had had this deacons' meeting where all the division was laid out before pastor and staff and deacons, and because people became aware and started praying, it was hoped that we could be brought together. That deacons' meeting had no effect. There were no efforts made to reconcile. The pastor took no efforts as the shepherd of this flock to reconcile the flock. There have been no efforts since that time towards any spiritual reconciliation. A month ago, a motion was made to ask for the resignation of the pastor. It was put off to give him an opportunity, as I under-stand—and this is only hearsay—it was stated that it was hoped that he would resign within this period of time. He has not resigned, although several people have advised him to resign. We are further divided because of that very thing. I say to you that in my judgment, we have no hope of harmony in this church if the pastor stays as the pastor of this church.

Now young people, let me say something to you. You say that there is a division between young people and old, and I agree with you. Many of you have said that we old people don't understand things, that we are not in favor of the new program, that if you believe the Bible, you cannot be a relevant group in these days and times. Well, here's one person who is saying to you that I believe in the program you are after, but I believe in the Bible, too, and I believe you've got to have a scriptural teaching before you can carry out that program. Now, there are a lot of other people out there who are in favor of the program of this church, but are against the pastor for the reasons which I have stated to you. I say to you, now I want you to understand this, that the program which you have started, which

161

we've been carrying on in this church, can be carried out by a church led by a pastor that preaches sound, conservative, evangelical, theological doctrines. I know two of them in this town that have been carrying on a program before we started a program in this church. I know of churches throughout the Southern Baptist Convention in which sound, conservative, theological doctrines are preached from the pulpit and there are examples of the type of program that you want to carry out. But we cannot do it when we are this disunified.

Now let me close. Many of you have heard mentioned from this pulpit and in conferences and in these committee meetings, about the Church of the Saviour, Washington, D.C. This is a church that is very much engaged in being relevant in the way that word is used these days and times, that believes in getting out from the church to minister to the world. Elizabeth O'Connor is a member of that church and she's written two or three books on the activity and the program of that church. I want to read you a portion of this book that fits what I'm saying right here. "Those congregations whose stress has been on the inward worship, small prayer groups and study programs, are thinking that the cause of holiness involves more than this. Those who have abandoned this part of the inward program to carve out in cities new forms of the church are receiving hints that all is not well with these missions. Perhaps more than anything else the story recorded here is a glimpse of our own struggling with what it means to be on both these journeys. Certainly we are convinced that one is shallow and lacks substance without the other. We are going to know little about the task of reconciliation in the world unless we are in touch with what goes on in that world within ourselves and know how difficult reconciliation is there. We cannot begin to cope with what it means to build a world community unless we understand how difficult it is to be a community even with a small group of people—a church, presumably called by the Lord to the same mission." We cannot have this in a church where there is disharmony, where there is no effort made to reconcile the groups.

I say to you that the fruits of Dr. Gilmore's ministry in this church are disharmony tested by the Scriptures. They are not to abide with those who could know and talk and carry on dissensions. I again want to say—perhaps it's superfluous—that I am in favor of the program of this church, but I am opposed to the pastor, and I am in favor of this motion on the basis that he is not theologically sound as tested by the Scriptures and on the fact that he—and not altogether but for the most part, I think—has been the cause of the dissension, the division, the disharmony that we find ourselves in tonight.

APPENDIX 6

Statement by Miss Betty Bock at the August 19, 1970, church conference, in response to the motion on firing Dr. Gilmore and firing her, that the question be divided and then be voted on separately.

I would have to oppose this motion on the basis that we all know why we are here tonight. There is one issue involved and that is the question of race. As evidence of this I would like to refer to the events of the past few months. I have been a member of this church four years as of last Sunday. I was here the night the church voted to call Dr. Landes [Dr. Gilmore's predecessor] and am familiar with his ministry. I have also been familiar, from the standpoint of being involved very much in the church program, of the ministry which has developed under the leadership of Dr. Gilmore.

There were a few questions and a few problems prior to February 1, but they were not major, at least they were not spoken of as being major. On February 1 we had five Negro boys who had been attending our tutoring program, come to Sunday School. There really was no great difficulty because we had had Negro visitors before. However, on the next Sunday they came back, bringing some friends. This is when some difficulty began, when it was realized that they were going to be coming on a regular basis. You will recall that at that point we had fourteen resignations in two weeks in the departments in which these children were involved.

The next thing which occurred was the deacons' meeting—I don't recall whether it was April or May—this deacons' meeting was referred to awhile ago by Mr. Brown. I had the privilege of attending that particular deacons' meeting along with the others as a staff member. I remember that Mr. Brown, and possibly one other person, said that the purpose of that meeting was basically theology and race. There were at least four others— whose names I could call—who said during the debate that there was one basic reason for the meeting and that it was [to consider] the racial question.

The next event to which I would like to refer was the vote on the morning of July 5 [the first vote on the black people]. The question there could have been none other but one which was very obvious. The same was true on July 22. However, it wasn't as obvious.

Now, I know my heart and I know what I have done. As a member of the church I got very excited when we voted the *Commitments.* I took it

163

seriously. At a church fellowship sponsored for the youth on the Sunday night following the vote on Wednesday night, we had a discussion. The young people wanted to know, since we had voted the *Commitments*, what they could do about it? I told them I didn't know exactly.

I had heard references made to the Ridgely Apartments, so we decided to take a survey there to determine a need for a Bible Study Class, and to talk to Mr. Starr, Principal of Powell School [an elementary school two blocks from the church] to determine what needs he saw in the community. It was in a conversation with Mr. Starr that he pointed out that a tutoring program was needed. Now, I have no feelings of regret about my involvement in the tutoring program, but I do know that I carried a major responsibility in this particular endeavor because I thought it was the right thing to do.

Now, these events all occurred before Dr. Gilmore ever put his foot on Birmingham soil; even before the Pulpit Committee had talked to him, the conversation had been held with Mr. Starr. Therefore, because of my involvement in this particular thing, I feel like to a degree I determined Dr. Gilmore's timetable before he ever got here. Now, if I did wrong, if I acted wrongly, if I misinterpreted the *Commitment* in any particular way, then I deserve to be fired. The vote here, I think, will prove this, or will sustain this basic concept.

Most of you, prior to tonight, have heard very, very little, other than Dr. Gilmore's sermons, as far as his theology is concerned. Only one reference in the charges has been made to any statement he has made in his sermons. Now, I have not heard every sermon he has given because, in my employment before coming on the staff, it required me to be out of town at times. However, I have heard I would say ninety percent of his sermons. I have no difficulty with the theology that he has expressed in his messages. I am also quite anxious to hear his interpretation of his theology, and I assume he will have an opportunity to do this.

Therefore, the reason for the vote on July 22, or the experiences of July 22, and the large crowd here tonight—I find it very difficult to believe there is only theology involved—the facts and the charges that have been presented were all stated on the basis of individual conversation in most cases. None of the rest of us heard that individual conversation. I have real difficulty in feeling that theology is the basic issue. Therefore, I would have to speak against this motion.

APPENDIX 7

Speech by Dr. John Sims, Associate Pastor—Minister of Music at First Baptist Church, in the special church conference, August 19, 1970.

Beloved in the Lord! I wonder what kind of response that gets. Some of you I don't know at all. The ones of you whom I do know, you are my beloved in the Lord. My father was a pastor so I feel like I've been in the pastorate all my life. He used to say of people in the church, "Some people you just love like a Christian until you like like a friend." So it's in that sense that even those of you whom I would disagree with most heartily, I do love you in the Lord. I love you enough to come and tell you the truth. This is something I almost said on July 22 and did not. Now I would be in violation against my conscience and my honor, and my personal loyalties and my professional loyalty to you, and above all, to what I hope to understand as the mind of Christ—and that is a very bold assertion that we make very easily sometimes. Now this is what I want to say, and I hope you will hear me with at least as much of this deliberate Christian love as I spoke of.

I came to First Baptist Church in Birmingham under what I construed to be the leadership of the Holy Spirit. Again, that is a bold assertion. I feel like I should take off my shoes when I speak of these words—but I won't take your time to take my shoes off. I really thought this is what God wanted me to do, and nobody understood it. What in the world was I coming to Birmingham, Alabama, for? But I knew, even though I could not tell them. I thought: what a remarkable thing to find a congregation where there are more than just a handful who really wanted to live a sacrificial, disciplined, daring life for Jesus Christ in this day of great self-indulgence and super-criticism and nihilism and self-destruction.

This is a terrible age we live in and a wonderful age, and to find a church where a group of people—pastorless—would dare to write such a thing down as your *Commitment*—and I know some of you wish that *Commitment* were damned to hell. You wish it had never been written and you could burn up every copy, and erase every word of it from the mind of everybody here and around the world. But we can't. You really did adopt that resolution and I praise you for it. I praise God for people who would do something like that. I bet there were not this many people here to vote on it. But I didn't expect to find a church where there were fifty percent of the people who were—I mean, fifty percent of this mythical

165

1800 we talk about—I never expected to find a church where half the people, or a majority, had a real notion of laying their lives on the line. I mean, all the time. Well, I didn't find a church where there were that many, not 900 out of 1800, but I did find a group of people, and I don't know how many—a couple of hundred, three hundred? That is an amazing number of people in a place like Birmingham, Alabama, to have caught a vision of something that is truly remarkable.

Now I'm taking longer than I wanted. Let me stop rambling and just say that I came here under what I thought was the leadership of God's Spirit. Now, to this moment, right now, I have had no change in signals, and God does not write in handwriting on the wall for me; I don't hear voices; I don't see visions; I just get a feeling. And for 42 years, which is not a long time, the feeling gets clearer and clearer that, as I yield myself to him and become a slave of Jesus Christ, he leads me and that is my reward.

Now, this is my personal testimony, if anybody's interested. The daily walk with Christ is what I am seeking for myself and seeking to help any who are interested in sharing this experience of discovery. It is dynamic; it is ever-changing; it is miraculous; it is glorious, and that is the kind of person I have tried to be in your midst. It is the kind of reality and fellowship I have tried to encourage, insofar as I could. Now, I have had no indication from God's Spirit that I should resign, that I should say, "Well, if you fire Herbert Gilmore, and Betty Bock, you should fire me too." Now, that feeling may come to me and when it does, then I'll beg for another point of personal privilege, and stand and make my final speech.

But I want to say to you in all honesty—now hear me—I'm not trying to be antagonistic; I want to be as winning and loving as I can. If you are firing Herbert Gilmore for his theology, or his social outlook, what he believes and what he preaches is certainly consistent with what I believe—not one hundred percent, as Johnnie McCracken said. I don't guess I agree with anybody one hundred percent, not even my wife, maybe most of all not my wife. But what he says and what he believes is compatible with what I believe. It is open, it is creative, it is solid, it is consistent. If you are firing Betty Bock for her concept of ministry, reaching out into the community without being a respecter of persons, and serving in every conceivable way all of the people that you can get hold of—if these are the reasons you are firing them, you really couldn't possibly want me—because theologically I am consistent with what Herbert Gilmore believes, and ministry and program-wise, I am one hundred percent behind what Betty Bock does. And everything I do is going to be consistent with that, as I do it myself, as I do it with you adults, as I do it with your young people, with your children—and I have been as open and honest as I can about this—but I am telling you who I am. You may want to fire me too, but the burden right now will have to be on you. I don't feel God telling me to do anything yet but to be honest with you.

Because I am a musician, I go in a lot of unusual places. Now, if I go over to the University of Alabama in Birmingham and talk to a group of students, and it is an interracial group, I might be talking about the church or the music ministry. I might be preaching, or I might be talking about music therapy—there is no telling what I'm liable to be talking about. But if I talk to them, I am always concerned about the condition of their "souls," as we put it in our standard vernacular. I am concerned about their "souls." I am witnessing even though I may be talking about music. I am concerned about their "souls."

Now, this church represents to me one manifestation of Christ's body. These are believers here. We disagree, and that's all right. I dream of a church where people can disagree and glory in their disagreement, not panic because of it. I've been in churches like that. But, now, if I go some place and a person responds to me personally and he says, "You really take this religion stuff pretty seriously," I say, "Yes, my whole life is given to it." "And where is it you are a minister?" "First Baptist Church." If this person is black or yellow or red, and he says, "May I come over there?", I'll say, "You'll be very welcome over there." "What about your choir? Would I be welcome in your choir?" "Of course, you would be welcome in my choir. Anyone, any human being who wants to serve the Lord, and who wants to serve in this church is welcome in my choir."

Now, you say, "Are you trying to integrate the church?" Christ's church is integrated. We just haven't gotten the word yet. All I am saying is that when I go to people I try—I'm prejudiced like everybody—but I am trying "to know no man after the flesh"—no man. And when I offer the Bread of Life through word or deed, I am no respecter of persons. I can't be. Don't you know I can't be? Now, I've been asked to come next door to the Girls' Club, and spend an hour a week working with the girls, maybe getting a chorus of girls. That is a mixed, that is an interracial group. Now if I go over there, I'm going to make friends with those children. I always make friends with children, and they are going to say, "Could we come over to your church?" And I'm going to say, "Yeah!" "Could we sing in the choir?" I'm going to say, "Yeah!"

Now, that really is all I want to say. I want to declare myself honestly to you so you will know. If you think that is wrong, if you think it is unscriptural, if you think it is Communist, or whatever you think it is, I have told you as completely and as sincerely as I can who I am and what I intend to do. And that's all I want to say.

APPENDIX 8

Speech by Mr. Hobart Grooms, Jr., law partner of Mr. Brown, at the special church conference, August 19, 1970.

All right, you have heard from half of the firm. The other half can speak just as long. What has been said by Mr. Brown has been said in sincerity. I have talked with him. We have talked with each other, and there is no use rehashing it here. He feels that this is God's hand leading him. I feel different—only the Lord can say who is right. I feel that I am compelled to speak for both of these staff members, but particularly Betty Bock. I know Herbert Gilmore is eloquent, and when he has a chance to reply, he hardly needs a lawyer to defend him. He can stand on the Word of God and on his ministry.

But I blush to think that I would be in a fellowship where a pastor would irritate us so much, that I would blindly destroy the reputation of one of the finest young women of our Convention, in an attempt to rid our staff of this "troublesome" pastor. It reminds me of the way that I have heard of fighting forest fires. When a fire gets out of control, we simply burn down an acre or two, and there's a back fire, and then the fire burns out. Of course, we lose quite a few trees that way, but, after all, we just wanted to stop the fire. It is like finding a snake in a hen house, and just killing every hen in there with a few stray blasts of a gun, because we want to kill a snake. This is the philosophy we are operating under now.

I have heard as I have sat in the deacons' meetings the reasons why we are here today. I have heard the theological reasons. I have sat through so many deacons' meetings and have listened to the people that I grew up with, and sat under, and had respect for, and had to sit there and listen to them vent their spleens on this issue of race. You are not kidding anybody as to what the issues are tonight. I know there are people who have gotten their feelings hurt; there are people who do not agree with certain things that [the pastor] has preached. The people that have come to you here tonight have heard two sermons that they disagreed with, one of them that Dr. Gilmore preached. Well, I haven't heard but one sermon from this young lady, and it was on a morning when we just about did not have church. [An ice storm had prevented the pastor from coming.] As far as I am concerned she is one for one, and that is 1.000 in my book. This has been one of the most inspirational and inspiring people to work with that I have ever come in contact with. And how we can, in an attempt to get at

168

someone we can't agree with, or that we feel threatens our own little existence, [act as though] it doesn't matter who we destroy, who we hurt—if this is Christ, then we've been fooled a long time from this pulpit.

I grew up listening to Christ preached from this pulpit, and I've heard pastors from Hobbs to Slaughter to everybody else, and I've heard politics preached from this pulpit no later than 1960 when the pastor then urged you to vote against a man because he was a Roman Catholic. Is that politics from the pulpit? It's politics from the pulpit when we don't agree with exactly what's being said. I agree with the NAM and my wife went to school on a DAR scholarship. She didn't appreciate Dr. Gilmore's remark about the DAR, but do you think we are going to go off and get up a bunch to start firing the pastor because he has stepped on a few toes? Ladies and gentlemen, when we get to the point where you can find a pastor to come in this pulpit and say something sweet and nice that will make everyone of you feel so good you'll go out of here having been told what wonderful Christians we are everyday, and nobody's feelings are hurt, you don't have a pastor, you have a "toady." And I can go hire those a dime a dozen. I've worked in the home mission fields and I've seen some of these; in the home mission fields as a summer student missionary. I have seen some of the people that are pastoring our Baptist Churches. We don't know. We've been spoiled. We've had so many good pastors that have passed through this great pulpit, we don't realize what a bad pastor we can get. And that's just about all we are going to be able to afford—some "ding-a-ling" who'll get up here and tell us what we want to hear.

Now, we've tried to explain to you people what's going to happen to this church, and people who have not been affiliated with the pastor or the other side have said, "Here's what's going to happen—do you realize what you are doing—here's what the young people are going to do." "It doesn't matter," you say, "it doesn't matter. We'll have enough money to run the church." Is this the mind of Christ? Is this Christ speaking in our hearts? If it is, I've been fooled. I've been fooled all those years that I was an RA. I've been fooled all those summers that I wasted at Young Men's Mission Conferences at Ridgecrest. I was fooled the summer I worked in Arizona as a summer student missionary. I was given a "big line" in BSU in college. I've been led astray in the ten years that I have been teaching young people and young adults here in the Sunday School.

We can do what we want to do. And if we can vote out this staff tonight, you can go home tonight and say, "All right, I have done it, I'm glad I finally got even with these people." You've gotten rid of a staff— you've gotten rid of a church also. But if you think that God is going to sit and let this happen without his will being done, and without his judgment being passed eventually, I think we are sadly mistaken. I think we are sadly mistaken! We're playing with eternal things, ladies and gentlemen. We're not playing with a club. If we want to make a religious club out of this church, that's all right, go right ahead; I can't participate in that. We are

169

playing with, and handling, and trying to manipulate the Body of Jesus Christ—no less!

And when you can get up to that microphone and say, "I object to Dr. Gilmore's program, his philosophy, or Betty Bock's ministry to something," this isn't something we just cooked up to feed our egos, or to get some good publicity in the newspaper. We got it here because you voted unanimously in this auditorium two years ago, before this good man came to this pulpit, without a dissenting vote, to pass these *Commitments*, and I ask you, "Are they confusing?" You say, "We don't understand them." You understood them then. They were read in every Sunday School class, every department; they were printed in the bulletin of the church; they were discussed at church conferences, and we decided to stay downtown. I was talking with my law partners the other day about this. And they said, "We want to get something straight"—these are not Baptists, but law partners and secretaries sitting around having coffee—"Just tell me one thing—did your church vote to stay in downtown Birmingham?" "Yes, we did." "Did your church vote to pass these *Commitments* we have heard about?" "Yes, we did." "And you mean you voted to stay downtown, and you voted to pass these *Commitments* where you said you'd minister to all people, rich or poor?"—we didn't say "black or white," but we said "all people," and that is a confusing word when you say "All." It's so confusing! It's susceptible to so many different interpretations! All. A-L-L! "You mean to say that you stayed downtown and you unanimously voted to pass these *Commitments*, and then when these people came—where did they come from?" "Right across the street." "When they came from across the street into your church, that your members were upset?" "Yes, they were upset, some have left." "You want to fire your preacher now—a lot of them want to fire the preacher—because they brought blacks into the church?" "That's exactly right." They said, "What are you down there—a bunch of naive people? What did you think was going to happen? You stay downtown, you lay out the welcome mat, and somebody believes you." We've tried so many things that failed, and we tried this one and people believed what we said.

I sat down with this good gentleman in a cafeteria in a place in Maryland. The first Sunday we sat down with Joyce and Herbert I didn't have one bit of hesitancy. I didn't have to say anything about the church in Birmingham [as to] what I believed they wanted to do. I said here's what they said they'll do. It speaks for itself. "I don't have to give you any hard sell—this is what our church said they'll do." It wasn't something Hobart Grooms said. I was running around getting a preacher that summer. I was not here pushing for these *Commitments*. I just happened to be in the Wednesday night conference where you passed them unanimously. And it wasn't something that the Pulpit Committee got up, or that Harry Baker saw in a vision one night, and decided we needed some church commitments. This church passed them! And I tell you that it has been said that the group that wants to get rid of the pastor, are those who want to destroy these *Commitments* as well as the ministry—they admit it. You just have to come face to face with "what am I doing to my church?" You are crucifying Christ to me if we turn our backs on the things that we have told the world that we are going to do down here, and I speak against the motion unequivocally.

APPENDIX 9

Response by Dr. Gilmore to his critics at the special church conference, August 19, 1970, called in an attempt to dismiss him from his job as Pastor.

Ladies and gentlemen: I want to ask you to hear me out. My spirit is not defensive, but I want to say several things to you. My heart knows no bitterness. I am the pastor of every one of you. As I stated last Sunday morning, you do not have to agree with me for me to love you. I am the pastor of *all* of you.

Now, first of all, I want to talk to you about my theology, because there has been the charge that I do not believe certain things, that my theological position is at variance with Baptist thought, and that I am heretical in some of my beliefs. I want to talk about my theology under two headings. First of all, I want to respond directly to Mr. Brown's charges, and then, secondly, to set forth in a systematic fashion, as carefully as I can, what I believe. Mr. Brown—I'm going to take the things that he has said, and respond to them, so that you will know and have both sides—has indicated to you that he came to me because he had disagreed with me theologically. That is so. He said that I suggested to him that he read certain books, and that one of those books was Dr. Harry Emerson Fosdick's *A Guide To Understanding The Bible*. That is also true. He did not tell you, however, that when I made the recommendation I said: "This is a representative example of a certain approach to scripture." At the same time I also suggested other books that represented other points of view. The one that I most pointedly stressed was H. E. W. Turner's book, *Jesus, Master and Lord*, about which I said, "This is where I stand." Unfortunately, the impression was left that because I suggested he read Fosdick's book, and he quoted the article dealing with Dr. Fosdick upon his death that "a great liberal voice was stilled"—citing from the article some of the doctrines which he had championed, namely the denial of the Virgin Birth, the second coming, and the like,—the implication was left that because I recommended he read this book as a certain approach to Scripture, this means I have agreed with all that Dr. Fosdick has taught.

Now, let me say categorically two things: first, there were two Fosdicks—an early Fosdick and a later Fosdick. Second, Dr. Fosdick, a truly great man—and I would count it a privilege to be identified with Harry Emerson Fosdick in terms of his spirit and the effect, the profound effect,

172

he has had on the religious scene in America—in his early days was so badgered by Fundamentalists that he made mistakes. He mellowed, however, and in his later years anyone who reads his volumes of sermons, and they are classics, will discover that no man could have been more in the main stream of classic Christianity than Harry Emerson Fosdick.

One of the last sermons he preached at the Riverside Church was "Christ Himself is Christianity," in which he set forth his basic understanding of the Christian faith. Now, what I am saying to you is this truth: just because I recommend a book, that does not mean I agree with all that is in that book. I wanted Mr. Brown to read that book because it represents a certain point of view which would help anyone who is grappling with how to interpret and understand the Scriptures. I believe profoundly—and I am going to get into this more in a moment, but just to say it here—I believe profoundly in the high authority of the Holy Scriptures. I believe in the Virgin Birth. I believe in the second coming. So that to imply that because I recommend this book, that this means that I agree with all the things that Dr. Fosdick said in his early years, is not necessarily so. It has been said by Mr. Brown that I do not believe that the Bible is the infallible Word of God. Dr. Dickinson said a moment ago that Mr. Brown's interpretation of what he says I believe is what he means to believe in the infallibility of the Word of God. I don't believe that there is a man in this world that believes the Bible more profoundly than I do. Now, what has happened is that I have tried to be honest. One thing marks my ministry, and I think those of you who have worked with me most closely know it, if you ask me a question, I'm going to give you an honest answer, and tell you exactly what I think. And this is what I have done, not only with Mr. Brown, but with many others.

Now, let's take this matter of Genesis. I want to appeal to your intelligence. What do you do if a Fundamentalist quotes Genesis—"In the beginning God created the heavens and the earth. . . . He labored six days and on the seventh day he rested"—and then says to you that you do not believe Genesis if you do not believe literally that the world was created in six days? And yet over here is a group of devoted Christian scientists, and others, who have abundant proof that this world of ours is literally millions of years old. Now, when you begin to interpret the Genesis account of creation, what are you going to say? Are you going to say, "I just believe the Bible," or are you going to look at the evidence that reverent science has that this world is millions of years old, and begin to ask some questions?

Now, what is important here? Oh, here it is! The main importance is that the Scriptures, the charter of the Judeo-Christian Faith, affirm that God did the creating. This world of ours did not just emerge out of "stuff." It did not come into being because ooze somehow was pushed by some electric current, and something crawled upon the land, became more diffused, and then emerged in ever higher forms. No! The Judeo-Christian faith takes the Genesis account seriously when it says: "In the beginning

God created." But, dear friends, did you notice there is not the first word as to *how* it was created. Not the first word! The important thing is that God began the process, he guides the process, he continues to guide the process. What is important—and this is what the Christian faith affirms—is that behind all that we see is not just matter—stark, faceless, impersonal, matter that has always been here and always will be here—but that behind all that we see there is one who is like Jesus Christ. Such an understanding prompted Robert Louis Stevenson to say, when he was really up against it, dying with tuberculosis: "The universe turns on the axles of love." When you talk about the doctrine of creation, the issue is not this business of "I believe the Bible—six days!" No, the issue is the *nature* of the creation. Now, one other word. Does it make you a scientist, no matter how devout you may be? It doesn't, does it? Do you think that the men who lived seven or eight hundred years before Christ knew the intricacies of the modern scientific world-view? No! And no matter how devout a man is, this does not give him special insight into scientific things. He has to pay the price to know this.

The Bible is not a book of science. Because I have said this I have been hit in the midsection with the charge that I don't believe the Bible. *The Bible is not a book of science!* It is a book that unfolds the revelation of God of himself to the world, culminating ultimately in Jesus Christ. I have had the privilege—and there is nothing I enjoy more—of trying to interpret the Christian faith in its essential themes on many university campuses across this nation. At state universities and Christian universities—and I don't mean to brag about this—I have seen time and time and time again, when I set forth the doctrine of creation in the light of Genesis in the way I have done for you here tonight—I have seen students literally weep for joy that they were taken off the hook, because they thought they had to believe a literalism, a fundamentalism, in order to be Christian. You don't have to crucify your mind to be a follower of Jesus Christ. Just the opposite!

Now, along this same line, it was said by Mr. Brown that I believe that some parts of the Bible are more inspired than others. Precisely! I do, because I believe that God has increasingly revealed himself, culminating in Jesus Christ. And if you want chapter and verse, in fundamentalistic style, read the prophet Isaiah who, as it were, becomes a signpost, talking about all things yet to come. Why, to make the Bible just a flatland of wooden interpretation, as though every word is on the same plane, and that the "begats" in the Old Testament are on the same plane as Matthew 5, 6, and 7, the Sermon on the Mount, is not to be biblical at all; it is to be totally unbiblical. Indeed, I believe there has been progressive revelation, moving ever higher, culminating in Jesus Christ. And, moreover, I would say that God is not through yet! As our Lord said he would, the Holy Spirit has been sent "to bring to our remembrance all that Christ taught and did." And as Paul, caught up in the reality of this, said, "It doth not yet appear

174

what we shall be, but we know that when he shall appear, we shall be like him." Our God is moving on! Now, that is a proper understanding of the Word of God as I see it.

The charge has been made that I have said that the Bible contains myths and fables. Now, let me explain something. I am going to be technical here with you a moment. Never in my life have I ever said that the Bible contained myths and fables, in the sense of fanciful fairy-tales that are not true. The German word translated myth or "mythos" does not mean—and has never meant—to communicate to people who understand that you are talking about something that is untrue. It is profoundly true. I like the way Gilbert Murray says this. Talking about myth, in the sense of its profoundness, he said: "Myth is the things that never were and always are."

Now, let's take the matter of Jonah and the whale. It has been said I don't believe the Bible because I don't believe the interpretation that Mr. Brown, or others like him, would give it. I believe profoundly the realism and the basic thrust of what the book of Jonah is talking about. It's a great foreign missionary story. An Englishman who wrote some 50 years ago about the Jonah story asked: "Do you think that a man could live three days in the belly of a whale?" Is that the point of the book of Jonah? Do you accuse a man of not believing the Bible when he raises questions about that? Is that the message? It is possible for a person to say, "I believe it just as it is," and yet miss the point of what the story of Jonah is all about as to what happens when a man is disobedient to what God tells him to do. That is the issue!

It has been said that I don't believe the Flood story. Now, notice, I'm not calling these things fables in the sense that they are not so, but rather, that the deepest things, the prehistoric things—before man was even there to observe—are expressed by "myth." In other words—remember, we are going to be literalistic here—in the creation account man came last, certainly in one of the creation accounts. So, there wasn't anybody there to observe what was done. I'm saying that in prehistory, the literary vehicle of "myth" is a profound vehicle for communicating the deepest spiritual insight and feeling of the human spirit. To talk about the Flood and say that because I raise questions about taking it literally, that I don't believe it, isn't true. I believe it profoundly.

It was said that Jesus' reference to the Flood proves that he accepted it in the way Mr. Brown interpreted it. No, not at all! Have you ever done a little mathematics on this matter? Take the size of the ark as it is spelled out in Scripture, and just from the sheer point of mathematics try to get all of the animals of earth in it, two by two, and the food they would require for the time stated, and see if it's possible. It is not! Now, is that to say that you don't believe what this story is really about? Not at all! The Flood story is profoundly true, and it will happen again and again and again to any nation or to any people who are disobedient to God.

175

Judgment will come! And it's quite possible, and you see it all the time, and I do too, for people to get so "hung up" on the literalism of the Bible that they miss its message and meaning.

I have never questioned the Scriptures as to their authority. And I must tell you that I am in an utter quandary that any people could hear me preach for two years and think that I do not hold the Word of God in the highest esteem; I don't know what to make of it. It was said that I do not believe that men are born sinners, but that society makes them sinners. That is not what I said. This is what I said: man is not a sinner until he has his own will, and exercises it for choice. I do not believe—and Mr. Brown has again expressed what I did not communicate—I do not believe that that tiny little babe lying there in his crib is a "sinner," in the sense of the New Testament. We are not sinners until first of all we exercise our will to make moral choices for which we are responsible. I'll stand on that!

Regarding the *Baptist Faith and Message*, it was said that I do not accept it, and then it was said that I do accept it. Let me explain to you where I am here. It really doesn't make any difference whether I accept it or not, to tell you the truth, because if there is any one thing that is true of Baptist Christians, it is that no one group of Baptist Christians can bind the conscience of another group of Baptist Christians. One of the priceless privileges which has been mine, because of my teaching role, has been to rub shoulders with different kinds of Baptists around the world— Australian Baptists, British Baptists, German Baptists (my major professor was a German Baptist), and it's the most amazing thing in the world that there is at the center an amazing unanimity. But in terms of peripheral matters there is an amazing disagreement and diversity. And I glory in that!

Now, as to the *Baptist Faith and Message*, what I have said about this is in light of just what I have finished saying about the Scriptures. I have no difficulty accepting the *Baptist Faith and Message*, as it affirms in the first part that the Bible is the Word of God, if you don't make me sign that that means infallibility which is wooden and unintelligent, such as I have been talking about. Rather, I believe the Bible is the infallible Word of God in the sense that I think it is the vehicle, indeed, *the* prime vehicle of God's revelation of himself. In this sense, I'll sign it and have no trouble.

Again, by implication—and this is not fair—I have been smeared by Mr. Brown because I have been and I am now a member of the E. Y. Mullins Fellowship, and I am proud of it. This fellowship is constituted by some of the finest ministers and laymen in the Southern Baptist Convention. (And I might tell you because it's no secret, that when E. Y. Mullins wrote his great book, *The Axioms of the Christian Religion*, he was dubbed by many as a heretic of the worst sort.) The E. Y. Mullins Fellowship is a group of men, laymen and ministers, who are trying to be responsible and bring a different point of view to our Convention life. Now, so much about responding to Mr. Brown's charges as they relate to the Bible. What about Christ?

I believe that Jesus Christ is God incarnate; that he is the Savior of the world; that he is my Savior; that he is the Lord of all life, and that the only way I can find my utter freedom is to become his slave, his servant. I have discovered in some measure that the more I become his slave, the more my life is really what it should be and is all about. I believe that Jesus Christ is not merely the Lord of the church, or that he is merely a religious figure that is to be done patronage by a religious people. I believe that Jesus Christ, being God incarnate, is the Lord of all things, as I have said many times. He is just as much the Lord of General Motors as he is of the First Baptist Church of Birmingham. He is just as much Lord of the White House as he is of any religious institution. And this leads me to say that—and I am jumping a little ahead, but this is the point to say it—those of you who would find fault with this minister, or any other, for talking about politics, simply do not understand the Lordship of Christ. There is no area of life outside the pale of the Lordship of Christ, and any minister who is going to be faithful to his task, and faithful to his Lord, must speak to all dimensions of life up to the limit of his vision.

What about salvation? I believe all men are in need of salvation, that no man can save himself, but that he can be saved only by commitment to Jesus Christ.

What about sin? I believe that "all have sinned and come short of the glory of God"; that no man escapes it. I believe there is a negative disposition in every man by which he prefers his own way to God's way. This is what the classic definition of "original sin" is about. While I do not say that a little child in the crib is a "sinner" in the sense that Paul was talking about in Romans, yet there is a negative disposition in man by which he prefers his own way to God's way. All are sinners and need a Savior.

What about the church? Here I talk with bated breath because I think the church was constituted by Christ, building on the best and deepest insights of the "remnant concept" of the Old Testament, whereby the church is to be the representative of Christ in the world. It is to be the reconciling body that breaks down the middle walls of partition; that destroys the walls that divide men religiously, politically, racially, economically, and socially. It is the one place under heaven where the rich man and the poor man, the learned man and the ignorant man, the crude man and the cultured man, the red man, the white man, the black man, the yellow man, the brown man—every class, color, and condition—can sit down side by side, because they have the one great fact in common, and that is the sharing of the treasure of Jesus Christ.

You see, that is what we need to do! If we could demonstrate such a reconciling power in our church, it would be a witness to the community that this is the way things are supposed to be in the world. The church is commissioned—made up of people who have had a genuine confrontation with Jesus Christ and have surrendered their life to his Lordship—to move out into every area that we can possibly think of to represent Christ, there

177

to become his light, his salt, and his leaven; a church that binds up people's wounds; that is angered in the presence of injustice; a church that has become color-blind and is concerned about one thing—that is, to bring the love and the redemptive mercy of Christ to as many people as possible.

The church, true to its essential nature, is inclusive. The church is not satisfied, if it is true to the Lord's intent, merely "to snatch souls from the burning." It is not content to go to one who is poor and in desperate need of medicine and food and encouragement, and talk to him about a narrow salvation whereby he gets his (now don't misunderstand me, I'm not making fun of the concept) "soul" saved. This is totally inadequate. Rather, as we minister to his spiritual needs, we must take into consideration—the church must—that he needs food, he needs water, he needs medicine, he needs love, he needs understanding, he needs education. Oh, my dear people, if we could catch a glimpse of what the church in all of its majesty is to be and do, we would be so caught up in the wonder of our task that we wouldn't have time to argue with each other. This is what I believe about the church.

What about the second coming? Let me emphasize it this way: not only do I believe in the second coming, in the classical traditional sense, that one day the Lord will sum up all things, but I am more concerned about the fact that I know this reality in my own life. I know the reality through Scripture that he comes again, and again, and again. "Behold, I stand at the door and knock." There is no more pressing message in the whole New Testament than Matthew 25, where the emphasis of the Lord is against the backdrop of the great judgment: "I was hungry, you gave me no meat, thirsty and you gave me no drink, naked and you clothed me not, in prison and you visited me not." What is he saying? That he comes again and again and again. I believe that if our eyes, our spiritual eyes, are open, we can see Christ come to us ever and again, sometimes in a black skin, sometimes in a broken, defeated man. When we have this point of view, we are always looking for Christ. And where do you think you will find him? As I read the New Testament, you will find him among the prostitutes, among the dispossessed, among those who are denied justice. And it is your task and mine, as Christians, as a Christian church, to do everything in our power, to the limit of our vision and our ability, to minister to these.

What about the Holy Spirit? The charge was made that I have only two gifts of the Spirit. I am utterly amazed by this, as to how anybody could discern what fruits of the Spirit one has and what he does not have. I do not have such sapience; I do not have such Godlike discernment. I believe profoundly in the reality of the Holy Spirit of God in the world, and in my own life. Your pastor is a man of devotion. Never a day passes but what I spend various times, sometimes a long time, in company with the Lord. Dear friends, one of the worst things we can ever do is to begin to schematize the works of the Spirit, on the basis of a narrow little interpretation of the fruits of the Spirit. It is on this basis that it is charged that I have but two of them. How can any man say that of any other man? I do not know what fruits of the Spirit you have. Only God knows that! Well, so much for theology.

Now, let me say two or three other things to you. I have done some of this, but even at the risk of repetition, I think that some of you here tonight need some basic information, some of you whom I do not know. (And let me stop to say parenthetically that I regret that, but I can honestly say before God that I have done about all that could be expected of any man in 23 months. I have worked like a Trojan. I wish that I had been able to get to your home, so that I would know you. Some of you, as I look into your faces, I do not know, and some of you here tonight have never heard me preach.) Now, let me tell you then, since you do not know me as a person, something of the way I came to this church. When I was first approached, and I told my friends that I was possibly coming to Birmingham, they thought I was crazy. I do not say this unkindly but, dear friends, you are not aware of what a terrible, terrible image Birmingham, Alabama, has in other parts of this nation. They thought I was crazy. But the same thing happened to me that Dr. John Sims mentioned a moment ago. When I talked with Hobart Grooms, Jr., and Harry Baker and Joe Travis, Katherine Williamson, and other members of the committee, and they began to talk about the *Commitments* that the church had just made, I was flabbergasted. I could not believe it! I said, "Do you mean what you say?" They said, "We do. These *Commitments* were passed without a single dissenting vote." As the conversation progressed, subsequently I came to Birmingham to talk at length with the committee—and we spent a whole Sunday afternoon in one of the conference rooms at the Baptist Medical Center—we talked and talked. The content of it was these *Commitments*. It got close to dinner time and Mr. Travis said: "Well, I guess we have said all we need to say; I guess we can go." I said, "Oh, no, wait a minute, I have a lot more questions." Remember, Hobart? So after eating we came back to the conference room, and we talked—my! I don't know how much longer.

Now, let me tell you this, and any one of the committee members will tell you, your pastor was almost brutal with these dear men and women. I did not want to come under any false pretense at all. At times I was brutal in the way I zeroed in and asked them: "What do you mean by that? Suppose that we do have Negroes come, and so forth, and so on, what then?" What I am saying to you is, as we say in East Tennessee, "you didn't buy a pig in a poke." Those of you who were here after I came know that on Sunday morning, in my first sermon in September, I declared my soul to you, and I explained to you something of just what I have said.

Now, why did I come? Let me show you something so that you will understand the "why" of my mind's set. This *Commitment* was placed in my hands which reads: "We, the members of First Baptist Church, recognize and accept the full responsibility of an extended Baptist ministry in

179

downtown Birmingham, which involves a ministry to the special groups around us such as the medical center, apartment-dwellers, the deaf, the elderly, the Y's, the internationals and others." Listen to this: "we will proceed with faith." Now, hear this statement in the light of the charge that was made a month ago that "we have had a losing season." It was this sentence, more than any other single thing, that made me aware that I was in the presence of men and women who understood a dimension of the Christian faith that is rare, indeed. Most of our Southern Baptist Churches—some of the same philosophy that has been expressed tonight— are so concerned about saving their own lives, about budgets and buildings, and all the rest, that they don't understand this sentence. Listen to this: "We will proceed with faith even though the fruits of our efforts, the normal signs of success, are not as spectacular as we might wish." That is an amazing statement. And it reveals spiritual maturity that is laudable. Buildings are important, and budgets are important, but I'm pretty sure that we are much more concerned about these things than God is. Let me tell you something; where you have a group of people who want to do the bidding of the Lord, whose pocketbooks have been baptized, whose minds are available, whose hearts burn within them, you don't have to worry about whether or not you have enough financial resources to do anything you want to do.

Where is the risk of faith? Listen to this: "We recognize that there are people in our area who need the love of God as expressed through our church of the Lord Jesus Christ, and a city which needs spiritual leadership." What does that mean? Listen to this: "We believe that we cannot abdicate the responsibility of giving what we have of dedication, of leadership, and love to the situation immediately around us." Listen: "Our members may differ in nationality, birth, position, possessions, education or affinity, but we do not differ in our unswerving desire to be more Christ-like, not than any other livng soul, but more Christ-like today than we were yesterday." And, then, when I came to Number 9, I could scarcely believe it: "We are maintaining here a small part of God's great democracy and we ask courtesy and tolerance for all alike." Now, listen to this staccato emphasis: "On these stern terms, we invite all who will, whether they be young or old, proud or plain, rich or poor, to partake with us of the love of God and to give themselves to the task that is before us." Now, what I have tried to do is to implement this. I thought you meant this. I took, literally, that you meant this.

Let me share with you a letter—and this will give you an insight into your pastor's personality. I received this letter yesterday from a dear friend to whom I was pastor at the First Baptist Church, Marshall, Missouri. She wrote because she had seen our difficulty. It says what I prize because it reveals my heart to you. "This past week you have been on my mind constantly. When I opened my *Newsweek* and saw your picture, and read the article, I began praying for you. I hope the prayers are answered. Almost the first thought that came to mind was the incident

180

that happened at the 1948 Democratic National Convention. After a bitter fight, Hubert Humphrey's liberal Civil Rights plank had been adopted. A group of Southerners, led by Strom Thurmond, revolted and walked out of the Convention. (I might say that this woman's husband was very much involved in politics.) A reporter asked Mr. Thurmond why he was taking this extreme step. President Truman is only following the platform that President Roosevelt advocated, the reporter argued. "I agree," Thurmond said, "but Truman really means it." Now listen to this, this I prize and I will put it as a memento that adequately reflects the way I see myself: "I know you mean everything you preach. . . ."

That is the way I see myself, dear people. Being a minister is not a job to me. It is not a means of merely making some money—it's a way of life. And I took with absolute, utter seriousness this document, because I thought you meant it, and I've tried to implement it. Now, were we so naive, are we so naive tonight that we did not recognize that if we labored faithfully in God's vineyard that he would give us fruit? And will give us some more? Some of you are complaining about the fact that we have lost membership. Where is the "field" for us to correct that? Are you going to say that we have to draw them from Mountain Brook, or that they have to be of a certain culture, or standard, or that they have to be white? Or, are we going to minister? Now, this is the point I want to make to those of you who have been offended by what I have said about race. I've said repeatedly, and the Lord knows my heart, I did not come with any idea at all, in terms of a theoretical thing, of saying that "I am going to integrate this church." I did not do that. What I have said always is: let's minister to anybody and everybody on the basis of need. And if that person that has need happens to be white or black or brown, it doesn't matter. I don't care if they are green! If they have need, let us minister to them. And then, if the quality of our ministry in love is sufficient to draw an answering response from them, let us rejoice in our spirits that it is that adequate. Now, it's in that sense I have preached and will always preach the inclusive gospel. But I didn't come with any idea of integrating this church.

The NAACP doesn't even know who I am—well, they might now. The Home Mission Board of the Southern Baptist Convention has never paid a dime of my salary—as has been rumored and told by some. Anyone who could accuse me of being a Communist—that is so ludicrous that it's ridiculous. My soul alive—I guess I have trained about as many students at the graduate level in terms of philosophy against Communism as perhaps anybody in the Convention. I have a master's degree in sociology, and I'm quite conversant with Communist theory and practice; and I am opposed to it in every detail. But, apparently, that doesn't matter too much to those of you who oppose me.

Now, what about this statement that the issue is not race? Let me ask you a question that any sensible person will have to face up to: if I'm being fired because of my theology, why did you tack Betty Bock onto that? And when you had a chance to bring charges against Miss Bock, why

181

didn't some of you charge her with theological errors? *The issue is race!* As Hobart, Jr., has said, and some others have said, and many of you men sitting here know it—at deacons' meetings and other committee meetings it was honestly admitted that it was race.

What about this charge that I have created disunity? I want to read you something that came into my hands the other day; it says what I want to say about this matter of disunity. A while back, after some discussion about the pros and cons in selecting a preacher for a certain church, the chairman of the pulpit committee read to the members of the diaconate this letter reported to have come from an applicant. It read as follows:

"I have many qualifications. I have been a preacher with much success and have had some success as a writer. Some say I am a good organizer. I have been a leader at most places where I've been and have traveled rather extensively. I am over 50 years of age and have never preached in one place more than three years. In some places I've had to leave town as my preaching caused disturbances and sometimes even riots. I admit I have been in jail at least three times, but not from any wrongdoing. My health is not good, but I still get a lot of work done. The churches where I have preached have been small, though located in large cities. I have not gotten along very well with religious leaders in the cities where I've preached, in fact some have threatened and even attacked me physically. I'm not good at keeping records. I've been known to even forget some of those I have baptized. If you can use me, I will do the best I can." Then the chairman said: "What do you think, shall we take a chance on him?" Another deacon said: "Hire an unhealthy, absentminded, trouble-making jail-bird? I should say not. Who is the applicant? What's his name?" "Well," said the chairman who had just read the letter, "it is just signed, 'the Apostle Paul.'"

Now, I'm not through. If that doesn't say it—maybe this will. This is a letter to the Rev. Saul Paul, Independent Missionary, Corinth, Greece:

"Dear Mr. Saul: We recently received an application from you for service under our Board. It is our policy to be as frank and open-minded as possible with all of our applicants and we have made an exhaustive survey of your case. To be plain, we are surprised that you have been able to pass as a bona fide missionary. We are told that you are afflicted with a severe eye trouble, which is certain to be an insuperable handicap to an effective ministry. Our Board requires 20-20 vision. At Antioch we learned that you opposed Dr. Simon Peter, an esteemed denominational Secretary, and actually rebuked him publicly. You have stirred up so much trouble at Antioch that a special board meeting had to be convened in Jerusalem. We cannot condone such action. Do you think it seemly for a missionary to do part-time secular work? We hear that you are making tents on the side. In a letter to the church at Philippi, you admitted that they were the only church supporting you. We wonder why. Is it true that you have a jail record? Certain brethren report that you did two years' time at Caesarea, and were imprisoned at Rome. You made so much trouble for the business men at Ephesus that they refer to you as 'the man that turned the world upside down.' Sensationalism in missions is uncalled for. We also deplore the lurid 'over the wall in the basket' episode at Damascus. We are appalled at your obvious lack of conciliatory behaviour. Diplomatic men are not stoned and dragged out of the city gate or assaulted by furious mobs. Have you ever suspected that gentler words might gain you more friends? I enclose a copy of Darius Carnagus' book on *How To Win Jews and Influence Greeks.*

"In one of your letters you refer to yourself as Paul, the aged. Our new mission policies do not envision a surplus of super-annuated recipients. We understand that you are given to fantasies and dreams. At Troas you saw a man of Macedonia, and another time were caught up into the third heaven and even claimed the Lord stood by you. We reckon that more realistic and practical minds are needed in the task of world evangelism. You have caused much trouble everywhere you have gone. You opposed the honorable women at Berea and the leaders of your own nationality in Jerusalem. If a man cannot get along with his own people, how can he serve foreigners? We learned that you are a snake handler. At Malta you picked up the poisonous serpent which is said to have bitten you, but you did not suffer harm. You admit that while you were serving time at Rome that all forsook you. Good men are not left friendless. Three fine brothers by the name of Diotrophes, Demas, and Alexander, accomplished men, have notarized affidavits to the effect that it is impossible for them to cooperate with either you or with your program. We know that you had a bitter quarrel with a fellow missionary, Barnabas. Harsh words do not further God's work.

"You have written many letters to churches where you have formerly been pastor. In one of these letters you accused a church member of living with his father's wife, and you caused the whole church to feel badly, and the poor fellow was expelled. You spent too much time talking about the second coming of Christ. Your letters to the people at Thessalonica were almost entirely devoted to this theme. Put first things first from now on. Your ministry has been far too flighty to be successful. First, Asia Minor, then Macedonia, then Greece, then Italy, and now you are talking about a wild goose chase into Spain. Concentration is more important than dissipation of one's powers. You cannot win the whole world by yourself, you are just one little Paul. In a recent sermon you said 'God forbid that I should glory in anything save the cross of Christ.' It seems to us that you ought to glory in our heritage, our denominational program, the unified budget, and the world of Federated Churches. Your sermons are much too long at times—at one place you talked until after midnight, and a young man fell asleep and fell out of the window and broke his neck. Nobody is saved after the first twenty minutes. Stand up, speak up, and then shut up is our advice!

"Dr. Luke reports that you are a thin little man, bald, frequently sick, and always so agitated over your churches that you sleep very poorly. He reports that you pad around the house praying half the night. A healthy

183

mind and a robust body is our ideal for all applicants. A good night's sleep will give you zest and zip so that you can wake up full of zing. We find it best to send only married men into foreign service. We deplore your policy of persistent celibacy. Simon Magus has set up a matrimonial bureau at Samaria where the names of some very fine widows are available. You wrote recently to Timothy that you had 'fought a good fight.' Fighting is hardly a recommendation for a missionary. No fight is a good fight. Jesus came not to bring a sword, but peace. You boasted that 'I fought wild beasts at Ephesus'—what on earth do you mean? It hurts me to tell you this, Brother Paul, but in all my twenty-five years experience, I have never met a man so opposite to the requirements of our foreign mission board. If we accepted you, we would break every rule of modern missionary practice. Most sincerely yours, J. Flavius Fluffyhead."

Now, why do I do this? You shake your heads and wag, because you think that has nothing whatsoever to do with the present situation. Now we have talked a lot recently about being biblical. What did they say about Christ? There are two kinds of disunity. I think that anyone here would have to admit that by human cussedness or by offending people because of ill-advised ways, I have not disunited you on this score. I am guilty of the charge, as Luther Easterwood said so eloquently, of disturbing you with the truth of the gospel. I have told you the truth, as I have seen it, up to the level of my ability. Whether you agree with me or not—(let me say immediately that I am the first to admit that I have made mistakes, and I will talk more about that in a moment)—if you are going to charge a man and fault him because he creates some discord, then you've got to rule out all the apostles. And you've got to rule out the Lord himself.

It's very interesting to note that when Christ's enemies came to the trials which led to the crucifixion, not a soul told the real reason why they killed him—not a one. "You are an upsetter of Israel," "you are a blasphemer," they charged. What did Jesus say? "I tell you, those who follow me will find that mother is against daughter, daughter against mother," so forth and so on, "and a man's foes shall be those of his own household." Apparently we have not understood that the gospel sometimes disturbs. Believe me, my dear people, I would do everything in my power, I would bend over backward, to be conciliatory. It's not my purpose to offend any person. But I don't truly love you as your pastor if I don't tell you the truth, as I see it. And, then, as we are in a covenant relationship, with the Holy Scriptures opened before us, if I have told you the truth, don't you get angry with me or any other pastor, but you ask the Lord to open your eyes and I'll do the same.

Now, one last word! Let me give you my personal testimony as to who I am and what I'm about. I'm no professional religionist. What I am at noonday I am at midnight. I could wish it were better. I wish that I had a countenance that was pleasing to everybody. I wish that my manner was such that everyone was drawn to me. But I can say to you with all honesty that there is no pastor anywhere that labors more urgently to be a faithful prophet and pastor than yours. I look upon that place [the pulpit] as holy ground, and up to the limit of my ability, I have never walked into that pulpit without the best effort of which I am capable. I know that I have blind spots; I am not God, but I try to do the best I can with what light I have.

As to mistakes, the following idea is a reality I wish you would add to your mental furniture. It's very easy for any person, or for the person himself, to sit in judgment on a decision that was made six months or a year ago, in the light of all that has come after it. If I had had the knowledge two years ago of all the dispositions and attitudes of the church that I have now, I would have made some different decisions. In fact, I wouldn't have come. But you see, to fault a man in the light of further developments for what he did back there, is to do what the Bible says is one of the worst sins—that is, to sit in judgment. I have made mistakes, I regret them. But they were honest ones. And they were not done in a corner. They were not done blindly; they were done with all the light I had at that time.

One final word! I can honestly tell you that my greatest concern is not for myself, although I have a family, and I recognize the full responsibility of this. It's at a time like this that I sometimes say I can appreciate Paul's counsel not to be married, though no man is more happily married than I am. I can put up with anything, but I sure do hate to see my wife and my children dragged about by such stuff as this. I am not primarily concerned about myself; I'll get by. But, oh! my dear people, I am deeply concerned as to what is going to happen to the cause of Christ here. Leave me out of it and let's face the issue at hand—to vote in such a way that we position this church as a racist church, or to vote in such a way that we position this church as being a rank fundamentalist church that is concerned about dotting every "i" and crossing every "t" theologically, is to mean great loss to the cause of Christ here in this city, and around the world. A letter came to my desk just a few days ago from a friend I made in Japan. She said, "I am praying for you and your church as you meet next Wednesday night." All over the world! I make no plea for myself—I come to you not in weakness, not in begging—but I come to you in great moral strength and earnestness, simply asking you to *be the church*. And may God have mercy on our souls!

Wallace Henley, "Distrust to Fear, Then Desperation," The Birmingham News, September 5, 1970.

How bitter the price of distrust. It breaks to fear, which in its horrendous way snowballs into those situations in which human beings fall in desperation. First Baptist Church has been plodding through the process and for some that point of desperation has been reached. We are told First Baptist's dilemma is a private one. It cannot be private if one believes the New Testament teaching of the Christian experience as one of familyhood, or community. All of those named "Christian" are involved negatively or positively in the action of others called "Christian," even as all those in the family of Dillinger or Churchill are impuned or exalted by the activities of others bearing the family name. First Baptist is no private matter.

Back to the distrust. Last Sunday, a prominent Birminghamian and his family sought to join the church. They were white, so there was no overt racial implication. But the family was not admitted to membership. One member suggested why he opposed admittance of the applicants: Their motives were to be questioned, since the man seeking membership was known to be a friend of Dr. Herbert Gilmore, First Baptist's pastor, and probably wanted membership only to sway votes to Dr. Gilmore's side.

The motive-question in Southern white church attendance and membership is as old as the first day Negroes sought to attend. Few churches were concerned with the motives that caused congregations to assemble until an out was needed to exclude unwanted people from church.

In fact, there was a time when the worse the motive, the more welcome a person might be in church since his need was apparently greater. But that was in the day of the heroic church.

If persons are to be barred from church on the basis of motive with any degree of Biblical justice, the matter must be consistent.

Bar all of those who come simply to show off Easter clothes (maybe churches would have to close on Easter); keep out people who come to church because it's the only place they can safely assert any power; don't let attend church those whose only motive is to assure they'll have a preacher to preside over their weddings and funerals; close the church doors to those who come because it is a step in getting them elected to political office or expedient in the operation of their business.

If such a motive-question process is initiated, there must be appointed some motive-questioners. In other words, there must be appointed some assistant gods since God can be the only judge of what goes on in the remotest cavern of a man's soul. As Jesus aptly put it, one shouldn't be too picky about the splinters in another man's eyes until he has gotten the two-by-four out of his own eye.

Can it be that a segment of a community of faith has deteriorated to such a level that it will not trust those who wish to become part of it?

APPENDIX 11

Statement by Federal Judge H. H. Grooms, Sr., to the church conference on September 2, 1970, called to discuss the motion not to accept or reject prospective members on the basis of race or color.

Brother Chairman and fellow Christians: There are lots of others here who have earned the right to address you as well as I have, and I hope I won't take too much time in doing so. The Psalmist said: "Enter into his gates with thanksgiving and into his courts with praise." I hope we have all come in that spirit tonight. He also said, "I was glad when they said, Let us go into the house of the Lord." Now, I must confess to you that I am not glad to be here tonight. I am not glad to be here tonight because the burden of this matter is just about more than I can take, and I know the same thing is true with many of you. But I have reached the conclusion that we can't work this matter out in our own strength. We are going to have to depend upon God. There is no solution to this problem unless God gives a solution. There have been all kinds of things said here. There have been dodgers that have been passed around, accusations have been charged, but I have not heard a single verse of Scripture cited. When I have a case to decide, I wouldn't think about deciding the case without looking up the authority before I reached a decision. I wouldn't think about deciding a case until I determined what the law was that was applicable to the facts of the case. Now, I am hoping tonight to sort of pave the way for more deliberate and thoughtful and prayer-provoking discussion than we have had heretofore. I have said my heart was heavy. To be frank about it, I had to take two milltown to get up here and I'm still leaning on this platform. When I look over this audience and I see men here that I have labored with in this church for forty or fifty years on the other side of this controversy, I say to myself, "Lord, what's wrong with us?" When I came to this church in 1927 we were in a controversy. Dr. Hobbs was pastor of the church at that time. Some of you remember that controversy.

I went through a controversy in 1941 and '42, and that's more vivid to some of you. And, then, we have had a succession of pastors; this is the sixth (in fifteen years). I have just begun to wonder if it's the pastor—now you don't have to answer out—if it's the pastors or if it is the people who are involved here. Have I been wrong or not? Some day we are going to

188

have to find where the fault lies. I don't think the fault has lain with these pastors. They may have been at some fault but you know, as I look at the Scriptures here—and I'm going to try to confine myself to the Scriptures—I find that Jesus said: "Think not that I am come to send peace on the earth, I am not come to send peace but a sword. For I am come to set a man at variance against his father, and the daughter against her mother, and the daughter-in-law against her mother-in-law. And a man's foes shall be those of his own household." I was reading from Matthew 10:34-36. I have all of these citations if you wish them. Then, over in Luke 12:51 this is said: "Suppose ye that I am come to give peace on earth? I tell you, nay; but rather division. For from henceforth there shall be five in one house divided, three against two, and two against three. The father shall be divided against the son, and the son against the father; the mother against the daughter, and the daughter against the mother; the mother-in-law against her daughter-in-law, and the daughter-in-law against her mother-in-law." Who is the real divider? Jesus Christ says he is the divider. Now, I think we should seek his will in these matters. And that's what I have tried to do in the remarks that I will make to you tonight. I wonder how many prayers have gone up to heaven and how many have searched the Scripture? Our strength is found in these Scriptures. Two weeks ago tonight we measured our pastor by the Scriptures. I'd like for us tonight to measure ourselves by what the Bible says.

Now, I'm not asking you to take my interpretation. I think that every man has his right to interpret the Scriptures for himself. These Scriptures have a meaning for me and I will try to translate that meaning. You may not have the same interpretation. The interpretation that I give may be foreign to your thinking. And I won't disabuse you or I won't bring down maledictions upon you if you don't agree with me. I do not propose to judge anybody's theology. I only know that God has given me certain light, and through forty years as a Sunday School teacher I have learned certain things. And these things have come to my mind.

What are the Scriptures in relation to this? I am only going to quote one Scripture from the Old Testament and that's from Isaiah: "For my house shall be called an house of prayer for all people." If you drive by the Jewish Temple over here, you will find those words written up across the building. Now let's turn a little further on—I am reading from the 8th chapter of Matthew, verse 11: "And I say unto you, that many shall come from the East and West, and shall sit down with Abraham, and Isaac, and Jacob, in the kingdom of Heaven." And over in the 10th chapter of Mark, verses 13-16, an incident occurred that parallels very closely what has happened in our church. "And they brought young children unto him" (and we have had young children brought *here*, and I heard one of the deacons get up and say, "Who brought these children here?") " . . . and they brought little children unto him, and his disciples rebuked those who brought them. And when Jesus saw it, he was much displeased and he said unto them, 'Suffer little children to come unto me and forbid them not;

189

for of such is the Kingdom of Heaven.' And he took them up in his arms, and he blessed them." And over there in the 18th chapter of Matthew, verse 5 he said: "Any one that receives one of these little ones in my name, receiveth me. But anyone who offends one of these little ones which believe on me, it is better that a millstone be hanged around his neck, and that he be drowned in the midst of the sea." "Take heed that ye despise not one of these little ones; for Jesus came to save those who were lost. And it is not the will of the Father that even one of these little ones should be lost." Now, we have before us these little children to be baptized and if you have seen the action that has been taken, and the lack of action, if there ever was a parallel, I want us to consider this. You may have an entirely different interpretation from what I have and that's your right. You can read these Scriptures as well as I can.

And then I read from the 23rd chapter of Matthew. It has been suggested that in lieu of taking black people in, we increase our gifts to foreign missions. This church has had a marvelous record in this area. It has helped build churches. Dr. Oliver built churches down in Brazil with money he had received from this church, and these churches had both black and white in them. But [Jesus] said to the Pharisees: "You shut up the Kingdom of Heaven against men," yet "you compass land and sea to make one proselyte." The last version that I have read on this reads this way: "You lock the doors of the Kingdom of Heaven in men's faces, yet you sail the seas and cross whole countries to win one convert." Now I am appealing to the women here who have labored so long and so arduously and so fine, and who have given so sacrificially in the missionary society, to read these things I am reading now.

In the 28th chapter of Matthew, verse 19 he says, "Go ye therefore, and teach all nations, baptizing them in the name of the Father, and of the Son, and of the Holy Spirit." The word "nations" there is translated in three different ways. It refers to people and it refers to races. "Go ye therefore and teach *all*" people, *all* races, "*all* nations." So we have our marching orders as Christians to do these things, and I hope that we will keep this in mind. I am going to try to, and I remind you again that I am giving you my interpretation.

In the 12th chapter of Mark, Jesus said this: "And thou shalt love the Lord thy God with all thy heart, and with all thy soul, and with all thy mind, and with all thy strength: this is the first commandment. And the second is like it, namely this, thou shalt love thy neighbor as thyself." And they asked him on one occasion who their neighbor was and he told the story about a man who went down from Jerusalem to Jericho and fell among the thieves, and a Levite came that way and passed on by, and a priest came and passed by, but a Samaritan—a man of another race—came by, and he took him and he poured in oil and wine as he cleansed his wounds, and took him to the inn. And Jesus said unto them, "Which of these three thinkest thou was neighbor to him that fell among the thieves?" And his reply was, "He that showed mercy." Are we—I'm asking myself now—are we showing mercy toward the little white boys and the little white girls and the little black girls and boys? I want us to think on these Scriptures.

Consider Luke 14—"But when thou makest a feast, call the poor, the maimed, the lame, the blind: And thou shalt be blessed; for they cannot recompense thee." And, then, there in the 3rd chapter, verse 16, which is the key verse of John's Gospel: "For God so loved the world, that he gave his only begotten Son, that whosoever believeth in him should not perish, but have everlasting life."

Jesus made a special trip on one occasion. He went to Samaria. The Jews didn't ordinarily travel through Samaria. They would have to purify themselves when they went through Samaria. But Jesus went through Samaria and he came to a woman at the well—not only a Samaritan woman, but a woman of the streets who had had five husbands—and Jesus said to her: " 'Give me to drink.' And the woman said to him, 'How is it that thou, being a Jew, ask a drink of me, which am a woman of Samaria?' For the Jews have no dealings with the Samaritans. And Jesus said, 'Whosoever drinketh of the water that I shall give him shall never thirst.' And the woman said to him, 'Sir, give me this water.' " And what was the reaction of his disciples? "And upon this came his disciples, and marveled that he talked with the woman: Yet no man said, What seekest thou; or, why talkest thou with her?"

Then, in the 6th chapter of John, Jesus said: "All that the Father giveth me shall come to me; and him that cometh to me I will in no wise cast out." Can I as a Christian, in the face of that injunction, cast out anybody who comes believing on the Lord Jesus Christ? That is the question that comes to me. It may not come to you. You may have an entirely different view of the application. In John 10, verses 9 and 16 are these words: "I am the door: by me if any man enter in, he shall be saved, and shall go in and out, and find pasture." In verse 16 he adds this, "And other sheep I have, which are not of this fold: them also I must bring, and they shall hear my voice: and they shall be one fold, and one shepherd." In Acts 1:8 Jesus says: "And ye shall be witnesses unto me both in Jerusalem"—and he was speaking in Jerusalem—"and in all Judea, and in Samaria, and unto the uttermost part of the earth." Now, our mission work doesn't begin in Africa or Brazil, it begins in Birmingham. It begins across Sixth Avenue if I read the Scriptures correctly. Now you may have a different interpretation of these Scriptures.

Then there was another occasion. It's recited in the eighth chapter of Acts, verse 27. He's talking about Philip. "And he arose and went: and behold a man of Ethiopia." The Ethiopians were first mentioned in the second chapter of Genesis. The word has come into our own language. You never refer to a white man as an Ethiopian. What does the word mean to begin with? It comes from the Greek word *ethios*, meaning the burned face one. So here was a man from the region of the burned face one. And what did the Holy Spirit tell Philip? The Spirit said to Philip, "Go near,

191

and join thyself to this chariot." And you remember what happened there—he was reading from Isaiah. And Philip asked him if he understood, and he said, "No, how can I understand when I have no one to interpret for me or teach me?" After Philip had opened the Bible to him, what did the Ethiopian say? "What doth hinder me to be baptized?" And Philip said, "Thou mayest if thou believest."

So at the very outset of the Christian ministry we find that the hand of the evangelist was extended to a black. But not only that, let's turn over a little further. Peter had a vision. They said, "Go down, there is a Gentile down here. He has a problem of the soul." Peter went. And he said unto them, "Ye know how it is an unlawful thing for a man who is a Jew to keep company with one of another nation. But God has shown me that I should not call any man common or unclean." Then Peter opened his mouth and said, "Of a truth I perceive that God is no respecter of persons, but in every nation he that feareth him and worketh rightly is accepted with him." Another translation . . . reads as follows: "I now realize that it is true that God treats all men alike. Whoever feareth him and does what is right is acceptable to him no matter whatsoever he belongs to."

Now, we say we are a New Testament church. We want to get back to the old-time religion. Let's look at the 13th chapter of Acts, the first verse, the first church outside of Jerusalem, of which it is said the disciples were called Christians first at Antioch. Who composed the leadership of that church? "Now there were in the church that was at Antioch certain prophets and teachers; as Barnabas, and Simeon that was called Niger, and Lucius of Cyrene, and Manaen, which had been brought up with Herod the Tetrarch." Now, you say, "What's significant about that?"—Simeon, called Niger. What does the Latin word *niger* mean? The Spanish word for black is *negro*. And the Latin word for black is *niger*. Now, if you take your modern version, it reads like this: "Now there were in this church that was at Antioch certain prophets and teachers: Barnabas, Simeon that was called the Black, Lucius," etc. So the hand of fellowship was extended to a Negro man who was searching for the truth on the way down to return to his country, and Philip baptized him. Are we going to refuse to baptize a little Negro girl and her mother? That's the question I'm asking you. Among the leaders of the first church of Antioch was a man called Niger, the Black.

Then, over in the seventeenth chapter of Acts, Paul is speaking on Mars Hill, and he said: "Neither is he worshipped with men's hands"—talking about God—"as though he needed anything, seeing he giveth to all life, and breath, and all things; and hath made of one blood all nations of men for to dwell on all the face of the earth, and hath determined the times before appointed, and the bounds of their habitation; that they should seek the Lord, if haply they might feel after him." In Romans 2:11 we read, "For there is no respect of persons with God." This is Paul writing to the church in Rome.

You know somebody has said that nothing good comes out of a fight

192

like this. Well, the short-range outlook is bad. It looks like the only one who can get anything out of this is the devil. But do you know that two of the greatest epistles we have in the New Testament were written because of a church dispute in the church of Corinth. Think about that. And here is what he says here—I Corinthians 1:13: "Is Christ divided? Was Paul crucified for you? Or were you baptized in the name of Paul?" Perhaps one of the greatest passages in the Bible is the thirteenth chapter of I Corinthians. In the 13th verse of the 12th chapter he says: "For by one Spirit are we all baptized into one body, whether we be Jews or Gentiles, whether we be bond or free; and have been all made to drink into one Spirit." And then he begins this wonderful 13th chapter by saying, "Though I speak with the tongues of men and of angels, and have not love, I am become as sounding brass or a tinkling cymbal." Now, we can give all the money in our possession to missions in Africa. But if we do not believe in missions across Sixth Avenue, how will God regard us?

There is this statement in Galatians 3:28: "There is neither Jew nor Greek, there is neither bond nor free, there is neither male nor female: for ye are all one in Christ Jesus." Are we all one in Christ? I hope that we are. In Ephesians 2:14 we read this: "For he is our peace, who hath made both one, and hath broken down the middle wall of partition between us." He came to break down the wall. I believe that Scripture tells me—I don't know what it tells you—that we ought not to build one. We know what the wall in Berlin has done and what it was put there for. And James, in the second chapter, verses 8 and 9 says this: "If ye fulfil the royal law according to the scripture, Thou shalt love thy neighbor as thyself, ye do well: but if ye have respect of persons, ye commit sin, and are convicted of the law as transgressors." Another translation reads: "But if you treat people according to their outward appearance, you are guilty of sin and the law condemns you as a lawbreaker." Now on top of these admonitions, what does he say? James 4:17 says: "Therefore to him that knoweth to do good, and doeth it not, to him it is sin." And in I John 4:20, 21: "If a man say, I love God, and hateth his brother, he is a liar: for he that loveth not his brother whom he hath seen, how can he love God whom he hath not seen? And this commandment have we from him, That he who loveth God will love his brother also." You notice I have referred to but one Old Testament Scripture. In Revelation 22:17, it says this: "And the Spirit and the bride say, Come. And let him that heareth say, Come. And let him that is athirst come. And whosoever will, let him take the water of life freely."

Now, the program of work that we have had here has brought us into contact with some Negroes, some black people, and you know if we are going to do anything, we are going to have to take some chances. I fought off this matter—this issue—for years. I fought it off in 1963. This isn't a new issue. It will not depart with Dr. Gilmore. It will be right on our doorsteps until we decide it the way the Lord wants us to decide it. But when it comes right down to scratch, we are going to have to decide the question. Which side are you going to come down on? That's the question I have asked myself. Are you going to say peace and harmony is above everything? Am I going to say that, or am I going to say that truth and right also count? And, maybe, that is what has divided our church. I'm not saying this. You may have an entirely different interpretation about the matter. Now, in this connection we have had accusations or have had statements—I won't characterize them as accusations because I don't want to be in the position of offending my brother, and I have many of them here—whom I love, whom I don't want to hurt personally, and I hope none of us will hurt anybody personally. I know families are divided over this issue, but I believe that what we have undertaken here is what God would want us to do. Now, if it has brought us in contact with colored people, why then, I think we should take the consequences of it.

In the great final judgment, what will be the hallmark of our Christianity? It is found in the 25th chapter of Matthew—"And he shall say to them on the right hand, 'Come, ye blessed of my Father, inherit the kingdom prepared for you from the foundation of the world: For I was an hungered and ye gave me meat; I was thirsty, and ye gave me drink; I was a stranger, and ye took me in; naked, and ye clothed me; I was sick, and ye visited me; I was in prison, and ye came unto me.' Then shall the righteous answer him, saying, 'Lord, when saw we thee an hungered, and fed thee? or thirsty, and gave thee drink? When saw we thee a stranger, and took thee in? Or naked, and clothed thee? Or when saw we thee sick, or in prison, and came unto thee?' And the King shall say unto them, 'Inasmuch as ye have done it unto one of the least of these my brethren, ye have done it unto me.' Then shall he say also unto them on the left hand: 'Depart from me, ye cursed, into everlasting fire, prepared for the devil and his angels: For I was an hungered, and ye gave me no meat; I was thirsty, and ye gave me no drink; I was a stranger, and ye took me not in; naked, and ye clothed me not; sick, and in prison, and ye visited me not.' Then shall they also answer him saying, 'Lord, when saw we thee an hungered, or athirst, or a stranger, or naked, or sick, or in prison, and did not minister unto thee?' Then he shall answer them saying, 'Inasmuch as ye did it not to one of the least of these'—he didn't say my brethren—'ye did it not to me.' And these shall go away into everlasting punishment: but the righteous into life eternal." Now, that, in my judgment, is the charter for what we have undertaken to do in this church. This is the first part of what I have to say. I have a few more things I wish to say to you and then I will conclude.

I want us to talk about the practical aspect of the matters involved here—the practical things. We have missionary work in seventy-three countries, I believe it is. And most of these countries are populated by colored people. If we vote this motion down here tonight, what will it do to the missionary work that we—you women in WMU work— have so generously sacrificed for all through the years? The eyes of the world are watching us here tonight. Are we going to say, "Lord, we are going to come down on

194

this question and let the world know where we stand?" Are we going to build the wall that divides us again? Those are my interpretations—the observations I have made for myself. I think the public relations of this matter will be catastrophic because we are the First Baptist Church. We are in Birmingham, which is known far and wide, and I think unjustly so.

Now, what are the further consequences of this? You can see that this church is split right down the middle on this issue. What is the future for the First Baptist Church? I am not a prophet; I can only predict. But I do predict certain things. There are certain alternatives. We will have to dissolve this church. That's one alternative. The second alternative—we might divide the church and let those who want to have a segregated church have a segregated church, and those who want to have an open church have an open church. And third, we might decide to move. Now, the program of work that we are working under, the very first article of this program of work says this: "We, therefore, make the following firm decision to remain in our present downtown location." I sincerely believe that we cannot do that and shield ourselves from the blacks indefinitely. We may settle the question tonight, but will it be settled next month, next year, five years from now? So, if you are going to repeal the whole program of the church as adopted, then it becomes an open question as to what we will do and where we will move. I want to see us stay here. We voted to do that and I want to back up the program of the church in that respect.

The fourth thing is this: I heard one of my brothers—and I respect him very highly—say that if we take these colored people in, this church will be overrun. He even predicted that since I wanted to be buried in this church, that my pallbearers would probably be Negroes. Now, I haven't seen any churches being overrun with Negroes. One of our brothers says he entered a church in an area of the North and there was a Negro family there. He stayed there fifteen years. I don't know how many Negro families were there when he left, perhaps he would be glad to tell us. Maybe this can cast some light on the decision we are trying to make.

Here's a fifth thing: I hope that nobody will say that I am giving you an opinion, or that nobody will say I am adjudicating a case, or this is the law. But you have been reading in the papers recently where private educational institutions have to get a clearance from the Internal Revenue Bureau. Now what is the purpose of this clearance? Well, the purpose of the clearance is this: if they do not get the clearance, any gift to a private school cannot be deducted in computing your income tax. Now, I am not saying that the Internal Revenue Bureau is listening in here tonight, but I say if we vote to segregate this church, they may do just what they are doing—or attempting to do—with private schools. One court has already held, and that is what the bureau is operating under right now.

Now I am concerned about this church. It breaks my heart and I know it does yours. I'm just about through. I hope I haven't trespassed unduly on your time. I've tried to confine my time that you have given me here to

195

not more than was taken two weeks ago by the featured speaker. I'm reminded of a story that I told my Sunday School class. There were two Arabs that grew rich in the caravan trade of Arabia. When they came near the end of their lives, they decided they wanted to do something to commemorate their lives. One of them by the name of Ahmed built a monument by the side of the road to commemorate himself. In the course of time the monument was torn down and weathered away. The other man dug a well, and through the centuries as travelers would come by, they have taken a dip from the well, quenched their thirst, and blessed the name of Acmar who dug the well. Now, we can have a monument of stone and glass and brick on this corner, but unless there is a well of living water that invites men to come to Christ, we might as well close the doors to the church. I don't want to do that. I have walked with too many of you too long. Too many of you are my friends. I wouldn't do anything to hurt your feelings, but in conclusion I want to say this. I was reading some of the eulogies after President Eisenhower's death. And in one of these by Senator Byrd of Virginia, he said that the Allied armies and the United States armies were advancing on the Rhine River. General Eisenhower and his staff were going down through the thirtieth division, and they came to a company of foot soldiers. There was a straggler at the end of the line who was having the greatest trouble carrying his pack. [And we are having the greatest trouble carrying this burden.] Ike got down from the jeep and walked over to the man, helped him shoulder his burden for a minute and said: "Soldier, you seem to be worried." He said, "I'm scared to death. I was wounded two months ago and I've just gotten out of the hospital and am nervous." Ike said, "I'm nervous, too. We'll just walk down to the river together and it'll be good for both of us." I hope that I can walk down to the river with you all—right down to the very end—and I believe that it will be good for both of us.

In conclusion, I want to read from this little book, *Look Up, Brother*, written by W. A. Criswell, who has just finished two years as president of our Convention. Criswell was a segregationist and he has a chapter in here on the race question. He has had a change of heart, and here's what he said: "Race, as such, had no place in the Christian message. It is irrevocable in dying for all men Christ dissolved forever the middle wall or the partition that would separate us from one another." And then he says this: "In fact, it had been my stated persuasion—and it was published in the paper four, five, or six years ago—that we ought to go our separate ways—the colored community and the white community, the colored church and the white church, the black Christian and the white Christian. But as I prayed and searched the holy Scriptures, preached the gospel and worked with our people, I came to the profound conclusion that to separate by coercion the body of Christ on the basis of skin pigmentation was unthinkable, un-Christian, and unacceptable to God."

Now, there is one other thing I wanted to read from Dr. Criswell's book on this question of our duty to minister. It has been said here that what we are doing in the way of our program is the social gospel; that what we need to do is to come here every Sunday morning and sing the old-time songs, preach the old-time sermons—and I'm for that 100 percent. But listen to what Dr. Criswell says: "The Christian religion has two sharp cutting edges: one is faith, the other is works. One is believing, the other doing. One is evangelism, the other is ministry. Together they are a glory before the Lord. Our ministry and message must be to the whole man. A theological dualism that separates the temporal from the eternal, the physical from the spiritual, the soul from the body, this world from the world to come, is alien to the mind of Christ. We seek a balanced ministry of evangelism and social responsibility. True pietism and social action are not opposite. Loving lost souls, we seek to minister to human needs. The Christian must express himself in two directions: vertical and horizontal, toward God and toward man. Faith and works are inescapable halves of the genuine Christianity. Neither is a substitute for the other." Now, the Scriptures command us: "Be ye doers of the Word and not hearers only." And James says, "Show me your works without your faith, and I'll show you my works by my faith."

This concludes my statement to you. I would like for anybody who has any Scripture that will cast any light on this question that we are so genuinely concerned about, to come forward and say that the Scriptures say this. I read the Scriptures to you. I have done the best I can, I'm going to abide by the will of God.

APPENDIX 12

Statement released by First Baptist Church of Birmingham, February 26, 1971, to the Birmingham News, the Birmingham Post-Herald, and subsequently to the Baptist Press.

Over the last several months, the First Baptist Church of Birmingham has received much publicity which the present members of the church neither sought nor wanted. The church has been silent until now, as we felt that our problems were problems to be decided within the church and not in the newspapers or on the radio or TV. In response to numerous requests throughout the nation, the church now issues the following statement:

1. Contrary to popular opinion, race was not the main issue. The church was severely divided about Dr. Gilmore before the black persons ever came forward for membership. This division involved his refusal to visit shut-ins and elderly members despite repeated requests to do so; his approach to child evangelism; problems with staff personnel which led to the resignation of several long-time staff members; his liberal and humanistic preaching which de-emphasized the Bible; and his failure to promote evangelism.

The church also had financial problems which included the moving of church staff offices to a new area with new furnishings at an expenditure of $27,000 when only $6,000 had been authorized by the deacons and the church.

2. These problems dragged on for several months and Dr. Gilmore was advised by several leaders that he should try to reach solutions. He made no effort to do so and a motion was made in July, 1970, to discharge him. Dr. Gilmore was then advised by the chairman and vice-chairman of the Board of Deacons, the leader of "The Company of the Committed" and a prominent local judge that they felt it was in his best interest and the best interest of the church for him to resign as pastor. Dr. Gilmore refused to accept the advice of these leaders who supported him.

3. Before the black persons came forward for membership, the church had never prayed about open membership; there were no church-wide Bible studies, seminars or conferences held on this question. Dr. Gilmore

was told by several leaders that the church was not spiritually prepared to vote on the membership of the black persons. He refused to listen to these leaders and insisted on a vote. Numerous members have stated they voted against the black persons because they felt this was another effort on the part of Dr. Gilmore to further divide the church.

4. Two hundred thirty-nine resident members of First Baptist withdrew their membership and formed another church under the leadership of Dr. Gilmore. Eight hundred forty-eight resident and 521 non-resident members remained at First Baptist. During January and February, 1971, 17 members joined First Baptist by letter and 10 were baptized.

5. Despite the loss of membership and staff leadership, there is evident at First Baptist Church a new willingness on the part of all members to serve wherever they are needed. Ministries to the deaf, senior citizens, and the people of Central City have continued. The tutoring program for both black and white students at the neighborhood school has been reorganized, and is under way again in a more effective manner.

Attendance at the Women's Meetings and at the Wednesday night family supper and prayer meeting has increased. Sunday School attendance is averaging 83 fewer per Sunday. We gave $6,400.00 to the December, 1970, Lottie Moon offering for foreign missions against a goal of $4,250.00. The church has subscribed $160,349.68 toward its 1971 budget.

6. First Baptist is deeply indebted to Dr. Gerald Walker of the Family Prayer Hour radio program; Dr. George Jackson, director of the Extension Department, Samford University, Birmingham; Dr. Gilbert Guffin, dean of the department of religion, Samford University; Rev. Sumner Wemp, president of Southeastern Bible College, Birmingham; and Dr. A. Ben Oliver, Southern Baptist missionary to Brazil for 32 years, for supplying our pulpit. Dr. Oliver, who was the adopted missionary of First Baptist for those years, has recently been called as our interim pastor.

7. We do not know all the reasons for that which has occurred in recent months. We do know that the Bible teaches us to forget those things which are behind and to reach forward to those things which are before. We believe the Bible to be the Word of God and the basis of our faith. We agree with the Apostle Paul in Romans 1:16 where he states: "For I am not ashamed of the gospel of Christ; for it is the power of God unto salvation to everyone that believeth; to the Jew first, and also to the Greek."

We ask for the prayers of all who believe as we do as we search out the pastor God has chosen to lead this church. We claim the promise in I Corinthians 2:9: "Eye hath not seen, nor ear heard, neither have entered into the heart of man, the things which God hath prepared for them that love him."

God honors those who honor His Son and His Word. God is not dead. Neither is the First Baptist Church of Birmingham, Alabama.

199

Statement by Dr. Gilmore in response to the February 26 statement of First Baptist Church.

I regret that the First Baptist Church of Birmingham has not yet faced up to the real issue that divided the membership. The simple truth is that when two black people, who were the fruit of the church's ministry, tried to join the church, they were rejected.

Whatever shortcomings the pastor may or may not have had, he had nothing to do with the church's rejection of the two blacks. The church voted to exclude the blacks. That was the issue. When the First Baptist Church opens its membership to black people, then everyone can take seriously the charge that the issue was not race.

It is strange that the First Baptist Church would now break its silence and its avowed belief in the Bible's teaching "to forget those things which are behind and to reach forward to those things which are before," and launch a personal attack on me.

It is even more strange that nearly 300 members, who manned ninety percent of the places of leadership in the First Baptist Church, would leave and follow a pastor who, according to their charges, "refused to visit shut-ins and elderly," and was guilty of "liberal and humanistic preaching that de-emphasized the Bible," and failed "to promote evangelism."

I have no disposition to fight or to downgrade the First Baptist Church. Any success which the church may have now or in the future will be a source of delight to me. I wish for the church God-speed.

APPENDIX 13

News article in the Washington Post, *November 8, 1970, describing the racial struggle of First Baptist Church from the perspective of a journalist from out of town.*

CHURCH DIVIDES OVER BLACKS
by Betty Medsger, Washington *Post* Staff Writer.

Birmingham, Ala.—That Sunday in June was a big day in the life of Twila Bryant, 11. Standing beside her mother, Winifred Bryant, she faced the congregation of First Baptist Church, one of Birmingham's most prestigious churches.

They stood there—just as thousands of persons who have joined the church in its 98-year history have stood there—and waited for the yes vote on becoming members. Usually it's a mere formality.

But it was different for the Bryants, the first black people to try to join First Baptist. As a majority of those present voted yes, a sizable number of others were saying, "No, no."

Twila Bryant, who is too young to know that perhaps hardly anyone would have voted yes a decade ago, cried that Sunday. She had been going to the church's tutoring program for over a year, and she could not understand why some people were saying, "No, no."

As the "no's" died down Deacon E. W. McKenney made an official objection. That tossed the Bryants into a controversy that ended in September.

The rejection resulted in another vote, this one resulting in the resignation of the pastor and nine members of the church staff, and more than 200 members plus their children, leaving First Baptist to form a new church, The Company of the Committed.

New Church Meets

The Company met last Sunday for the first time. About 20 black people were among the 375 present at the service in the chapel of the Alabama Baptist Association's offices. If it follows through in its promise, after it is incorporated The Company of the Committed may be the first white church in the state to open membership to blacks.

Federal Judge H. Hobart Grooms Sr. called the number of persons who have indicated they will join The Company of the Committed "a real sign of hope."

201

"Seven years ago I doubt if I could've done this myself," said Grooms, the federal judge who ruled, in the Autherine Lucy case of 1956, that the University of Alabama must admit Negroes.

"A lot of us have moved considerably in the past seven years," said Grooms, who is 70. "Now I think there's more than unity and peace that should exist in a church. We who are left are concerned more about principles than about our prejudices, more about people than about property."

Causes of Split

First Baptist also held Sunday services last week. "There's one big difference between us and them," Deacon J. R. Derieux said afterward.

"They had 20 'niggers' in church, and we had none. And we're going to keep it that way."

In the months before the split, First Baptist became a symbol of several problems that beset churches across the nation.

* The exodus to the suburbs that, for nearly two decades, has accelerated the decline of downtown churches.

* The charges of "theological liberalism" against pastors used to camouflage apparent racist attitudes.

* The fragile job security of clergymen who press for application of moral principles to social issues, especially racial prejudice.

Deacon Derieux was one of the leaders of the campaign against the Bryants.

"Why you never saw anything like it," he recalled recently. "My wife, and I think it was five other women, worked round the clock in July calling every member on the rolls."

Although about 750 regularly attended the church, there were several hundred more inactive members.

"What we did," Derieux said, "was ask them if they believed in the 'Commitments' of '68. If they did believe in them, we didn't call them again.

"In the end, we had 450 votes we could command at any time."

Like downtown churches throughout the nation, First Baptist has been faced with declining membership—down from a peak of 3,443 in 1953 to about 1,200 now—as members moved to the suburbs.

In 1968, members of First Baptist approved the "Commitments," a series of mission principles aimed at correcting a situation in which the church was virtually ignoring service to its own neighborhood while spending heavily on mission work overseas.

"We are maintaining here a small part of God's great democracy, and we ask courtesy and tolerance for all alike," the "Commitments" said in part. "On these stern terms, we invite all who will, whether they be young or old, proud or plain, rich or poor, to partake with us of the love of God, and to give themselves to the task that is before us."

The Bryants live in a housing development next to First Baptist.

Winifred Bryant, 38, charwoman and mother of six, gets up at 3 a.m. five days a week to mop floors in a recreation center for the aged, a job she has held for 11 years.

Her daughter Twila entered First Baptist's tutoring program when it began in October, 1968, and Mrs. Bryant recalls that she became curious about "this church that had been so good to my children." She went to a service last May.

"I remember the first time I went in. I looked around and thought, 'Oh, my goodness,' when I saw that everybody was white. But I liked the service and got lost in the sermon and forgot who was around me." She kept coming back.

She liked the sermons preached by the Rev. Dr. J. Herbert Gilmore, 45, former pastor of Chevy Chase Baptist Church in Washington. A blunt man, he says of himself that "people either like me or despise me." He usually slipped something about racial prejudice into his sermons.

No Compromise

"I'd rather sell shoes than compromise," Dr. Gilmore said last week. "I'm going to live and preach the Christian faith to the limit of my vision and ability. If this creates conflict, then I'm sorry, but so be it."

There was conflict aplenty this summer after the Bryants' membership was initially blocked.

"They were a product of our mission," said Mrs. H. Hobart Grooms, Sr., wife of the judge and like her husband a 43-year member of First Baptist. "If you can't receive the product of your own mission work, then you are blind."

Mrs. Grooms, her husband and their lawyer son and his wife were among those who ultimately left to join The Company of the Committed.

At times the battle centered on whether the "Commitments" of 1968 had promised open membership to persons other than whites.

"We didn't mean open membership when we passed those 'Commitments,' " maintains First Baptist Deacon Derieux. "What's more, if we had known those 'Commitments' had anything to do with Negroes there would've been no way to get them passed."

Another part of the battle was fought on theological grounds.

Ollie Blan, 39, a local lawyer, who describes himself as a Christian fundamentalist, led this fight with the admitted purpose of ousting Dr. Gilmore as pastor.

Blan says he rid himself of his once-strong conviction that churches should be segregated a year ago by searching through Scriptures. He recommends the same means for others; prayer and Bible study.

"God has to be the author of this in a man's heart," Blan maintains; "it can't come by a man saying from the pulpit that it's an obligation."

At meetings of the First Baptist congregation this summer, a move to oust Dr. Gilmore failed by a narrow margin, as did another move to oust the entire staff.

203

A third area of contention was the Bryants themselves.

Some members of First Baptist said in recent interviews that Mrs. Bryant wasn't "the right Negro" for First Baptist. "Why couldn't they have gone out and gotten a good, educated Negro?" one asked. Accusations were made that her children, "however many it is she has, were each fathered by a different man."

Mrs. Bryant, who says she was divorced around the time the youngest of her six children was born eight years ago, responds:

"They've been saying a lot of things like that. I just try to elevate myself above it."

First Baptist's deacons have confirmed that a prospective member's marital status has never been used as a criterion for acceptance. There are divorced members in the church.

The final vote on the Bryants' membership came on Sept. 27. They received more than a majority in a standing vote—but two-thirds was needed.

250 Walked Out

More than 250 members of First Baptist walked out. Dr. Gilmore and Betty Bock, Minister of Youth, resigned that day. Other members of the staff subsequently followed suit, and all have been retained at full salary by The Company of the Committed.

"I know it's been awful for the Bryants, but, you know, what has come out of this is wonderful," Mrs. Grooms said the other day. "Some of us were able to make a big decision—First Baptist meant a lot to us, so it was hard—and say, 'We are not willing to see Negroes treated that way any more.' "

Dr. Byrn Williamson, 57, is the surgeon who led the walkout of Sept. 27. Down at his clinic, they call him Moses because he "led the children out of the wilderness."

"It didn't really surprise me," said Dr. Williamson, "that some people were against their joining. But neither did it surprise me that a lot left the church. A lot of us have changed.

"It's still hard. I'm still prejudiced, but I'm working on it. Five years ago I would not have taken this stand. . . . No, it was nothing sudden. . . . I've just been growing.

"I guess what really did it for me were the times I spent overseas in mission hospitals. They were short-term experiences, but they showed me a lot. . . . It struck me that we were sending money to people in Africa we didn't even know or see, but we weren't willing to walk across 6th Avenue to help Africans in Birmingham."

Perhaps the change is best explained by Billy Austin, 36, vice president of Birmingham's First Saving and Loan Association:

"I just came to think that if there's one place where anybody ought to be able to be somebody, it's in the church."

Dr. Gilmore admits he is a "burned" man who, in the end, fulfilled the wishes of an opposition movement when he resigned.

But he's also a hero. Those who took a stand and moved out of the old church thank him for leading them.

"We were looking for a pastor who could really lead us," said Dr. Williamson.

Cautious Assessment

A local black pastor, the Rev. Wilson Fallin, was cautious in assessing The Company of the Committed: "I'm impressed with their sensitivity. I think it's good that a group is trying to be a real church.

"But I don't think their action will have much impact on giving blacks, poor whites and other minorities much power. . . . I'll get excited if these people—The Company of the Committed—say, 'We're willing to give up some of our money and power to bring justice to poor people.'

"We'll have to wait to see what they are willing to do, to see if they're willing to keep moving."

Back at First Baptist, leaders of the opposition to the Bryants have dropped their earlier public denials that race was back of the dispute.

Deacon Derieux said in an interview that the movement to oust Dr. Gilmore started back in April "when we were first certain he wanted to bring 'niggers' in. We were determined to get him sooner or later."

Derieux confirmed that in a telephone campaign to bring people to last Sunday's service, the first without Dr. Gilmore, callers told some people: "Come to First Baptist Sunday for good old gospel preaching, good singing and no 'niggers.' "

"We couldn't say that to everybody," Derieux said. "But we said it to some people."

Last Monday, Derieux, who is a civil engineer, was at the church early in work clothes. He and a locksmith had just finished changing 25 locks on the stone church and the adjoining seven-story brick education building, to keep out the former staff.

"We don't trust them," Derieux said. "They might come back and steal the music and the handbells."

Derieux called the Washington *Post* Thursday to bring the report up to date. He had just changed the locks on "The Crossroads," a coffee house operated for teen-agers in a store front operated by the church, he said. The congregation voted Wednesday evening to close it.

"We'll rent it to some store," said Derieux. "We had to close it. Too many colored people live near that block. It's cheap coffee. They'll all come in if we don't close it."

Derieux pointed out that the coffee house was in a building that "when we first owned it was a pretty good night club with a nice striptease."

The two-year-old tutoring program for neighborhood children also was closed last week. Deacon E. W. McKenney said the church didn't have adequate facilities for the tutoring and that it should be done in the public schools. The program has been operated in the education building.

Ollie Blan, the fundamentalist Christian, who thought integration should come through prayer and Bible study, was asked whether First Baptist would start such a program now.

"This is not the time to discuss it," Blan said. "We're still in a period of waiting."

P 15 Christian faith c
81750 *papers* 3 *pack* , 15 yr 6 m (about him
of supreme court d.
Hamburg drop 1 *km*

Date Due
